GEN

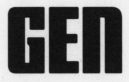

GEN

ONE IS ENOUGH, AUG 2014

ONE IS ENOUGH™ GEN™ & GEN MANGA™ ARE TRADEMARKS OF GEN MANGA ENTERTAINMENT, INC./
© 2014 GEN MANGA ENTERTAINMENT, INC. ALL RIGHTS RESERVED.

FOR INFORMATION, CONTACT GEN MANGA ENTERTAINMENT, INC.

COVER ART . . . . LOVE
COVER AND INTERIOR DESIGN . . . . RICHARD RODRIGUEZ
ONE IS ENOUGH . . . . LOVE

PUBLISHED BY
GEN MANGA ENTERTAINMENT, INC.
250 PARK AVENUE, SUITE 7002
NEW YORK, NY 10117 USA
WWW.GENMANGA.COM

PRINTED IN CANADA

MANGA

Japanese Style

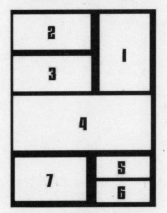

**Remember to read
from right to left**

One is Enough

art and story by

love

translated by
Julianne Neville

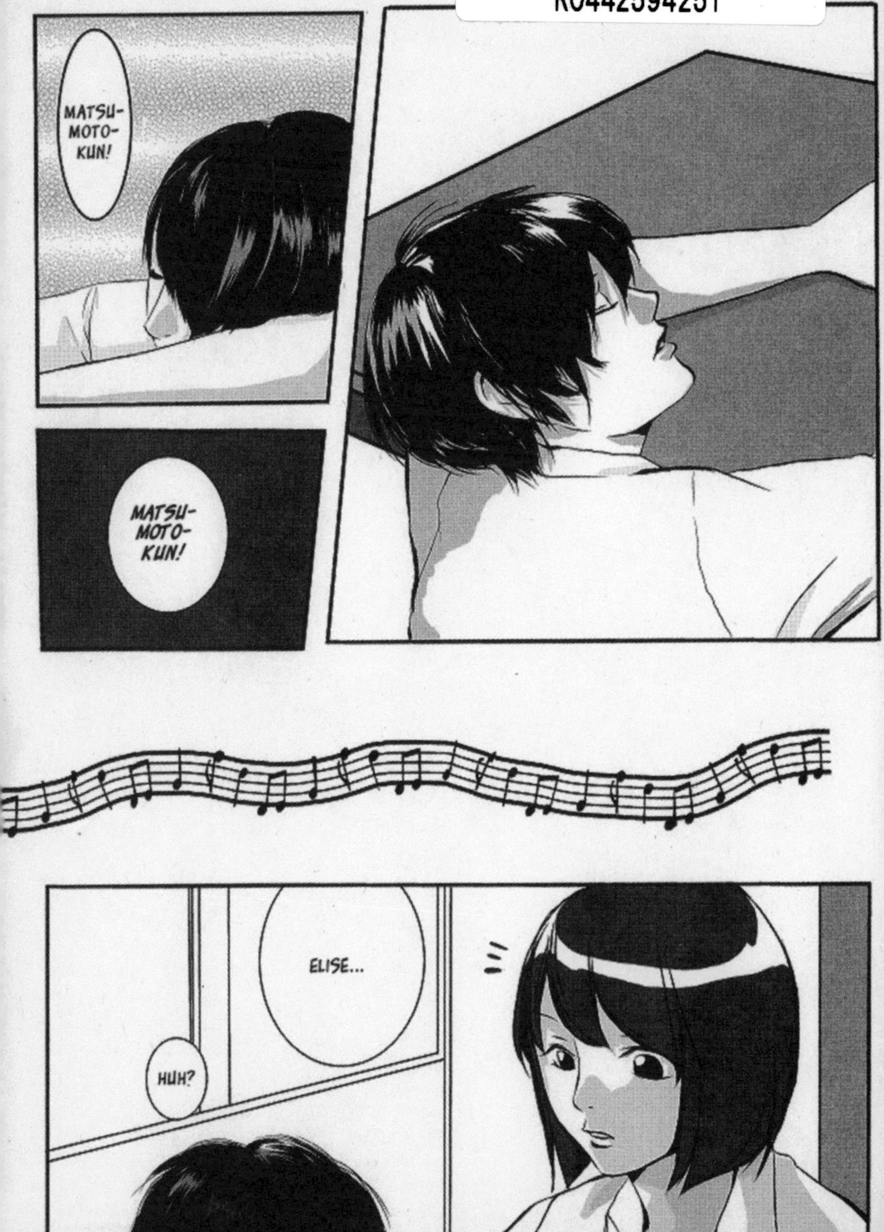
MATSU-MOTO-KUN!
MATSU-MOTO-KUN!
ELISE...
HUH?

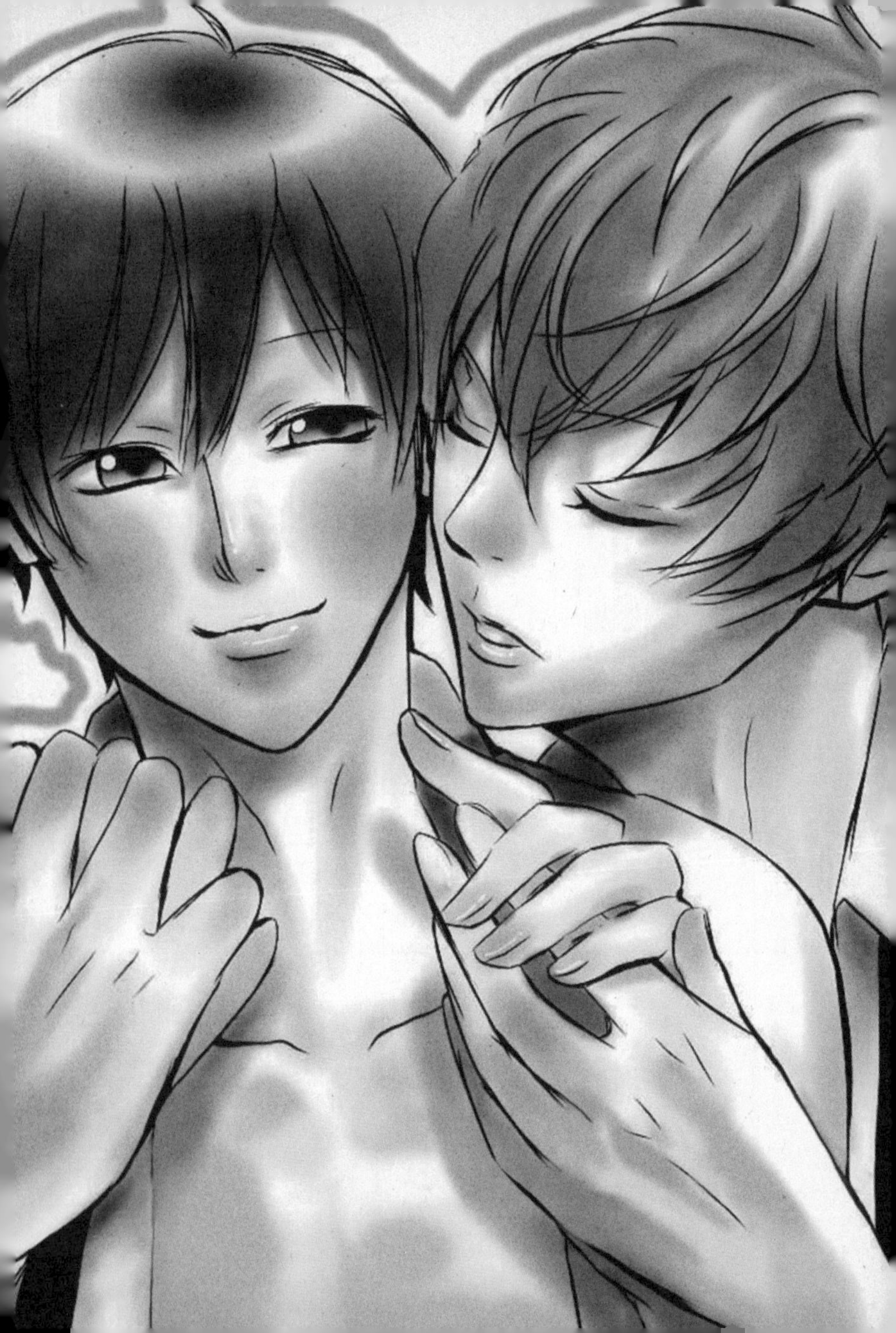

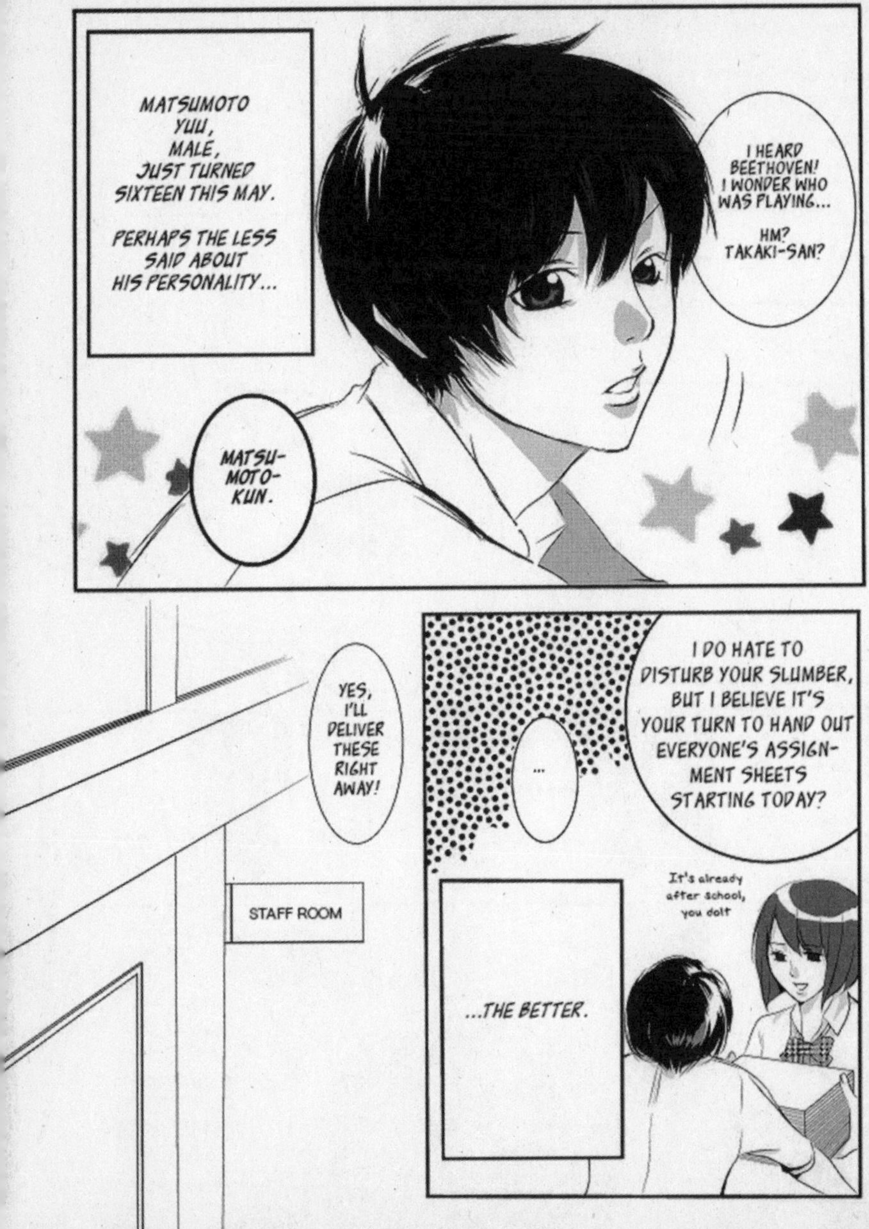
I HEARD BEETHOVEN! I WONDER WHO WAS PLAYING... HM? TAKAKI-SAN?
MATSUMOTO YUU, MALE, JUST TURNED SIXTEEN THIS MAY.
PERHAPS THE LESS SAID ABOUT HIS PERSONALITY...
MATSU-MOTO-KUN.
I DO HATE TO DISTURB YOUR SLUMBER, BUT I BELIEVE IT'S YOUR TURN TO HAND OUT EVERYONE'S ASSIGN-MENT SHEETS STARTING TODAY?
...
It's already after school, you dolt
...THE BETTER.
YES, I'LL DELIVER THESE RIGHT AWAY!
STAFF ROOM

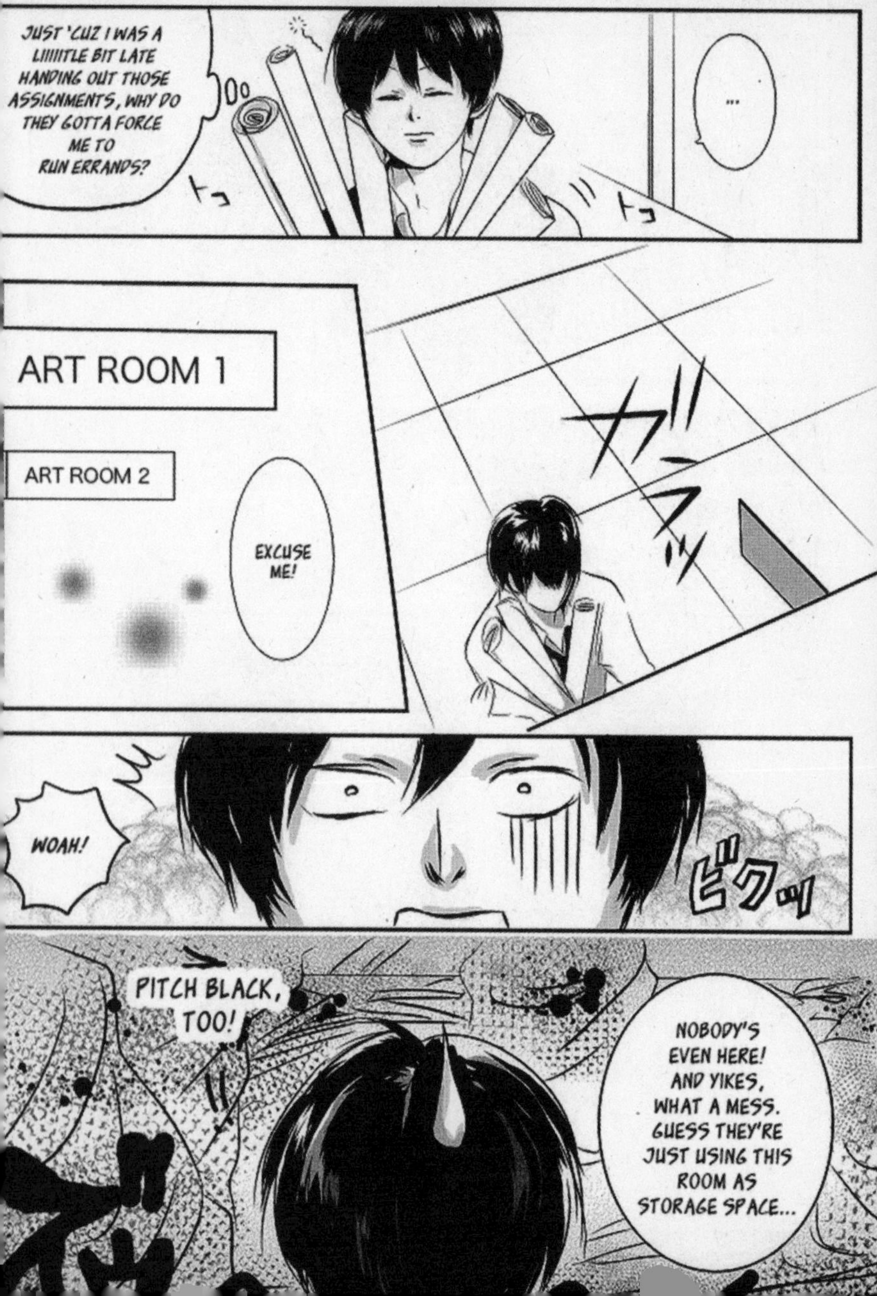
...
トコ
トコ
JUST 'CUZ I WAS A LIIIIITLE BIT LATE HANDING OUT THOSE ASSIGNMENTS, WHY DO THEY GOTTA FORCE ME TO RUN ERRANDS?
ガラッ
ART ROOM 1
ART ROOM 2
EXCUSE ME!
ビクッ
WOAH!
NOBODY'S EVEN HERE! AND YIKES, WHAT A MESS. GUESS THEY'RE JUST USING THIS ROOM AS STORAGE SPACE...
PITCH BLACK, TOO!

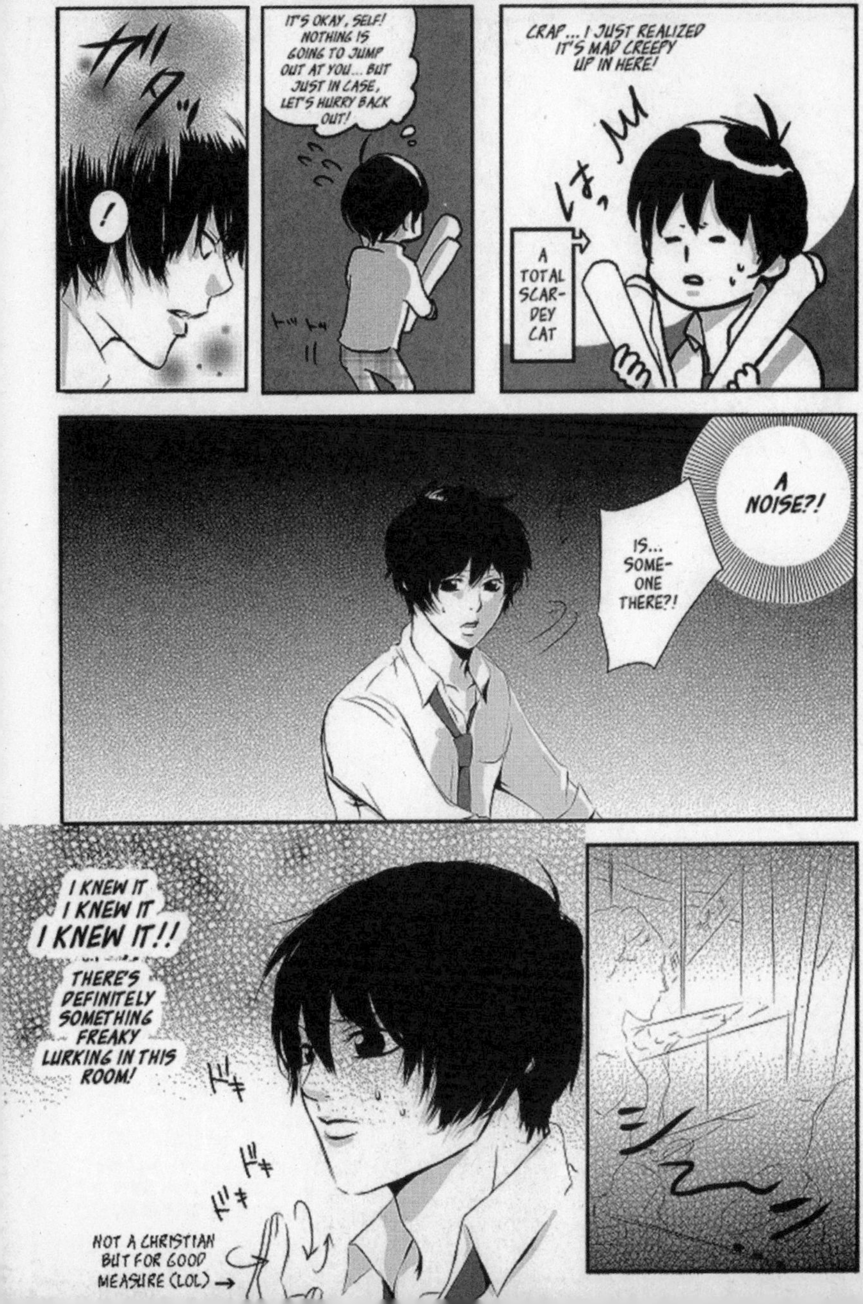
CRAP... I JUST REALIZED IT'S MAD CREEPY UP IN HERE!
はっ
A TOTAL SCAR-DEY CAT
IT'S OKAY, SELF! NOTHING IS GOING TO JUMP OUT AT YOU... BUT JUST IN CASE, LET'S HURRY BACK OUT!
ガタッ
!
A NOISE?!
IS... SOME-ONE THERE?!
I KNEW IT I KNEW IT I KNEW IT!!
THERE'S DEFINITELY SOMETHING FREAKY LURKING IN THIS ROOM!
ドキ
ドキ
ドキ
NOT A CHRISTIAN BUT FOR GOOD MEASURE (LOL) →

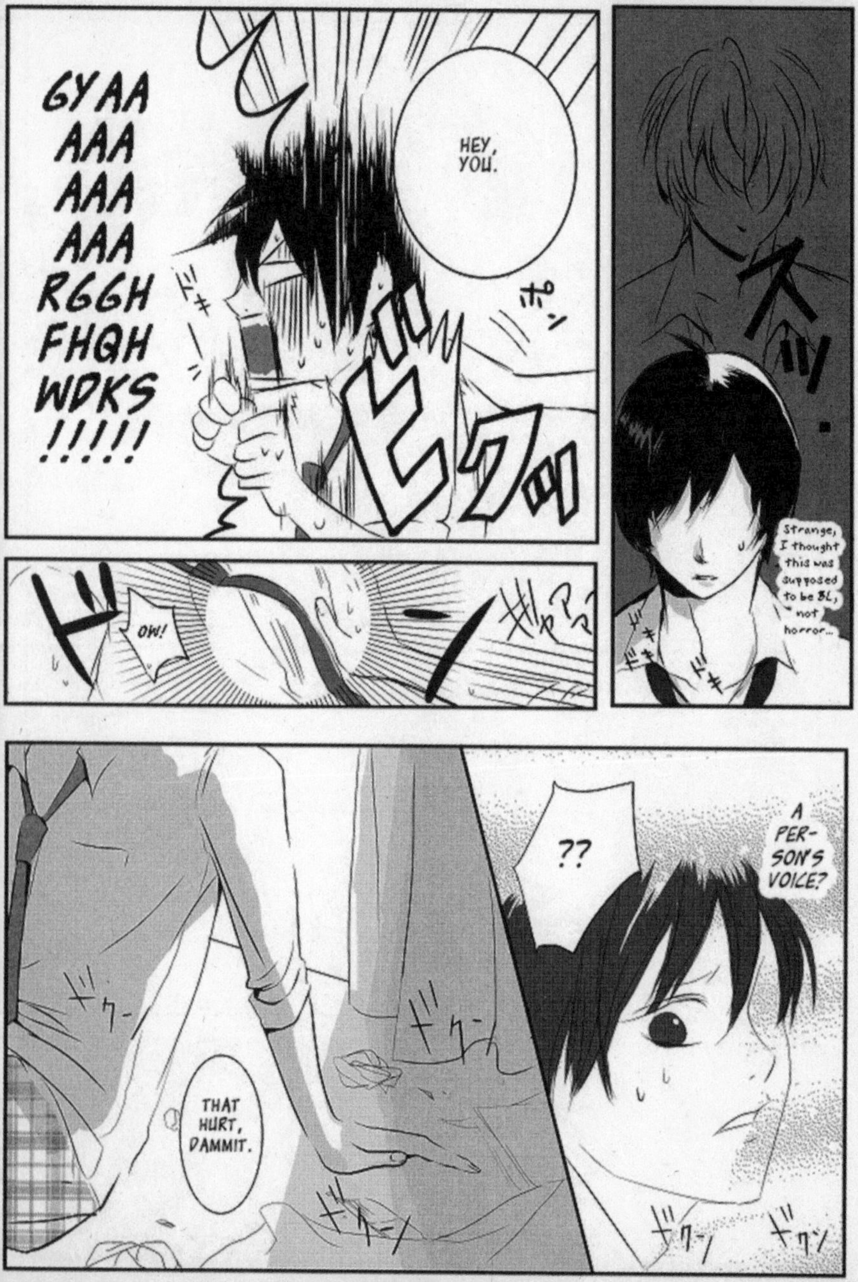
Strange, I thought this was supposed to be BL, not horror...
HEY, YOU.
GYAA AAA AAA AAA AAA RGGH FHQH WDKS !!!!!!
OW!
A PER-SON'S VOICE?
??
THAT HURT, DAMMIT.

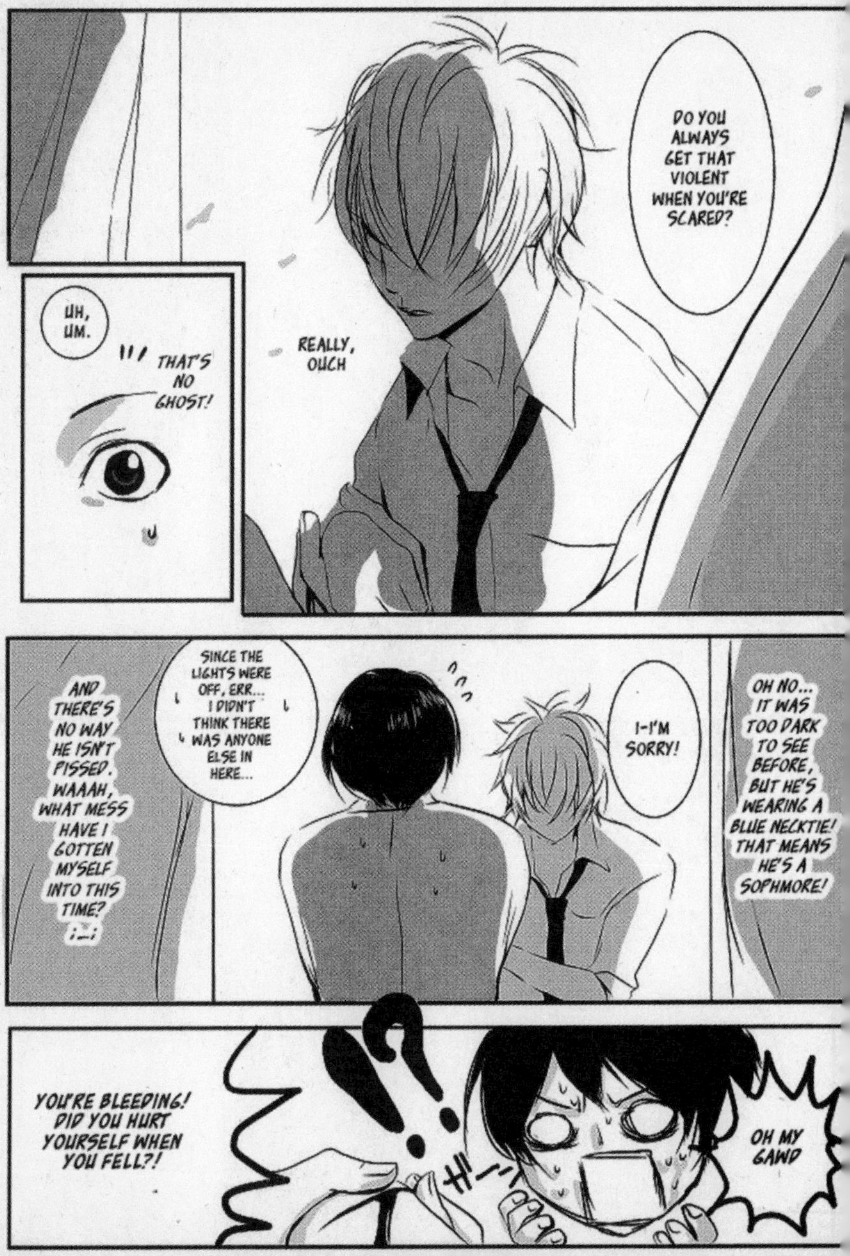
DO YOU ALWAYS GET THAT VIOLENT WHEN YOU'RE SCARED?
REALLY, OUCH
UH, UM.
THAT'S NO GHOST!
OH NO... IT WAS TOO DARK TO SEE BEFORE, BUT HE'S WEARING A BLUE NECKTIE! THAT MEANS HE'S A SOPHMORE!
I-I'M SORRY!
SINCE THE LIGHTS WERE OFF, ERR... I DIDN'T THINK THERE WAS ANYONE ELSE IN HERE...
AND THERE'S NO WAY HE ISN'T PISSED. WAAAH, WHAT MESS HAVE I GOTTEN MYSELF INTO THIS TIME? ;_;
OH MY GAWD
YOU'RE BLEEDING! DID YOU HURT YOURSELF WHEN YOU FELL?!

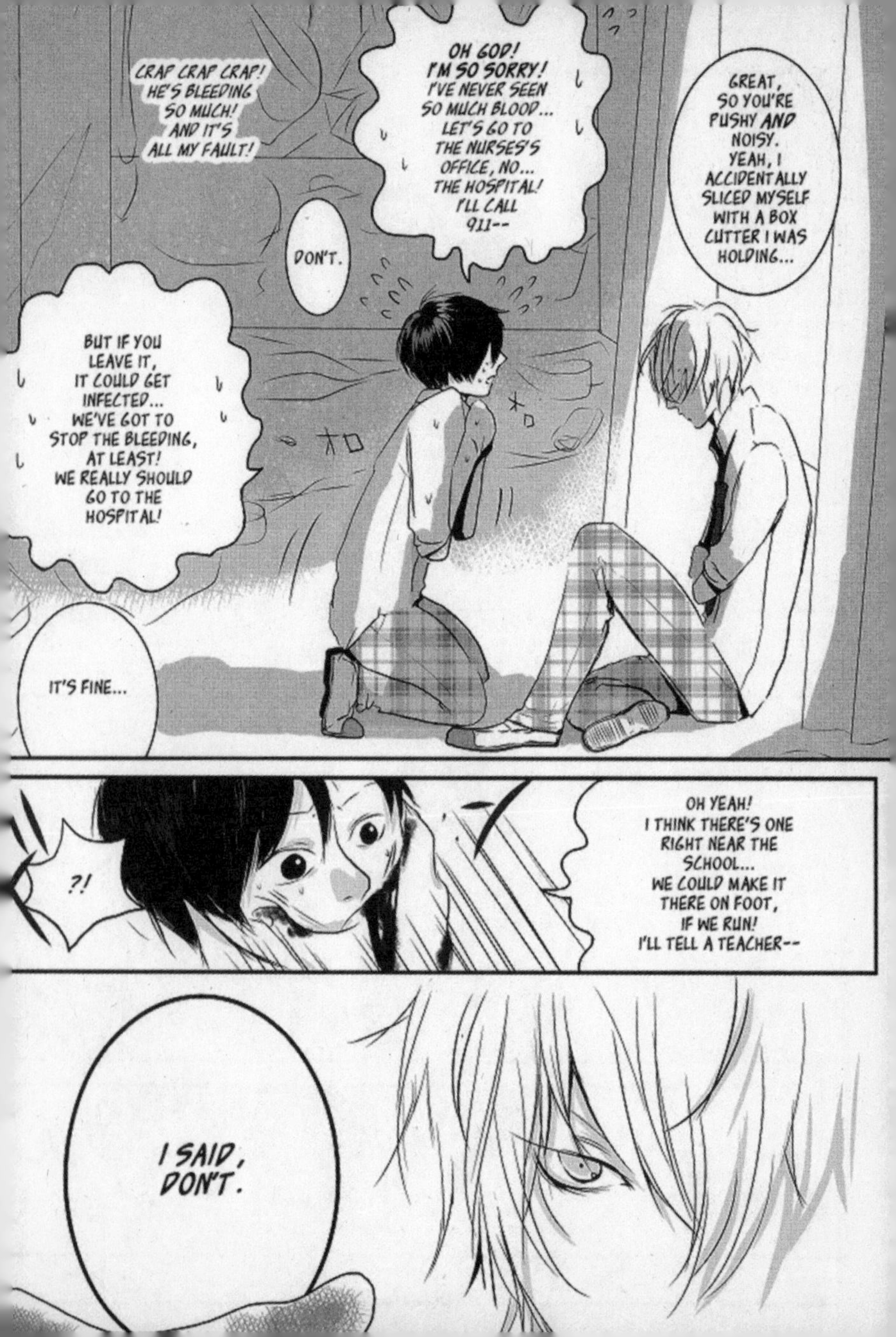
GREAT, SO YOU'RE PUSHY AND NOISY. YEAH, I ACCIDENTALLY SLICED MYSELF WITH A BOX CUTTER I WAS HOLDING...
OH GOD! I'M SO SORRY! I'VE NEVER SEEN SO MUCH BLOOD... LET'S GO TO THE NURSES'S OFFICE, NO... THE HOSPITAL! I'LL CALL 911--
CRAP CRAP CRAP! HE'S BLEEDING SO MUCH! AND IT'S ALL MY FAULT!
DON'T.
BUT IF YOU LEAVE IT, IT COULD GET INFECTED... WE'VE GOT TO STOP THE BLEEDING, AT LEAST! WE REALLY SHOULD GO TO THE HOSPITAL!
IT'S FINE...
OH YEAH! I THINK THERE'S ONE RIGHT NEAR THE SCHOOL... WE COULD MAKE IT THERE ON FOOT, IF WE RUN! I'LL TELL A TEACHER--
?!
I SAID, DON'T.

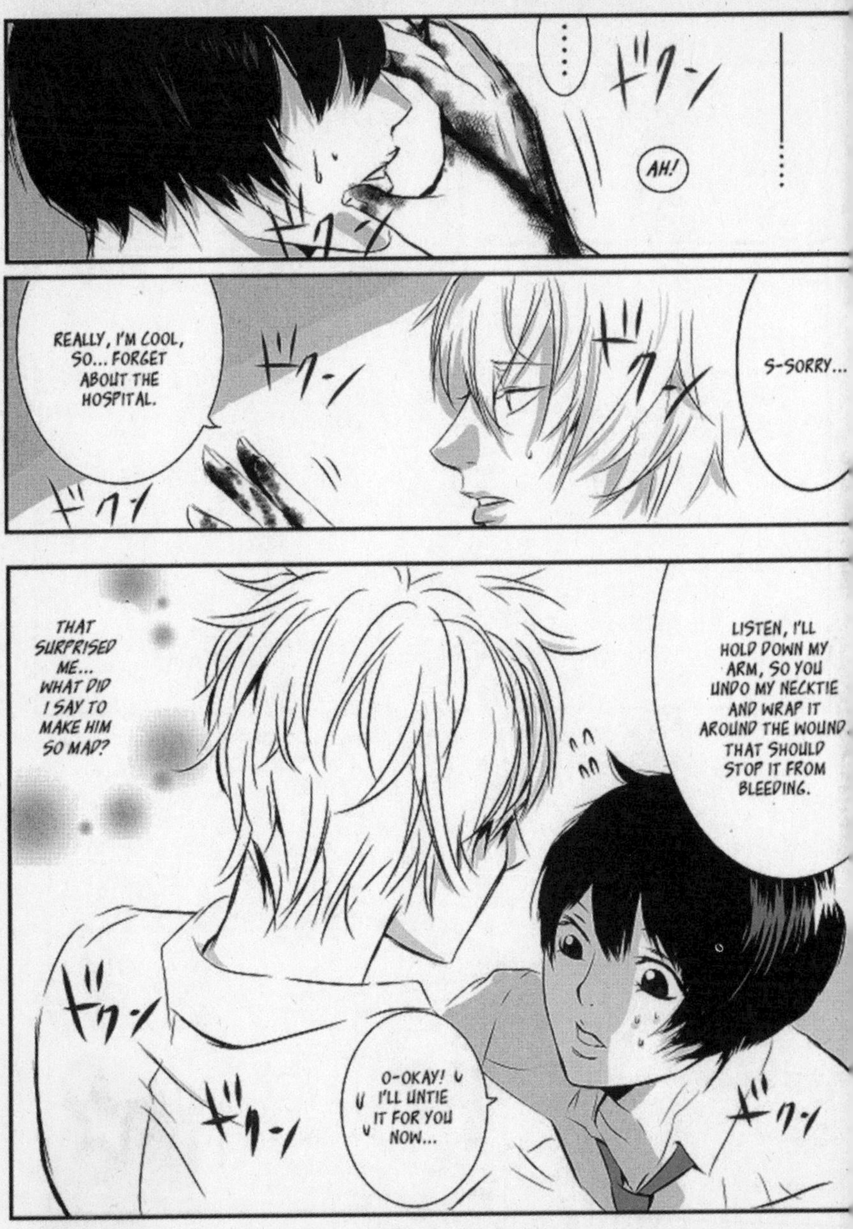
......
AH!
......
S-SORRY...
REALLY, I'M COOL, SO... FORGET ABOUT THE HOSPITAL.
LISTEN, I'LL HOLD DOWN MY ARM, SO YOU UNDO MY NECKTIE AND WRAP IT AROUND THE WOUND. THAT SHOULD STOP IT FROM BLEEDING.
O-OKAY! I'LL UNTIE IT FOR YOU NOW...
THAT SURPRISED ME... WHAT DID I SAY TO MAKE HIM SO MAD?

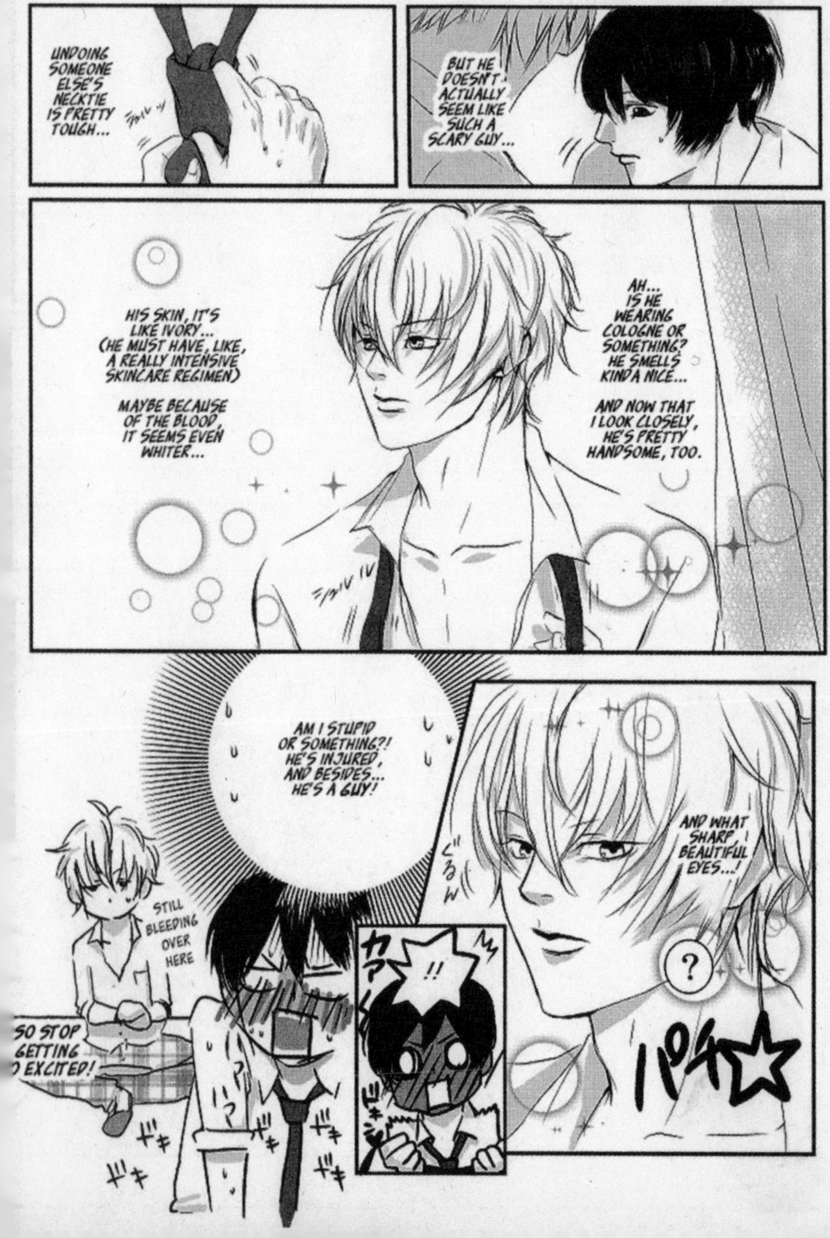
BUT HE DOESN'T ACTUALLY SEEM LIKE SUCH A SCARY GUY...
UNDOING SOMEONE ELSE'S NECKTIE IS PRETTY TOUGH...
AH... IS HE WEARING COLOGNE OR SOMETHING? HE SMELLS KINDA NICE...
AND NOW THAT I LOOK CLOSELY, HE'S PRETTY HANDSOME, TOO.
HIS SKIN, IT'S LIKE IVORY... (HE MUST HAVE, LIKE, A REALLY INTENSIVE SKINCARE REGIMEN)
MAYBE BECAUSE OF THE BLOOD, IT SEEMS EVEN WHITER...
AND WHAT SHARP, BEAUTIFUL EYES...!
パチ☆
AM I STUPID OR SOMETHING?! HE'S INJURED, AND BESIDES... HE'S A GUY!
STILL BLEEDING OVER HERE
SO STOP GETTING
O EXCITED!

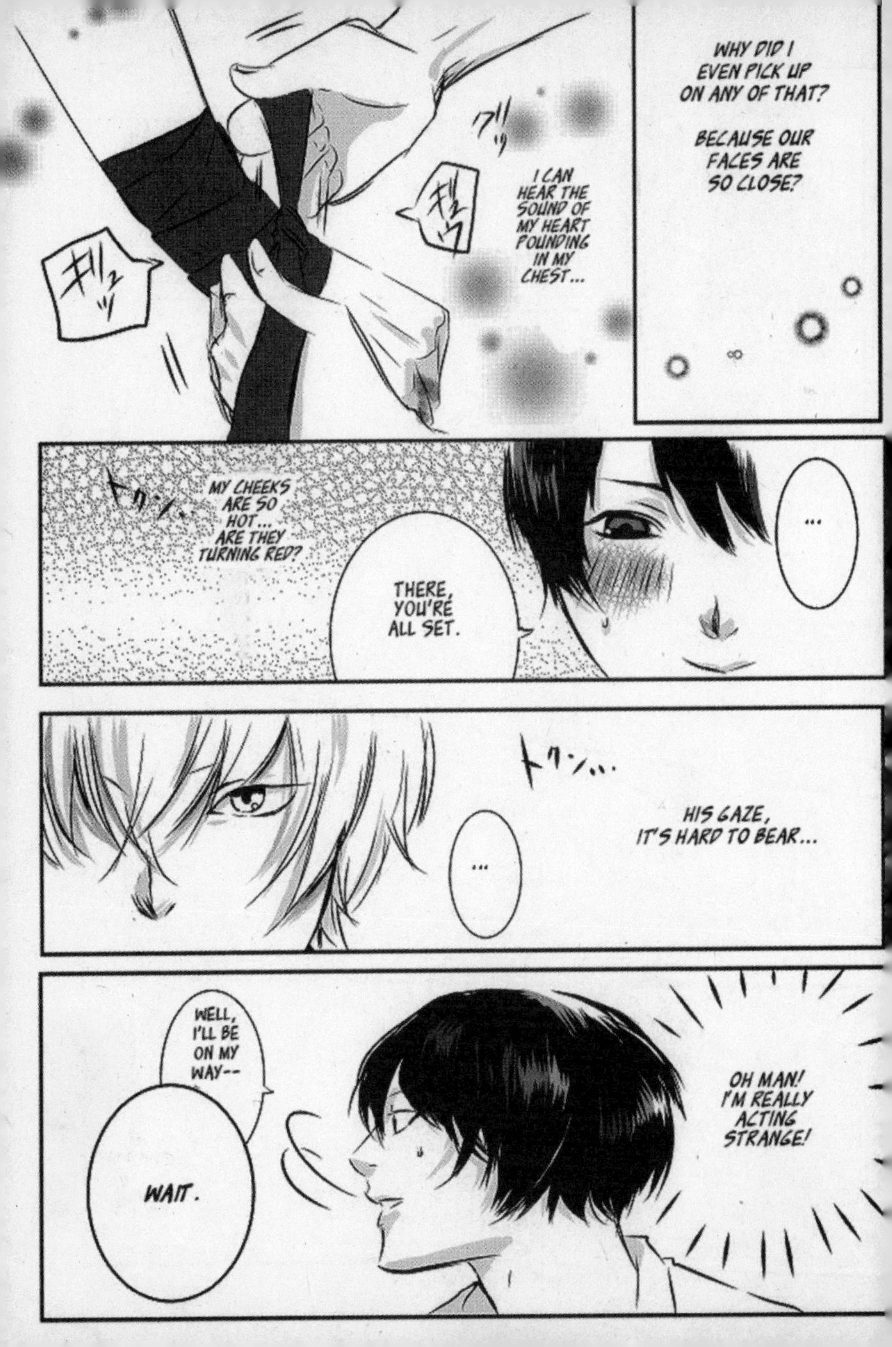

WHY DID I EVEN PICK UP ON ANY OF THAT?
BECAUSE OUR FACES ARE SO CLOSE?
I CAN HEAR THE SOUND OF MY HEART POUNDING IN MY CHEST...
...
THERE, YOU'RE ALL SET.
MY CHEEKS ARE SO HOT... ARE THEY TURNING RED?
HIS GAZE, IT'S HARD TO BEAR...
...
OH MAN! I'M REALLY ACTING STRANGE!
WELL, I'LL BE ON MY WAY--
WAIT.

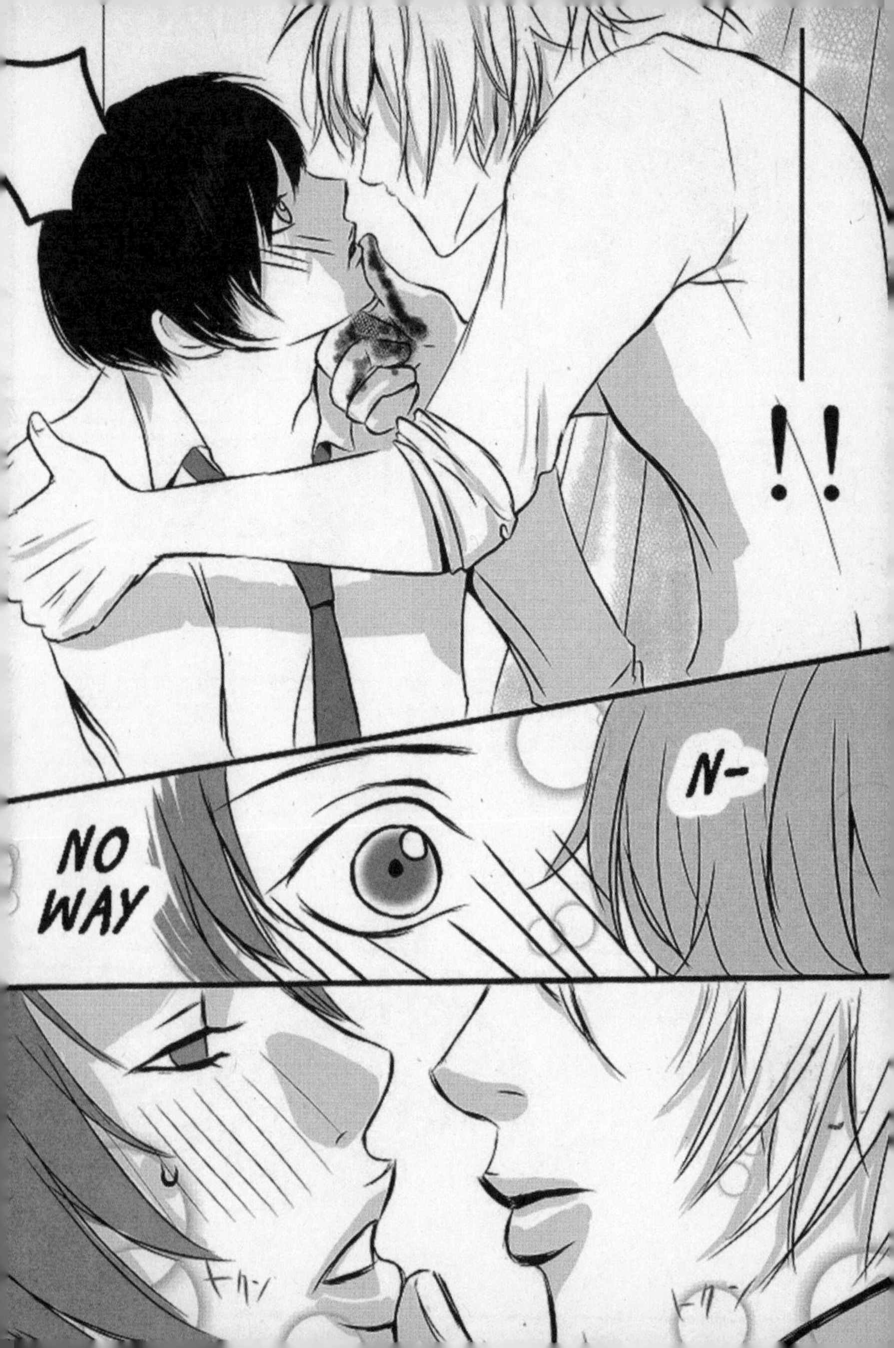
!!
N-
NO WAY

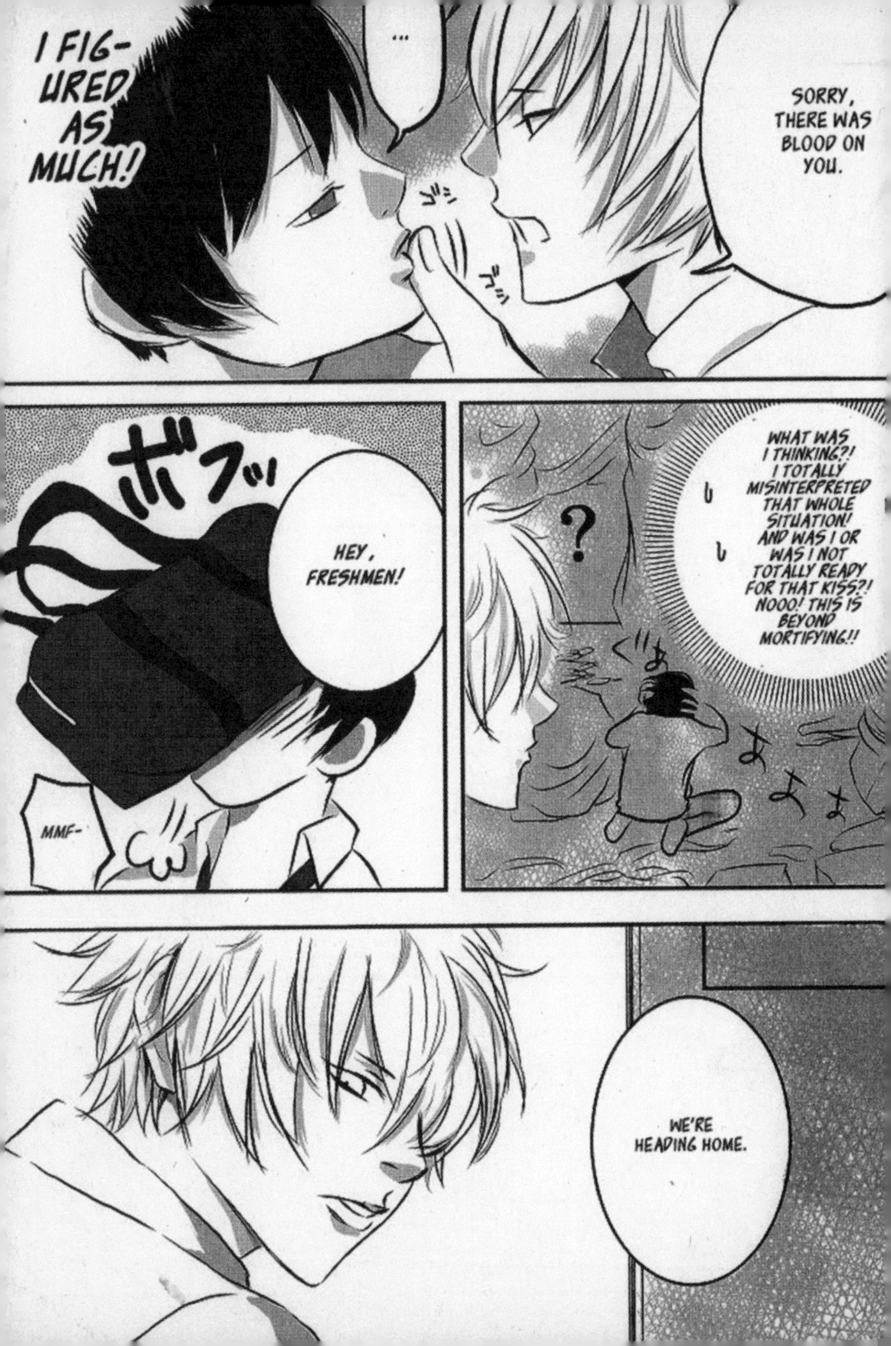
SORRY, THERE WAS BLOOD ON YOU.
...
I FIG-URED AS MUCH!
WHAT WAS I THINKING?! I TOTALLY MISINTERPRETED THAT WHOLE SITUATION! AND WAS I OR WAS I NOT TOTALLY READY FOR THAT KISS?! NOOO! THIS IS BEYOND MORTIFYING!!
?
ボフッ
HEY, FRESHMEN!
MMF-
WE'RE HEADING HOME.

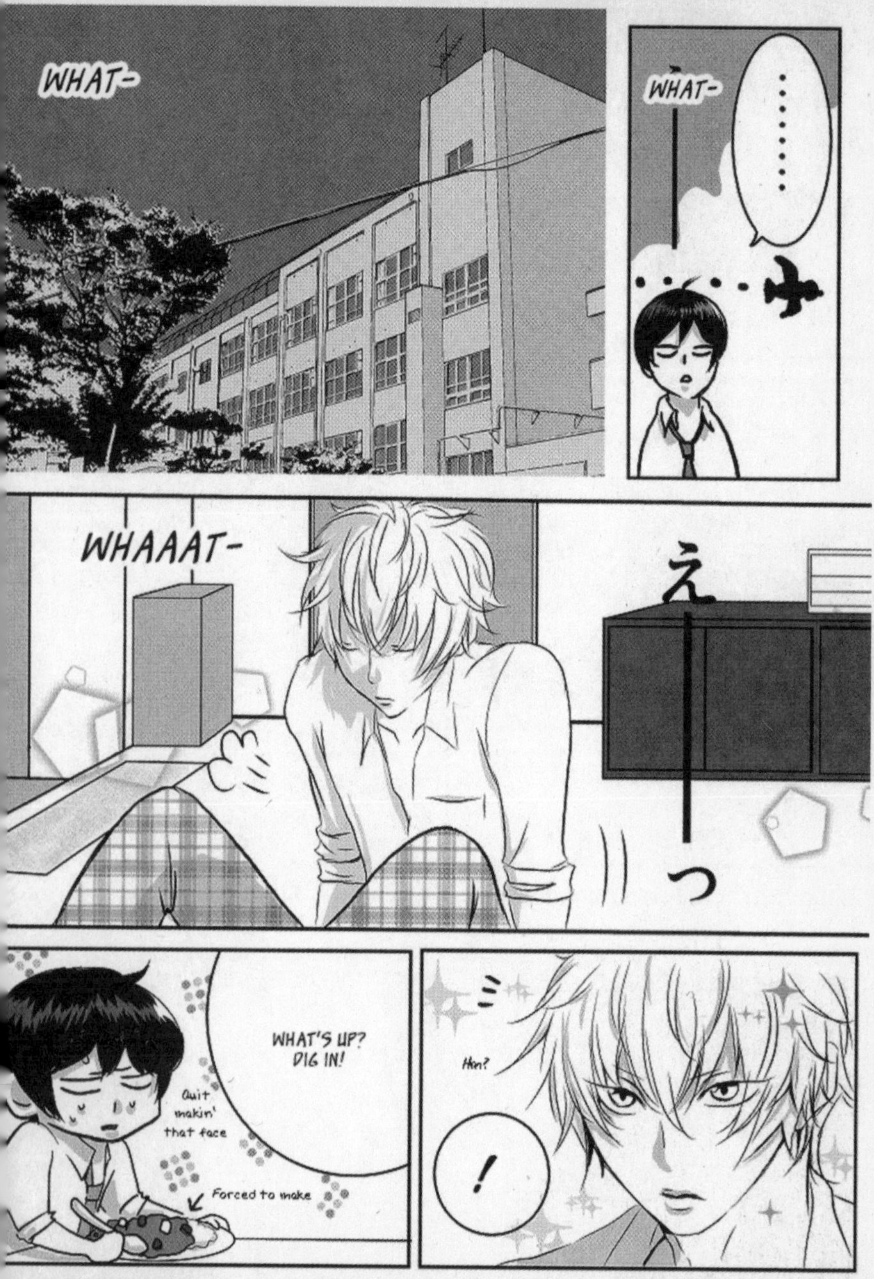

....
WHAT-
WHAT-
えーっ
WHAAAT-
Hm?
!
WHAT'S UP? DIG IN!
Quit makin' that face
Forced to make

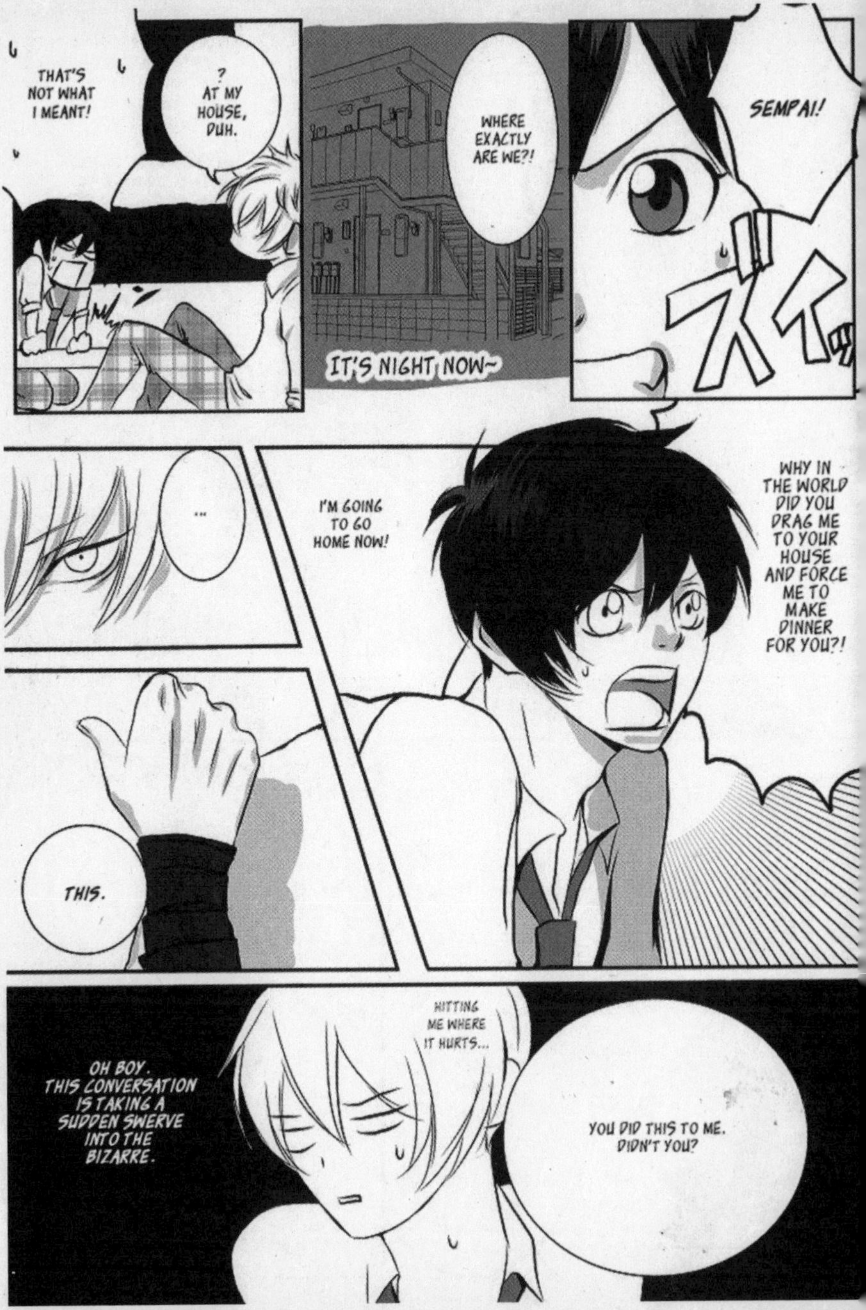
SEMPAI!
WHERE EXACTLY ARE WE?!
IT'S NIGHT NOW~
? AT MY HOUSE, DUH.
THAT'S NOT WHAT I MEANT!
WHY IN THE WORLD DID YOU DRAG ME TO YOUR HOUSE AND FORCE ME TO MAKE DINNER FOR YOU?!
I'M GOING TO GO HOME NOW!
...
THIS.
YOU DID THIS TO ME. DIDN'T YOU?
HITTING ME WHERE IT HURTS...
OH BOY. THIS CONVERSATION IS TAKING A SUDDEN SWERVE INTO THE BIZARRE.

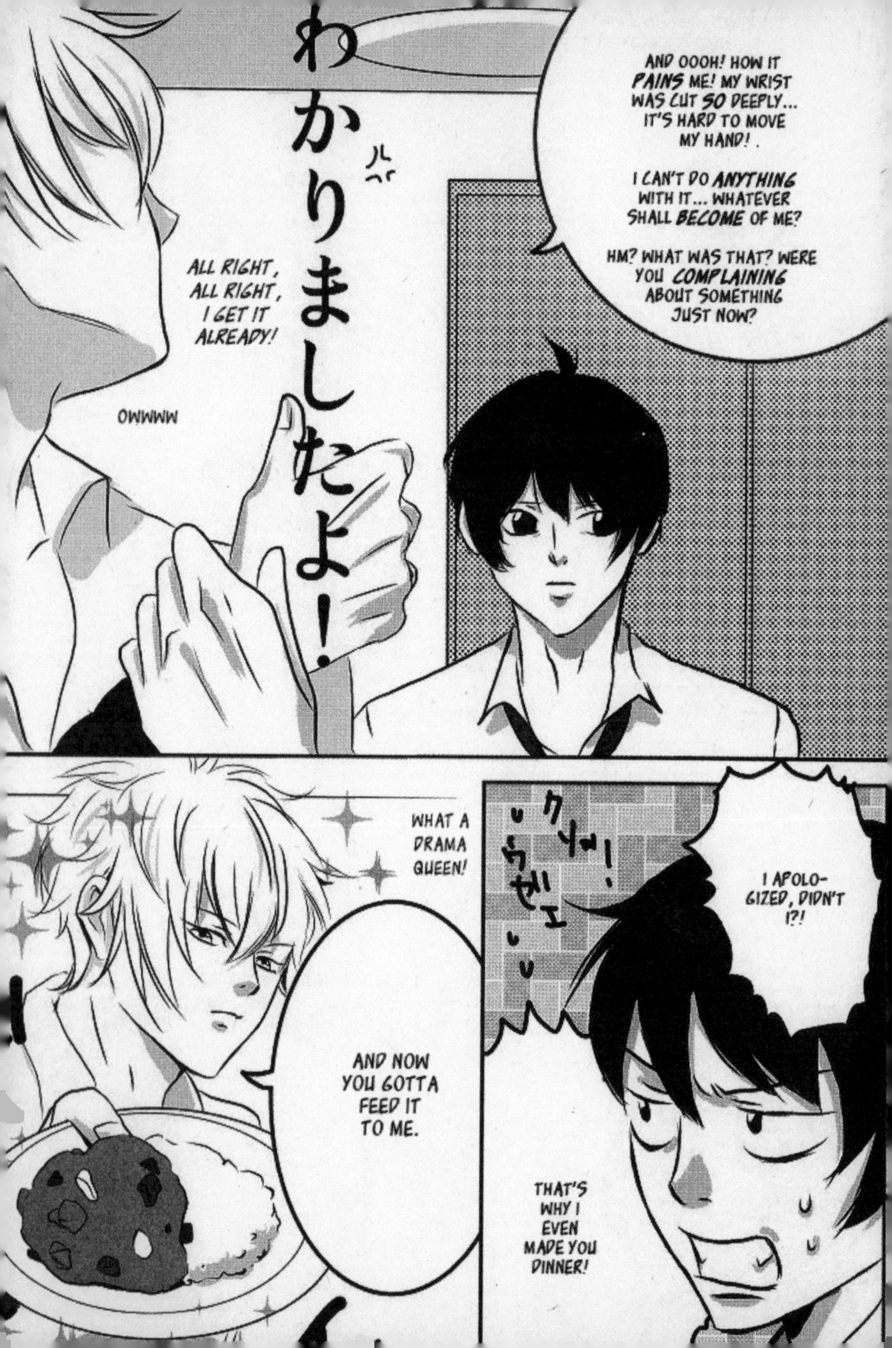
AND OOOH! HOW IT PAINS ME! MY WRIST WAS CUT SO DEEPLY... IT'S HARD TO MOVE MY HAND! I CAN'T DO ANYTHING WITH IT... WHATEVER SHALL BECOME OF ME? HM? WHAT WAS THAT? WERE YOU COMPLAINING ABOUT SOMETHING JUST NOW?
わかりましたよ!
ALL RIGHT, ALL RIGHT, I GET IT ALREADY!
OWWWW
I APOLOGIZED, DIDN'T I?!
クソッ!
うぜェ
THAT'S WHY I EVEN MADE YOU DINNER!
WHAT A DRAMA QUEEN!
AND NOW YOU GOTTA FEED IT TO ME.

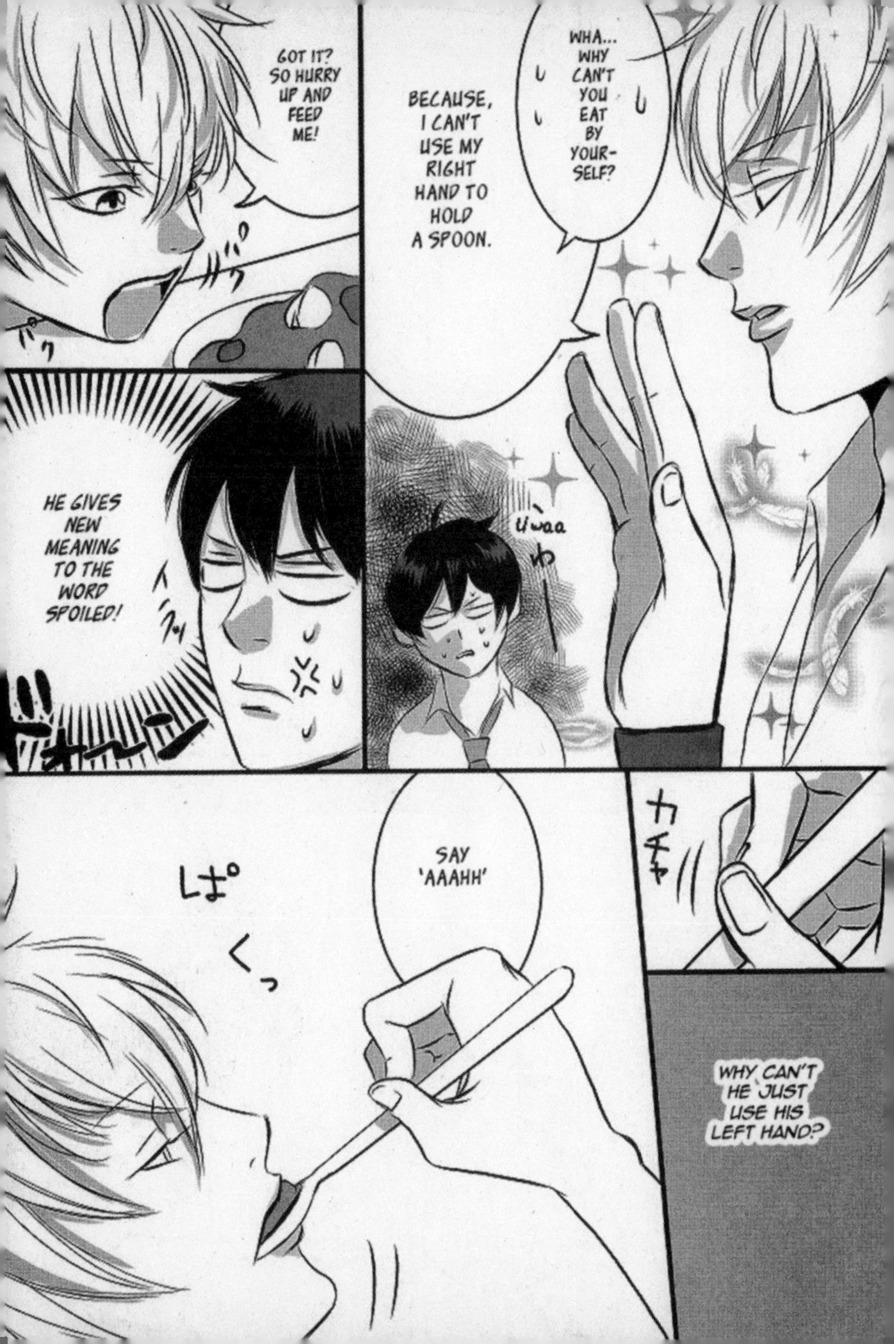
WHA... WHY CAN'T YOU EAT BY YOUR-SELF?
BECAUSE, I CAN'T USE MY RIGHT HAND TO HOLD A SPOON.
uwaa
GOT IT? SO HURRY UP AND FEED ME!
HE GIVES NEW MEANING TO THE WORD SPOILED!
カチャ
WHY CAN'T HE JUST USE HIS LEFT HAND?
SAY 'AAAHH'

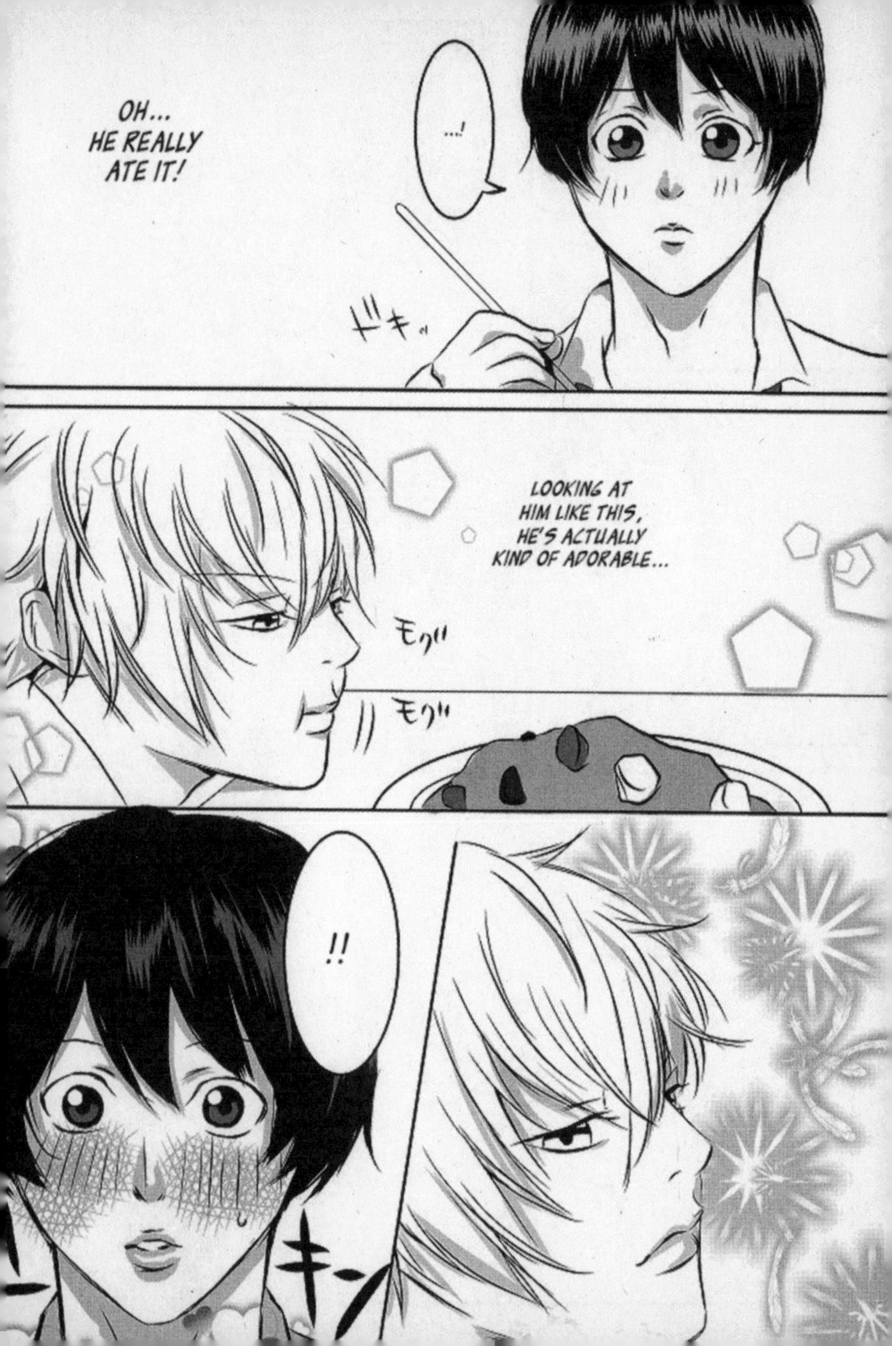

...!
OH... HE REALLY ATE IT!
ドキッ
LOOKING AT HIM LIKE THIS, HE'S ACTUALLY KIND OF ADORABLE...
モグッ
モグッ
!!
キー

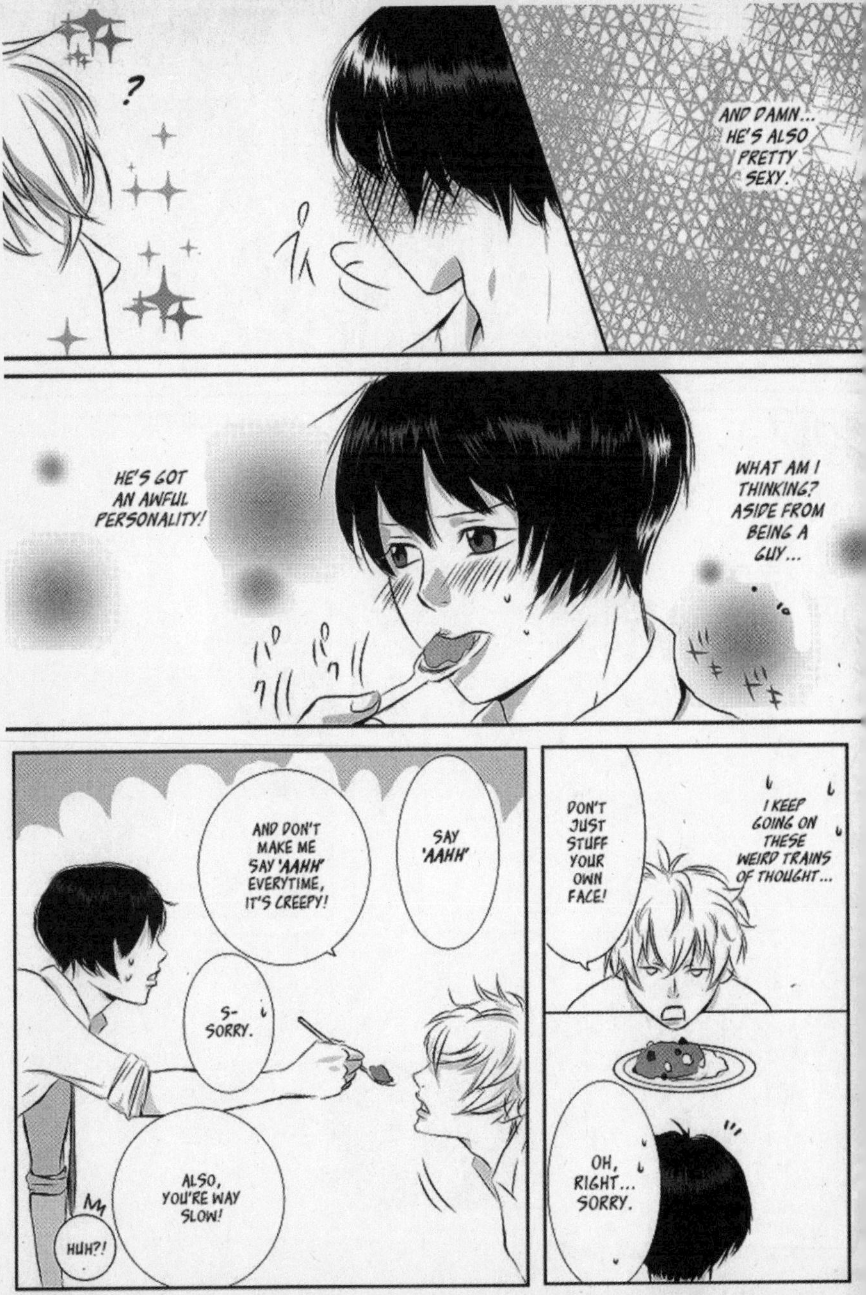
AND DAMN... HE'S ALSO PRETTY SEXY.
WHAT AM I THINKING? ASIDE FROM BEING A GUY...
HE'S GOT AN AWFUL PERSONALITY!
I KEEP GOING ON THESE WEIRD TRAINS OF THOUGHT...
DON'T JUST STUFF YOUR OWN FACE!
OH, RIGHT... SORRY.
SAY 'AAHH'
AND DON'T MAKE ME SAY 'AAHH' EVERYTIME, IT'S CREEPY!
S-SORRY.
ALSO, YOU'RE WAY SLOW!
HUH?!

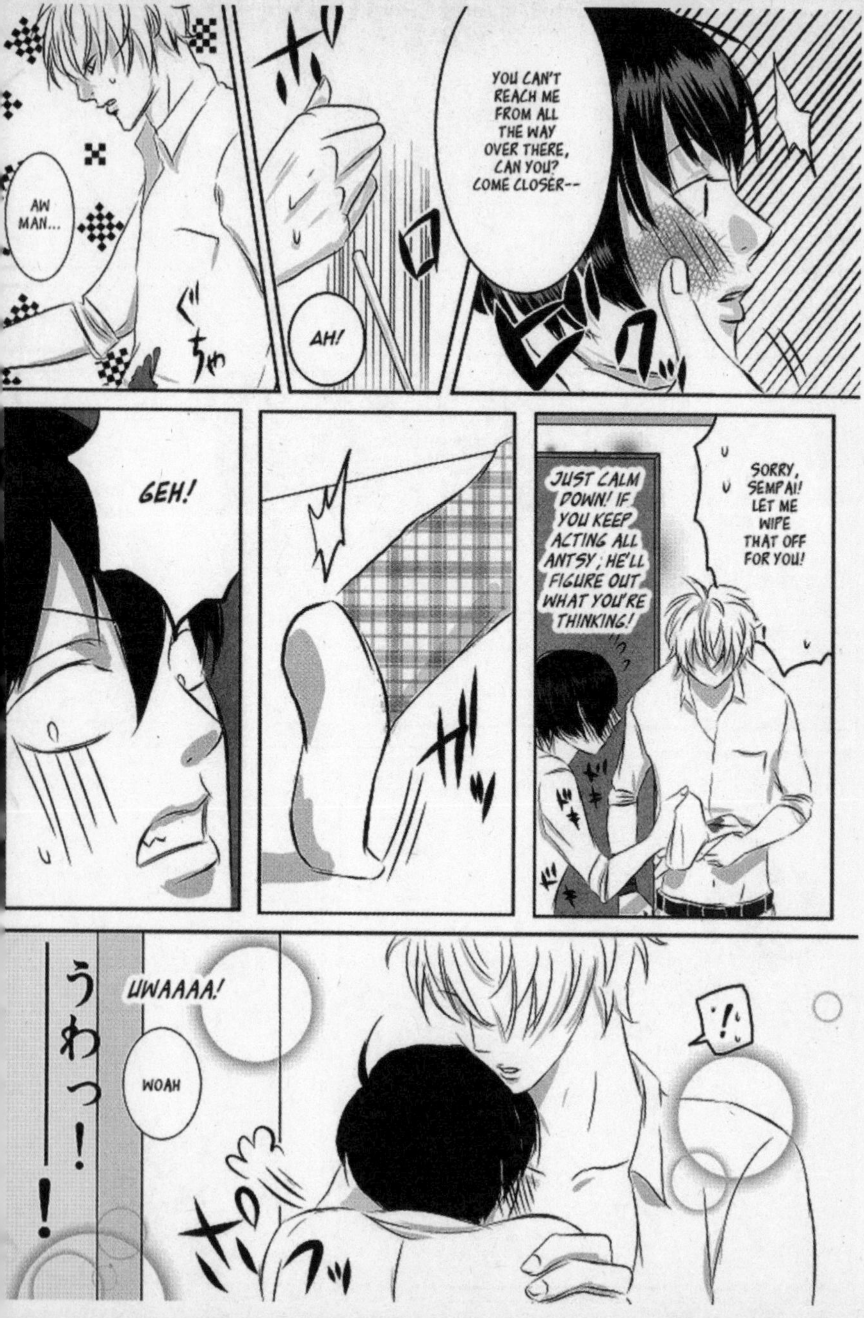

YOU CAN'T REACH ME FROM ALL THE WAY OVER THERE, CAN YOU? COME CLOSER--
AH!
AW MAN...
ぐちゃ
SORRY, SEMPAI! LET ME WIPE THAT OFF FOR YOU!
JUST CALM DOWN! IF YOU KEEP ACTING ALL ANTSY; HE'LL FIGURE OUT WHAT YOU'RE THINKING!
GEH!
!?
UWAAAA!
WOAH
うわっ!!—!

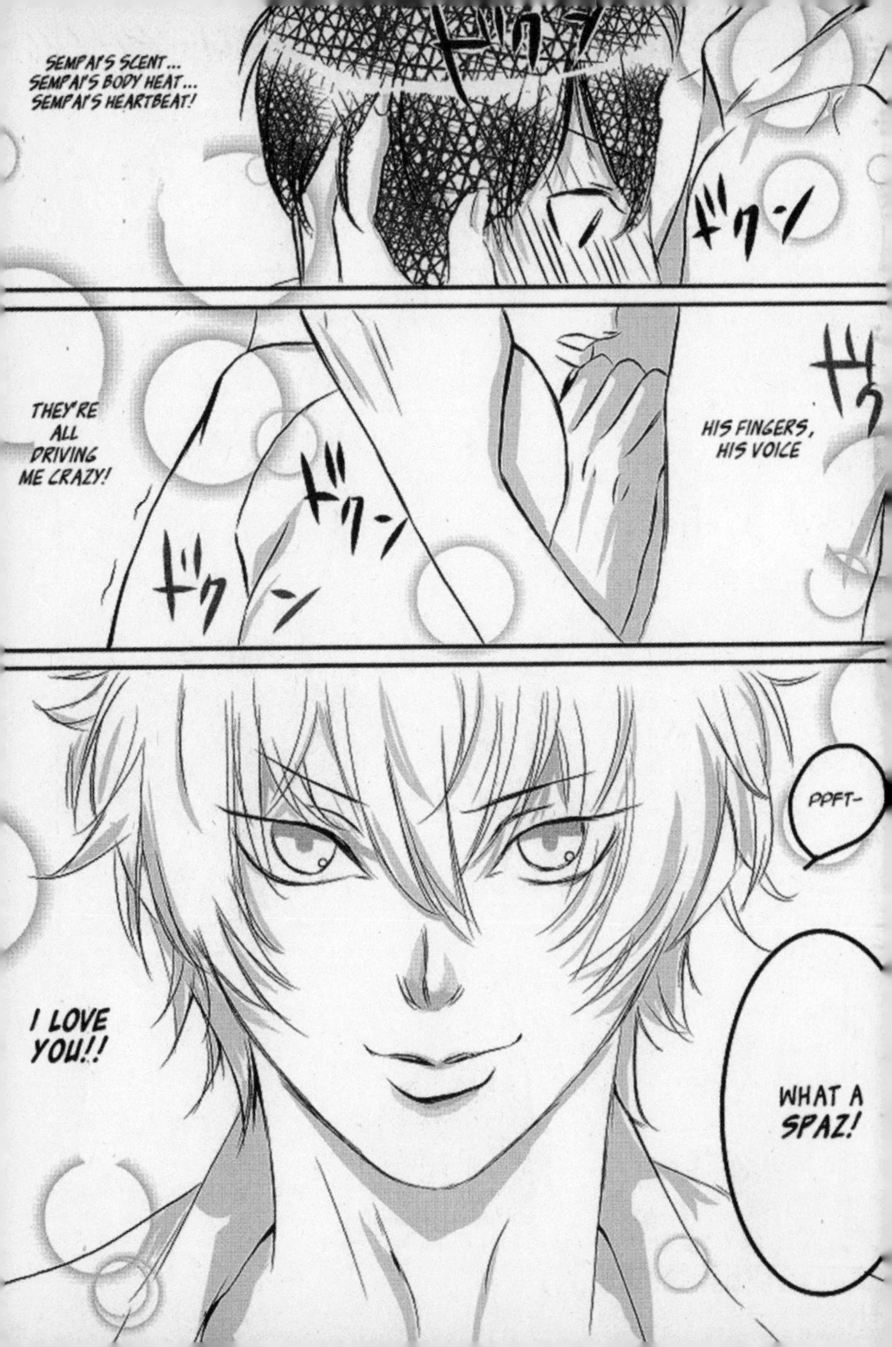
SEMPAI'S SCENT...
SEMPAI'S BODY HEAT...
SEMPAI'S HEARTBEAT!
ドクン
HIS FINGERS, HIS VOICE
THEY'RE ALL DRIVING ME CRAZY!
ドクン
ドクン
PPFT-
WHAT A SPAZ!
I LOVE YOU!!

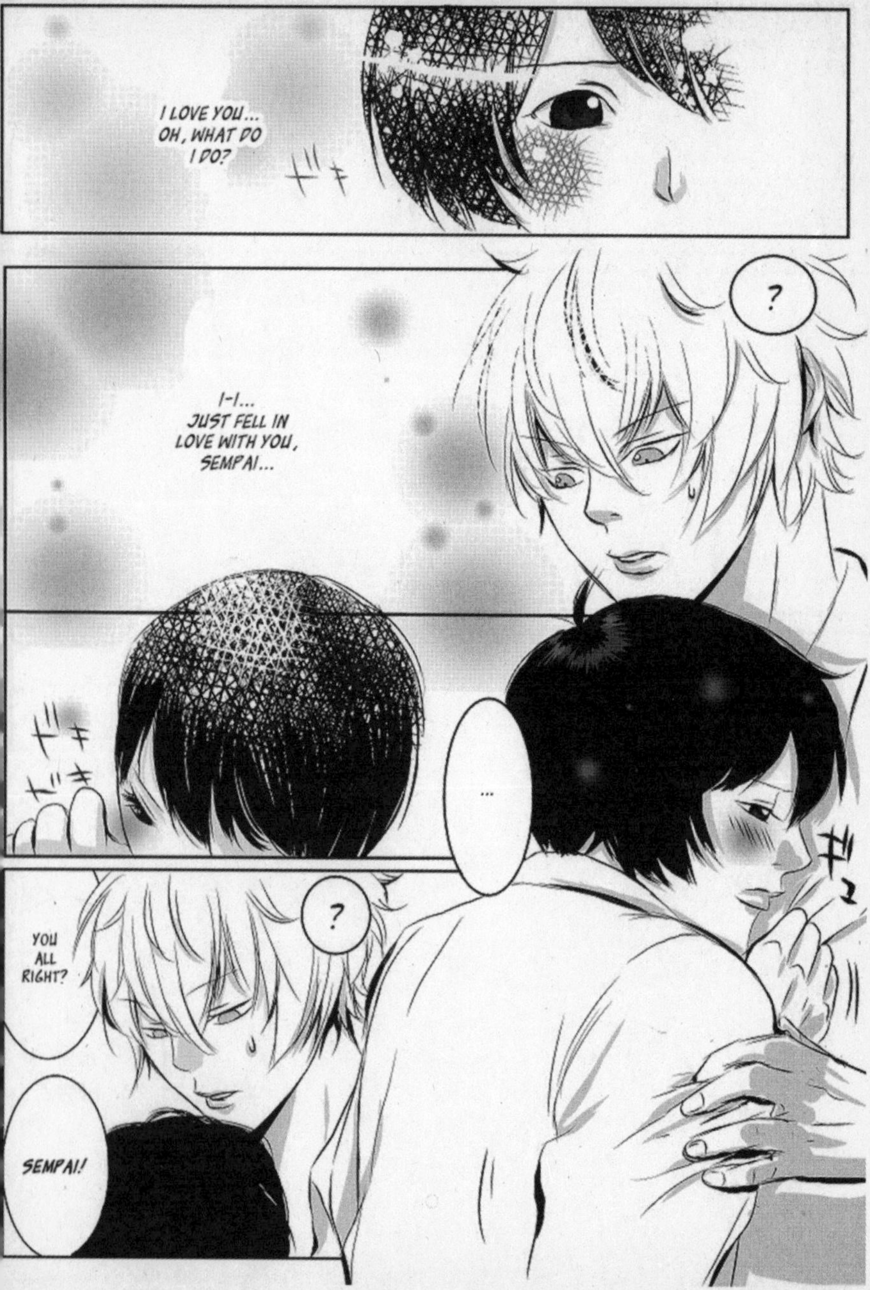
I LOVE YOU... OH, WHAT DO I DO?
?
I-I... JUST FELL IN LOVE WITH YOU, SEMPAI...
...
?
YOU ALL RIGHT?
SEMPAI!

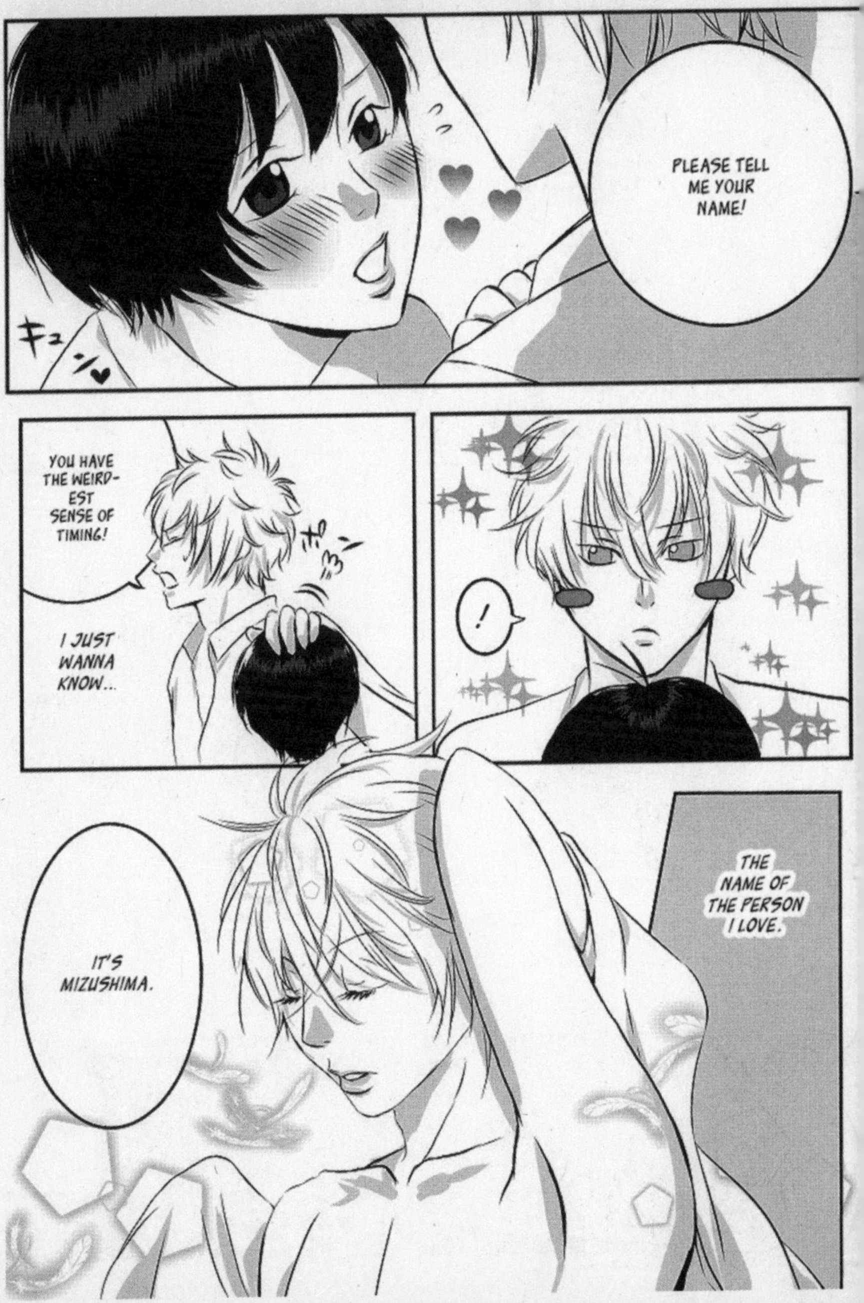
PLEASE TELL ME YOUR NAME!
キュン♥
!
YOU HAVE THE WEIRD-EST SENSE OF TIMING!
I JUST WANNA KNOW...
THE NAME OF THE PERSON I LOVE.
IT'S MIZUSHIMA.

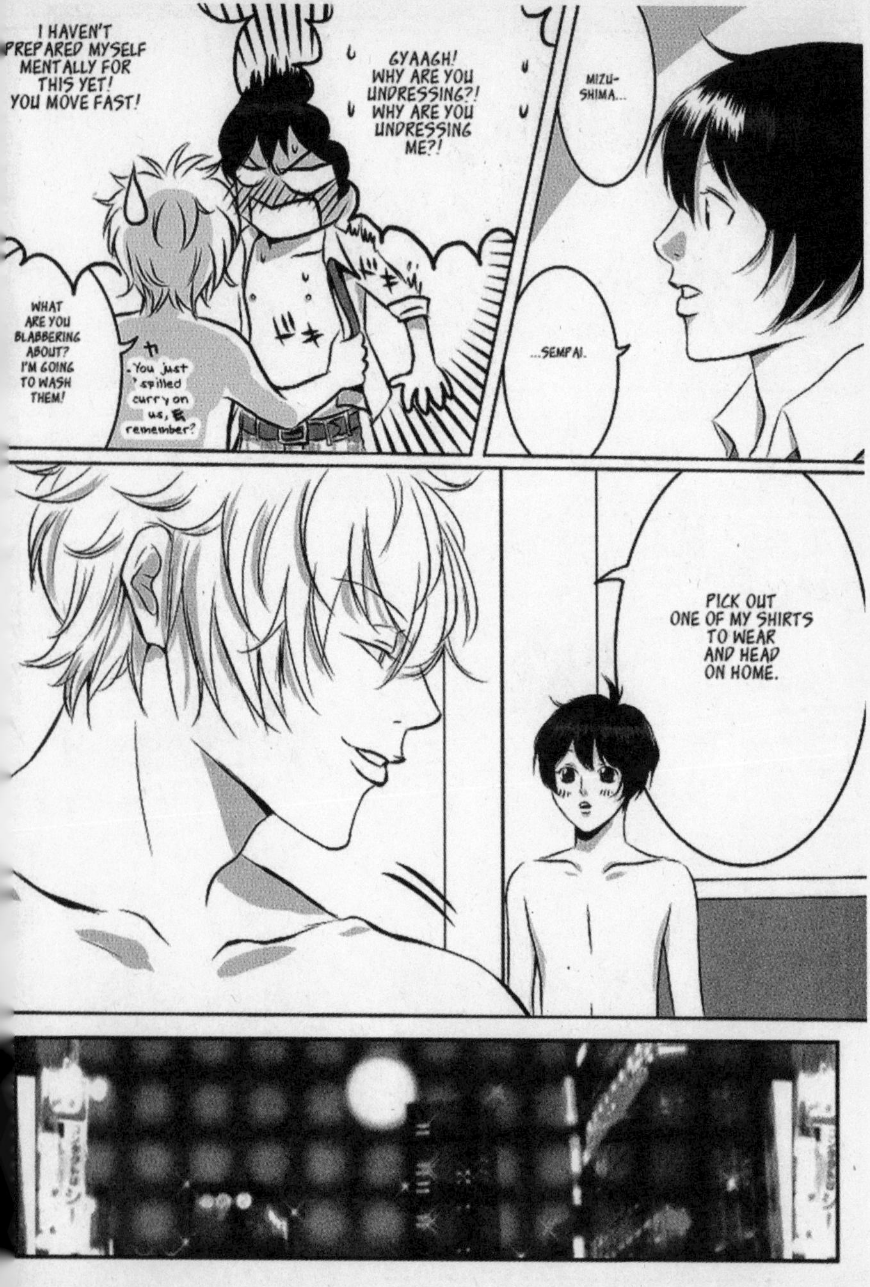
MIZU-SHIMA...
...SEMPAI.
GYAAGH! WHY ARE YOU UNDRESSING?! WHY ARE YOU UNDRESSING ME?!
I HAVEN'T PREPARED MYSELF MENTALLY FOR THIS YET! YOU MOVE FAST!
WHAT ARE YOU BLABBERING ABOUT? I'M GOING TO WASH THEM!
You just spilled curry on us, remember?
PICK OUT ONE OF MY SHIRTS TO WEAR AND HEAD ON HOME.

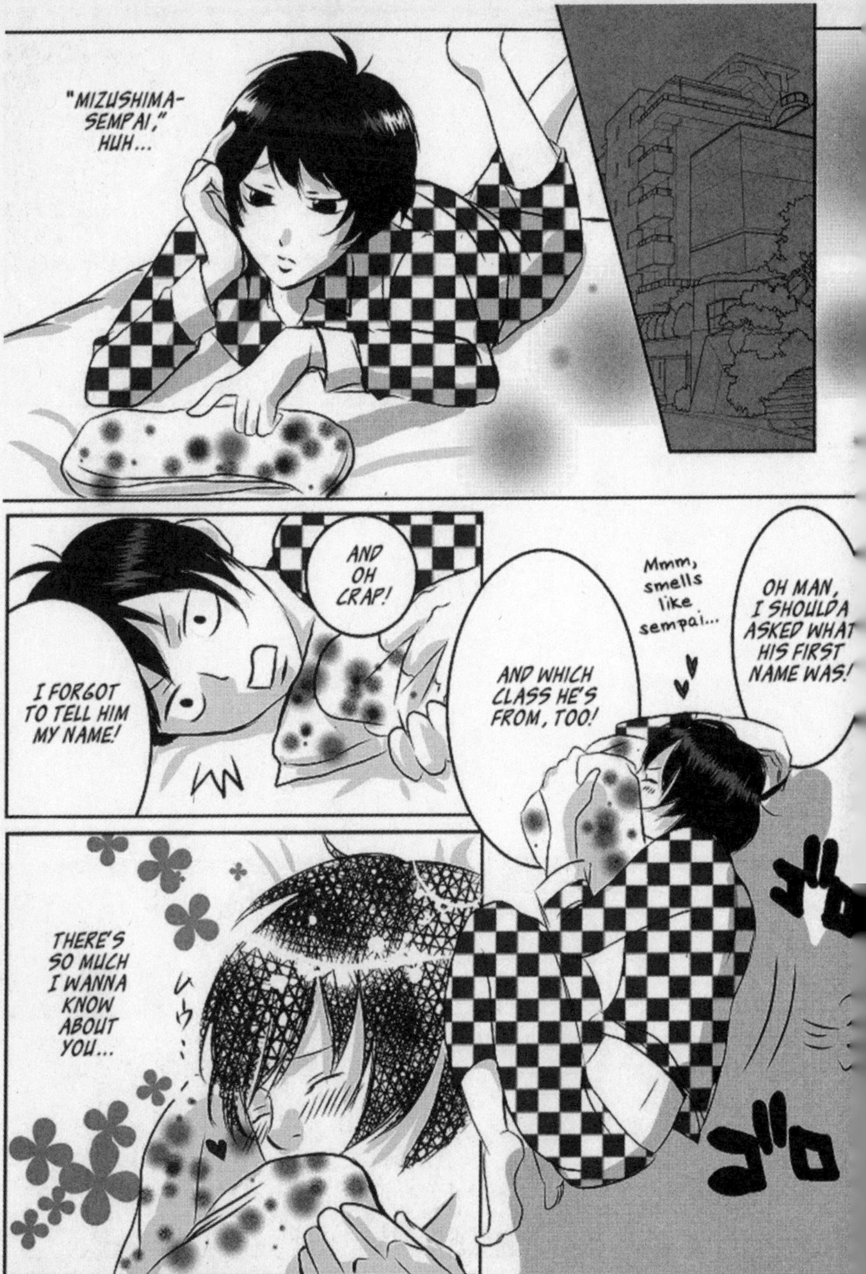
"MIZUSHIMA-SEMPAI," HUH...
OH MAN, I SHOULDA ASKED WHAT HIS FIRST NAME WAS!
Mmm, smells like sempai...
AND WHICH CLASS HE'S FROM, TOO!
ゴロ
ゴロ
AND OH CRAP!
I FORGOT TO TELL HIM MY NAME!
THERE'S SO MUCH I WANNA KNOW ABOUT YOU...

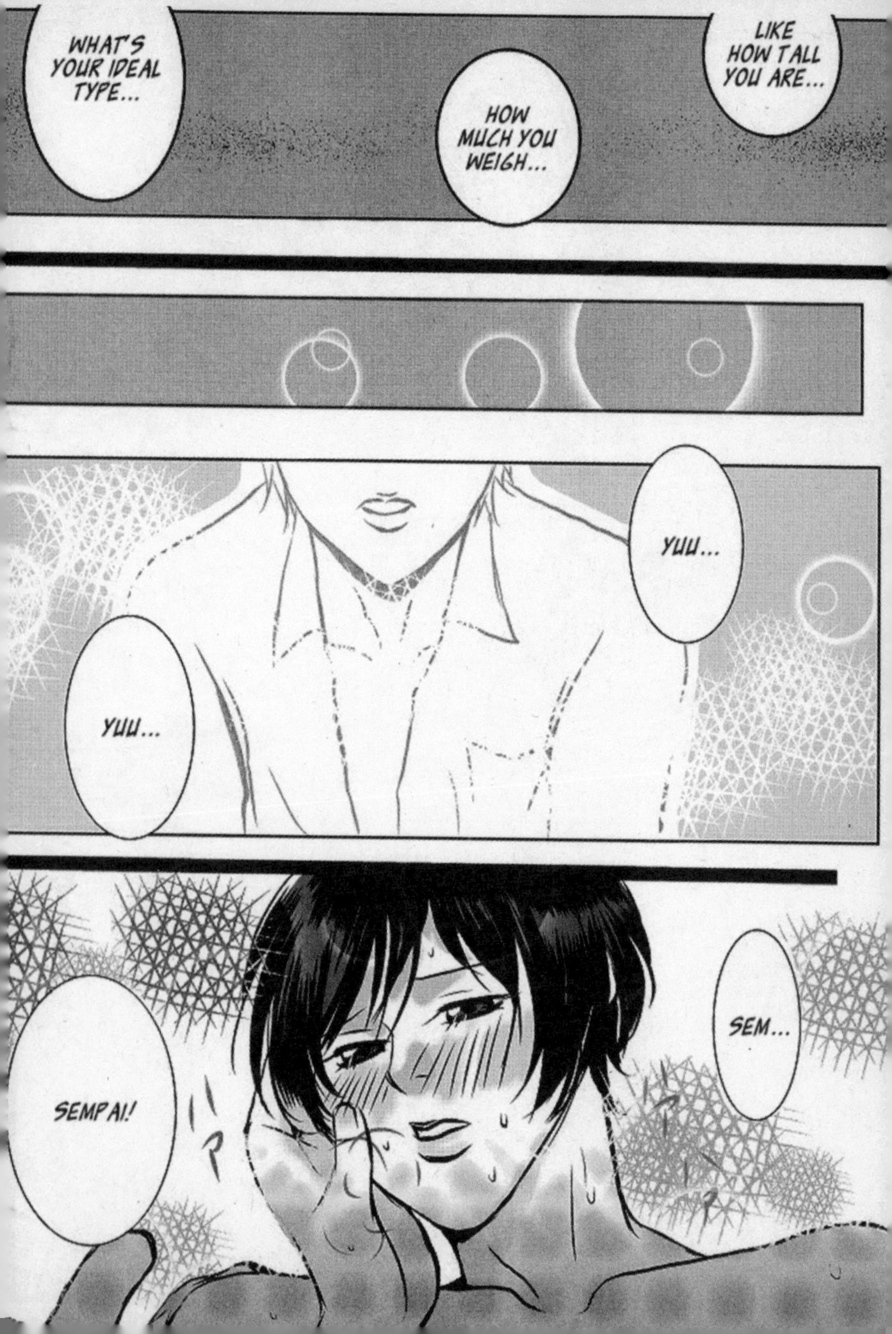
LIKE HOW TALL YOU ARE...
HOW MUCH YOU WEIGH...
WHAT'S YOUR IDEAL TYPE...
YUU...
YUU...
SEM...
SEMPAI!

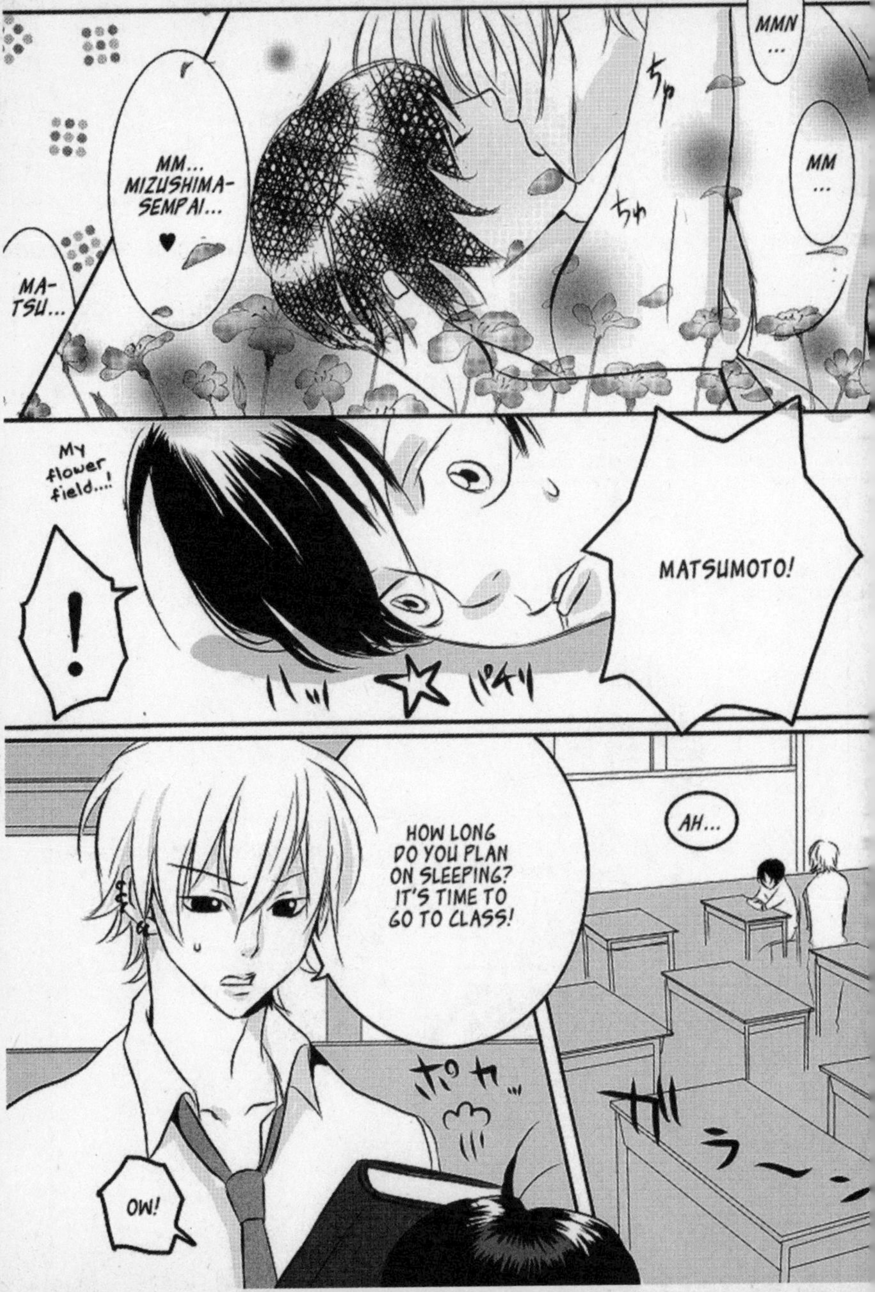
MMN ...
ちゅ
MM ...
ちゅ
MM... MIZUSHIMA-SEMPAI... ♥
MA-TSU...
MATSUMOTO!
パチリ
ハッ
!
My flower field...!
AH...
HOW LONG DO YOU PLAN ON SLEEPING? IT'S TIME TO GO TO CLASS!
OW!

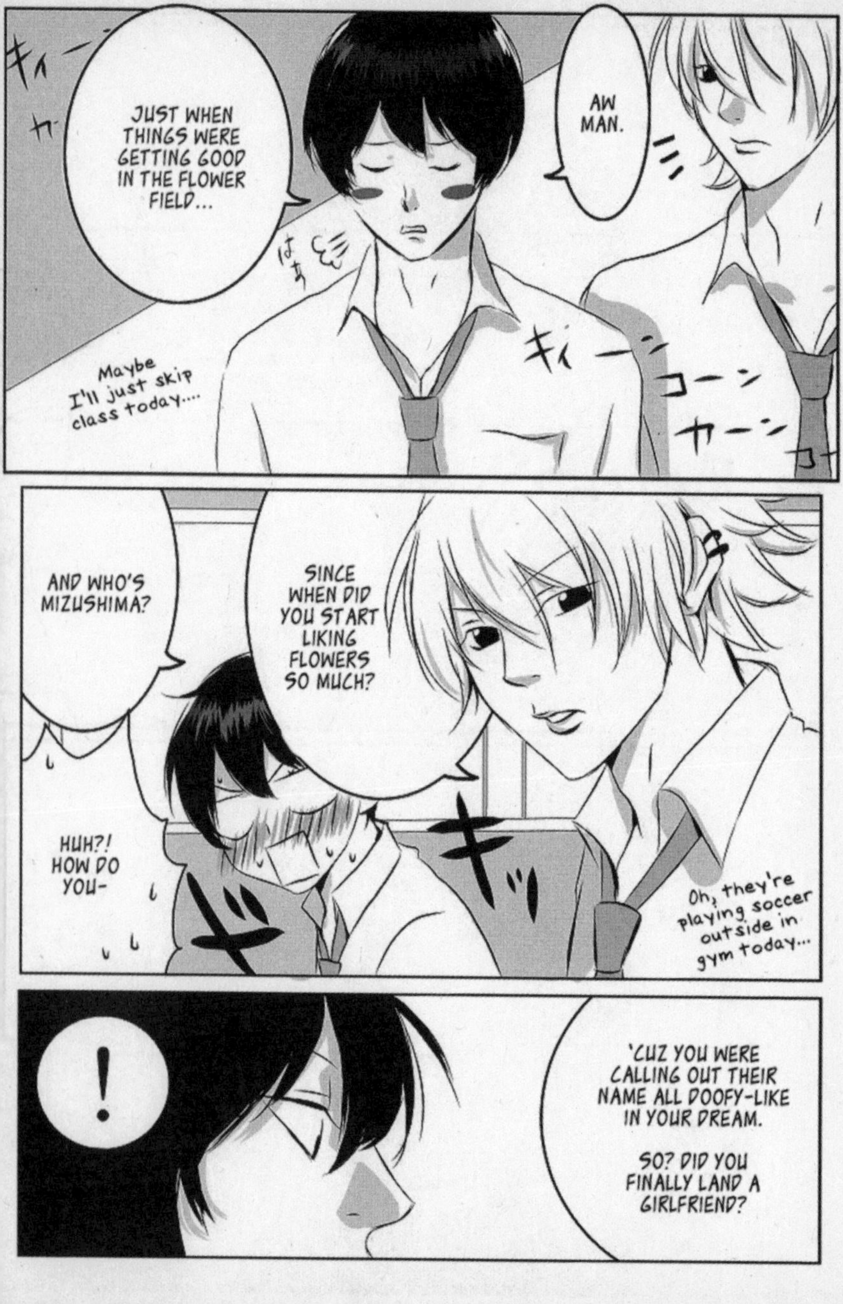
AW MAN.
JUST WHEN THINGS WERE GETTING GOOD IN THE FLOWER FIELD...
Maybe I'll just skip class today....
SINCE WHEN DID YOU START LIKING FLOWERS SO MUCH?
AND WHO'S MIZUSHIMA?
Oh, they're playing soccer outside in gym today...
HUH?! HOW DO YOU-
'CUZ YOU WERE CALLING OUT THEIR NAME ALL DOOFY-LIKE IN YOUR DREAM.
SO? DID YOU FINALLY LAND A GIRLFRIEND?
!

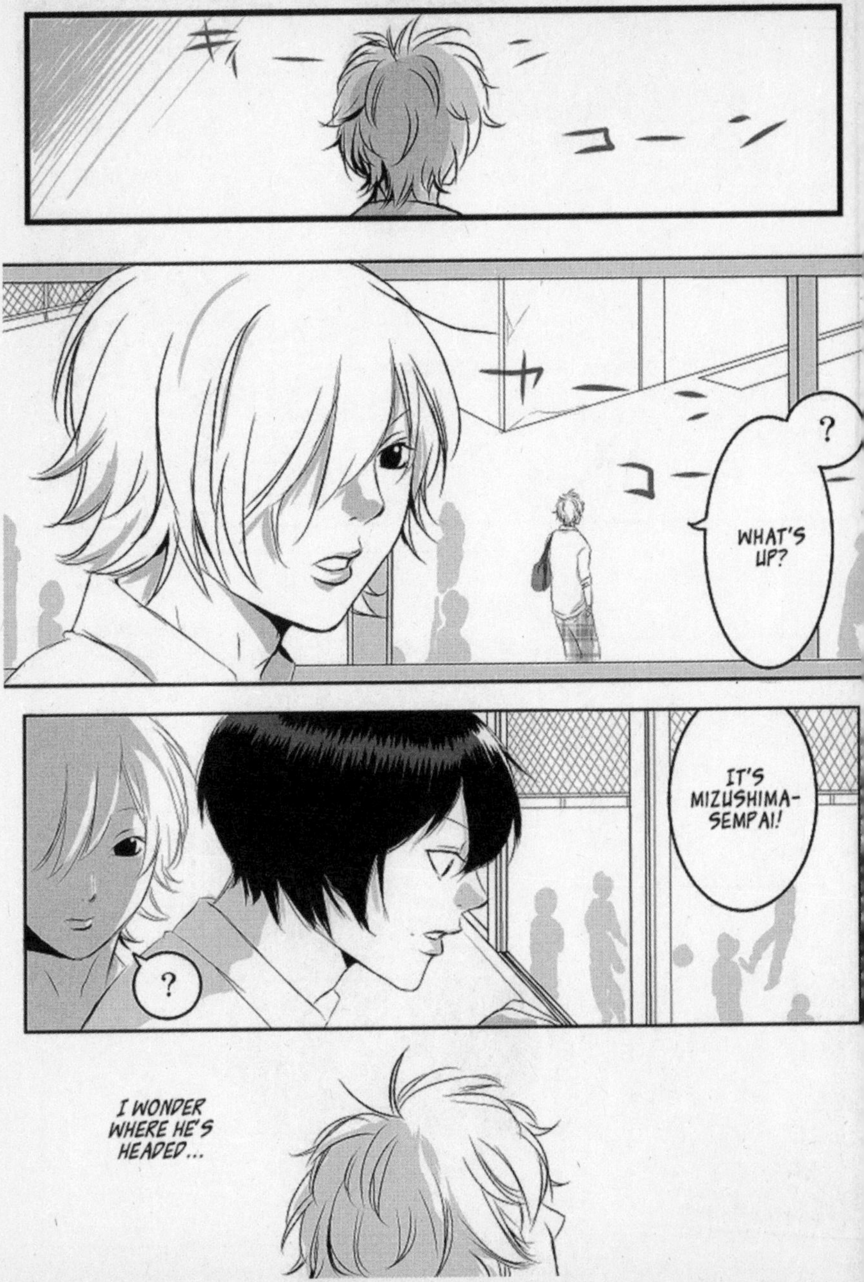
?
WHAT'S UP?
IT'S MIZUSHIMA-SEMPAI!
?
I WONDER WHERE HE'S HEADED...

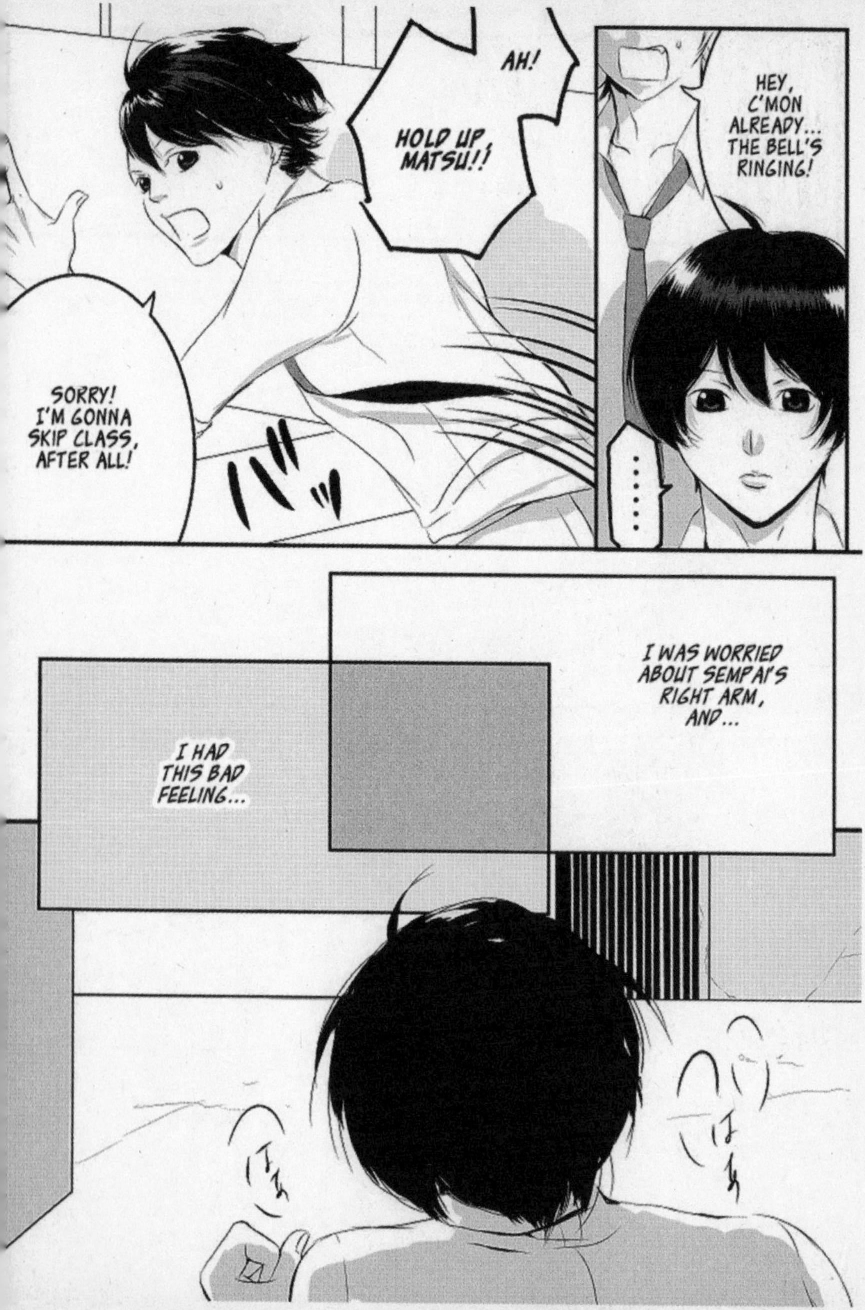
HEY, C'MON ALREADY... THE BELL'S RINGING!
......
AH!
HOLD UP, MATSU!!
SORRY! I'M GONNA SKIP CLASS, AFTER ALL!
I WAS WORRIED ABOUT SEMPAI'S RIGHT ARM, AND...
I HAD THIS BAD FEELING...

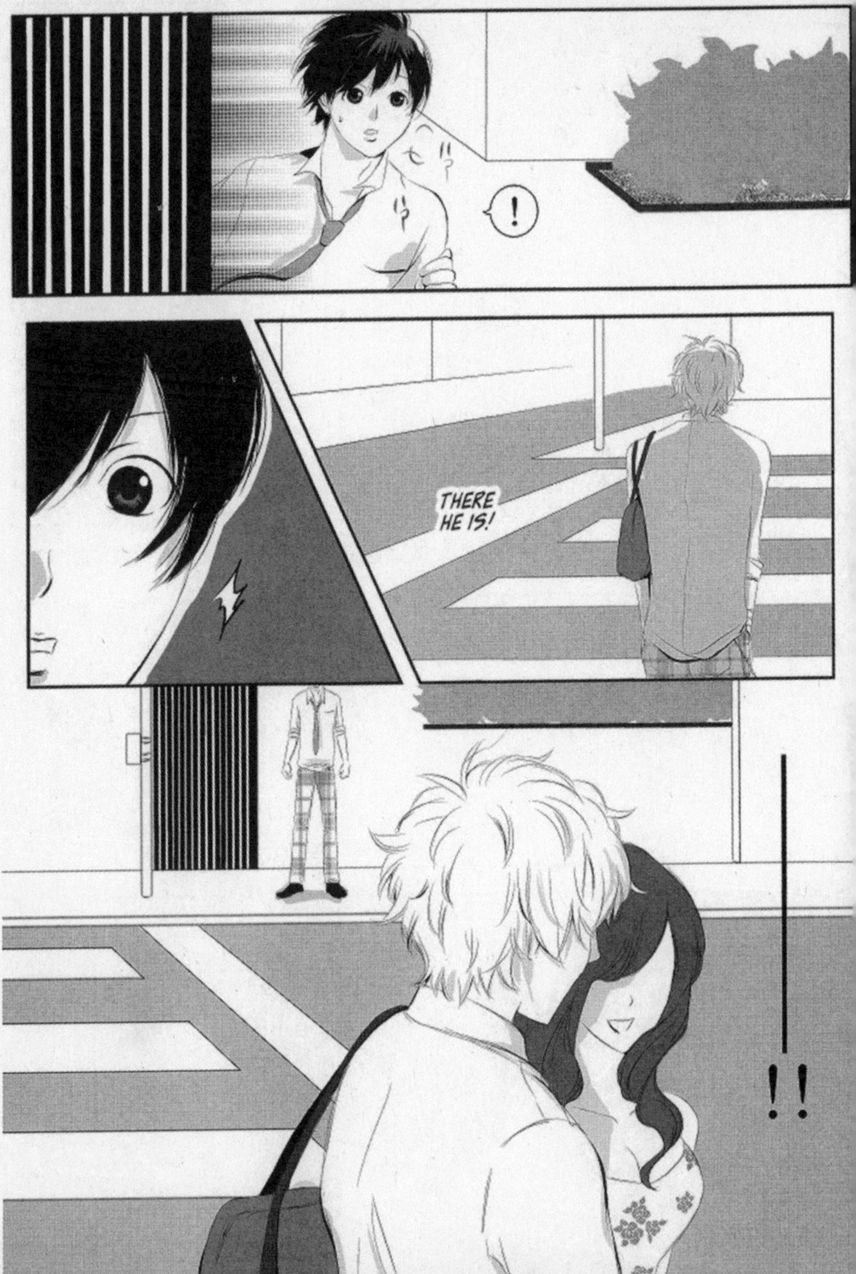
!
THERE HE IS!
!!

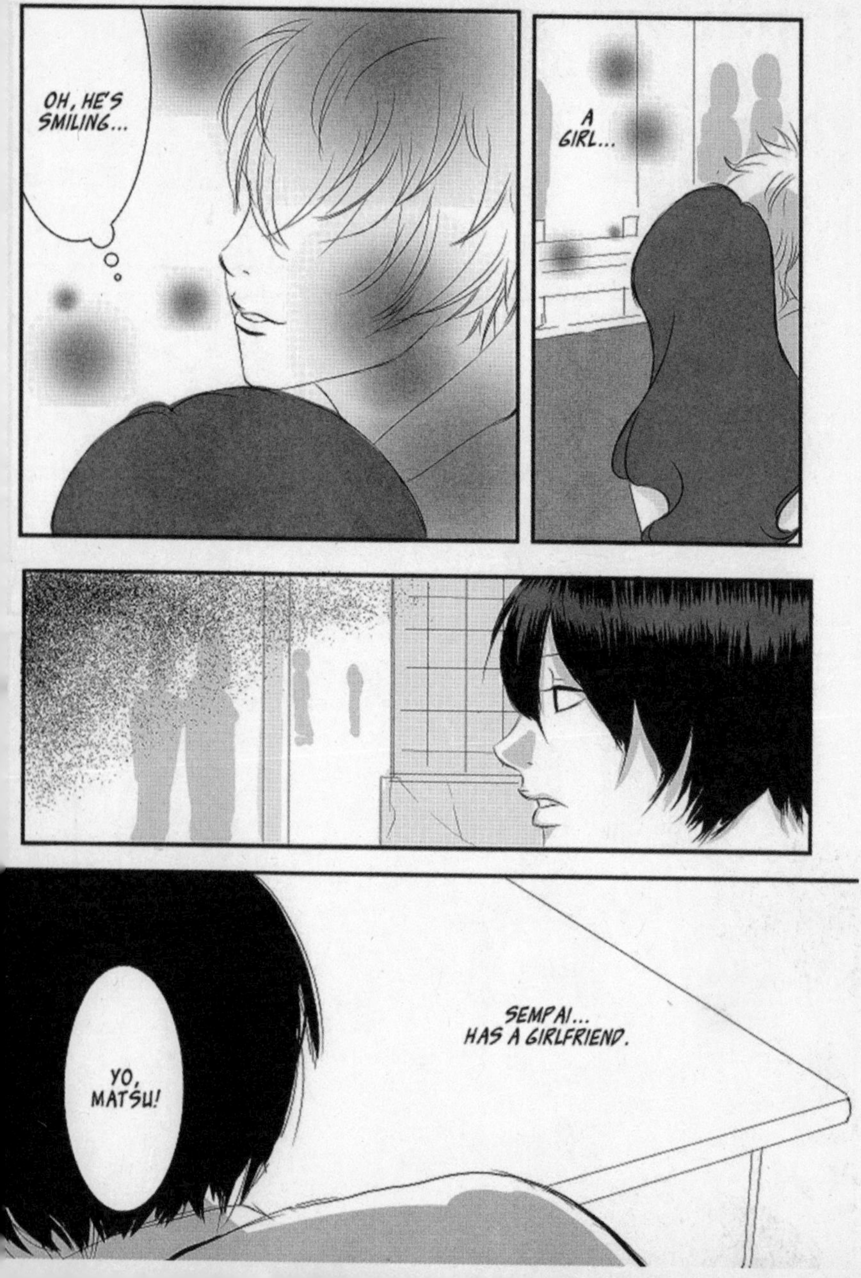
A GIRL...
OH, HE'S SMILING...
SEMPAI... HAS A GIRLFRIEND.
YO, MATSU!

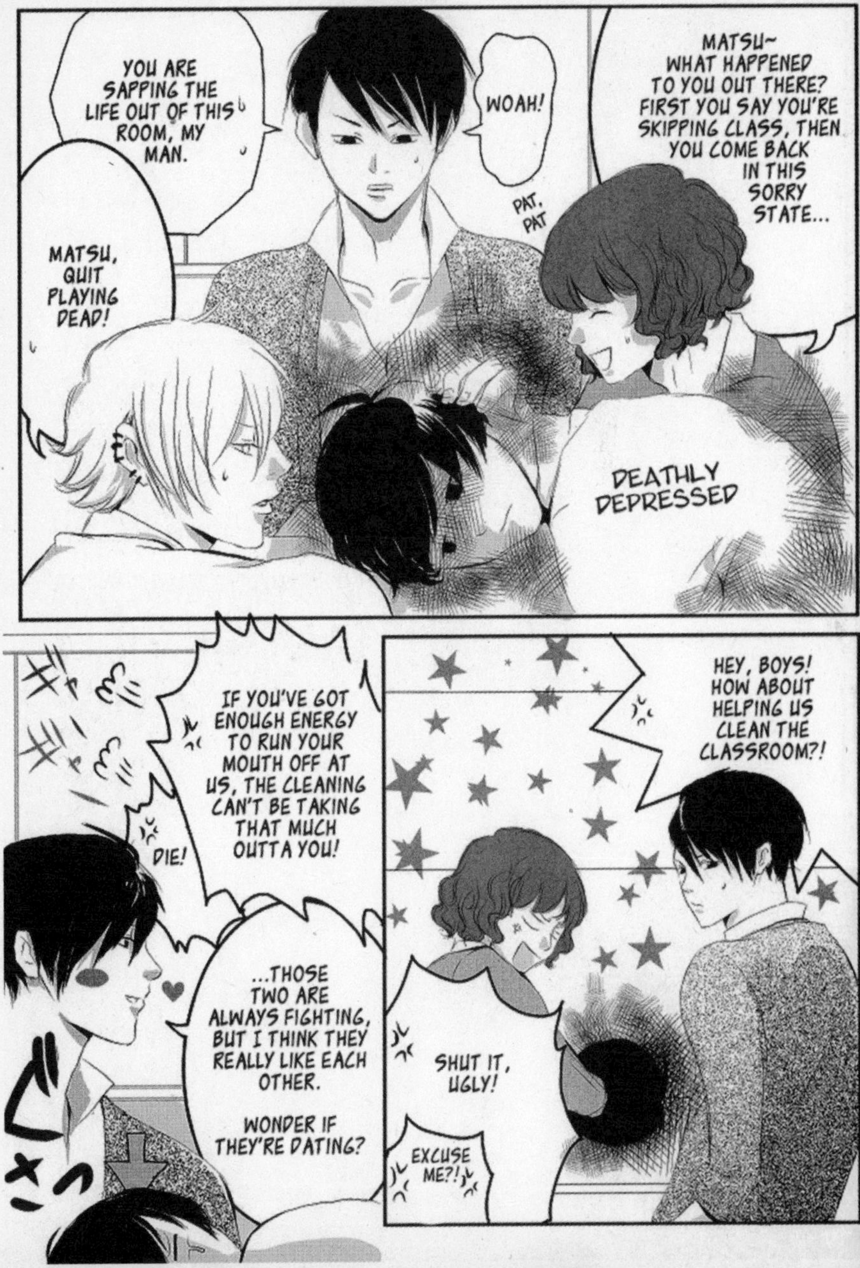
MATSU~ WHAT HAPPENED TO YOU OUT THERE? FIRST YOU SAY YOU'RE SKIPPING CLASS, THEN YOU COME BACK IN THIS SORRY STATE...
PAT, PAT
WOAH!
YOU ARE SAPPING THE LIFE OUT OF THIS ROOM, MY MAN.
DEATHLY DEPRESSED
MATSU, QUIT PLAYING DEAD!
HEY, BOYS! HOW ABOUT HELPING US CLEAN THE CLASSROOM?!
SHUT IT, UGLY!
EXCUSE ME?!
IF YOU'VE GOT ENOUGH ENERGY TO RUN YOUR MOUTH OFF AT US, THE CLEANING CAN'T BE TAKING THAT MUCH OUTTA YOU!
DIE!
...THOSE TWO ARE ALWAYS FIGHTING, BUT I THINK THEY REALLY LIKE EACH OTHER.
WONDER IF THEY'RE DATING?

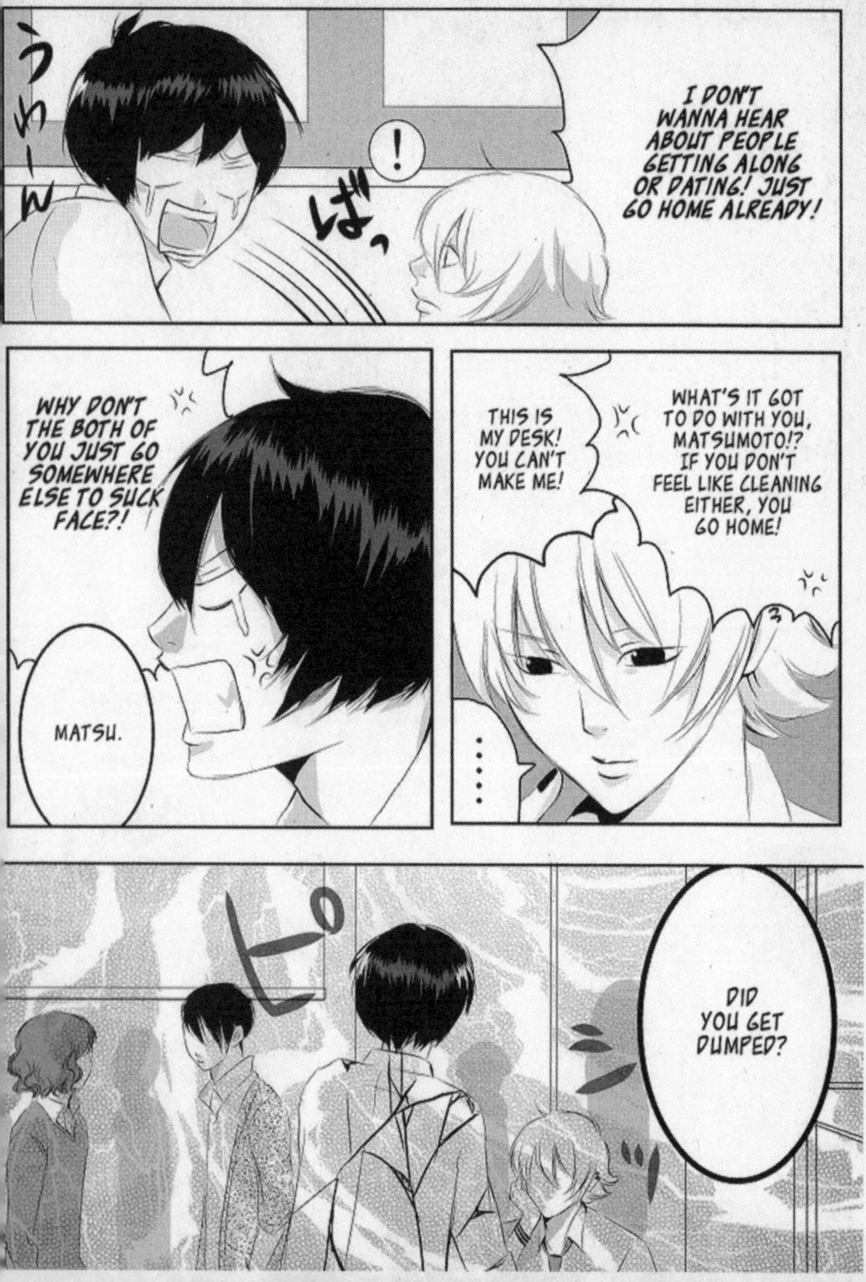

I DON'T WANNA HEAR ABOUT PEOPLE GETTING ALONG OR DATING! JUST GO HOME ALREADY!
!
ばっ
うわーん
WHAT'S IT GOT TO DO WITH YOU, MATSUMOTO!? IF YOU DON'T FEEL LIKE CLEANING EITHER, YOU GO HOME!
THIS IS MY DESK! YOU CAN'T MAKE ME!
......
WHY DON'T THE BOTH OF YOU JUST GO SOMEWHERE ELSE TO SUCK FACE?!
MATSU.
DID YOU GET DUMPED?
ピ

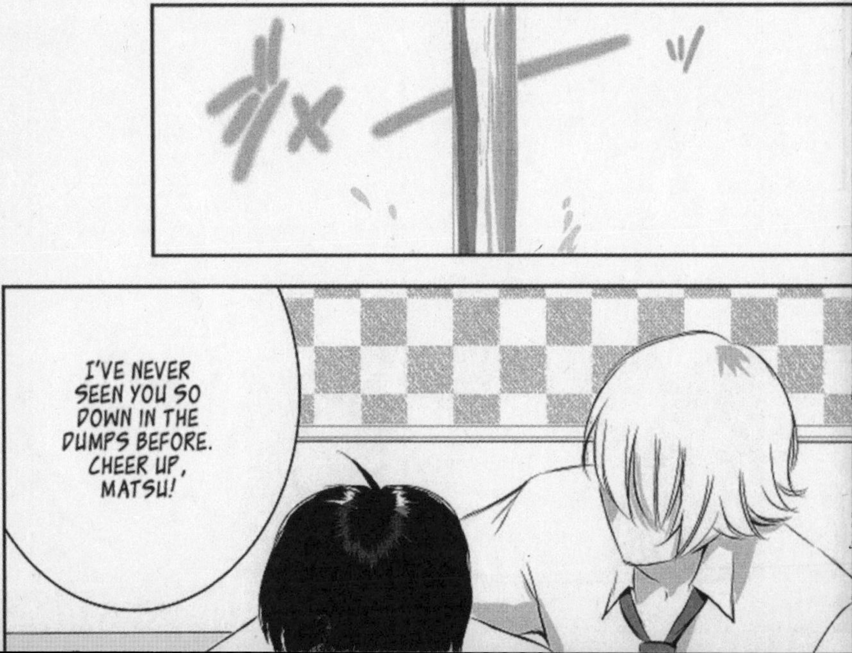
I'VE NEVER SEEN YOU SO DOWN IN THE DUMPS BEFORE. CHEER UP, MATSU!

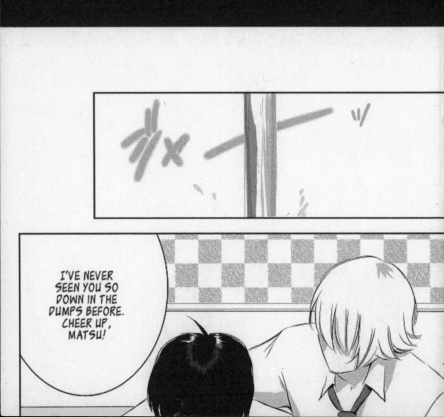

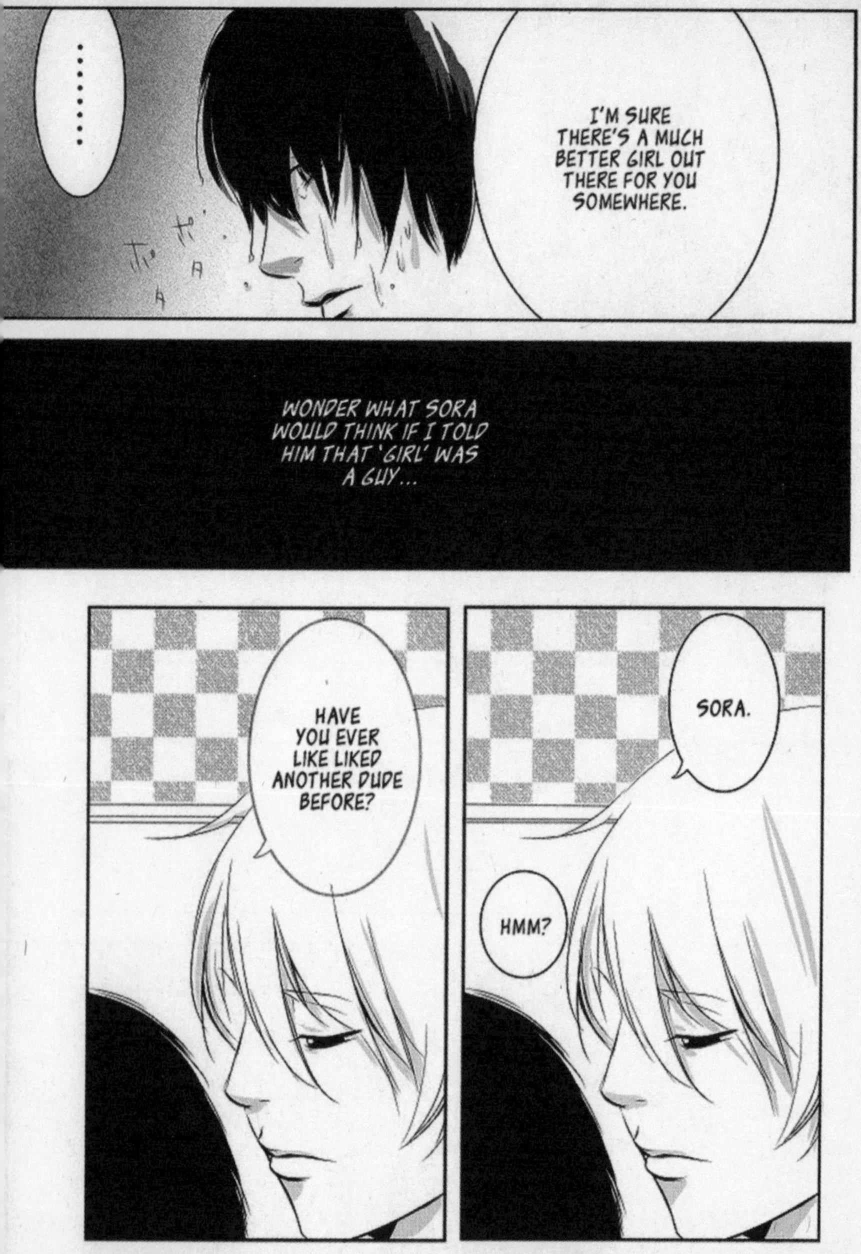
I'M SURE THERE'S A MUCH BETTER GIRL OUT THERE FOR YOU SOMEWHERE.
......
WONDER WHAT SORA WOULD THINK IF I TOLD HIM THAT 'GIRL' WAS A GUY...
SORA.
HMM?
HAVE YOU EVER LIKE LIKED ANOTHER DUDE BEFORE?

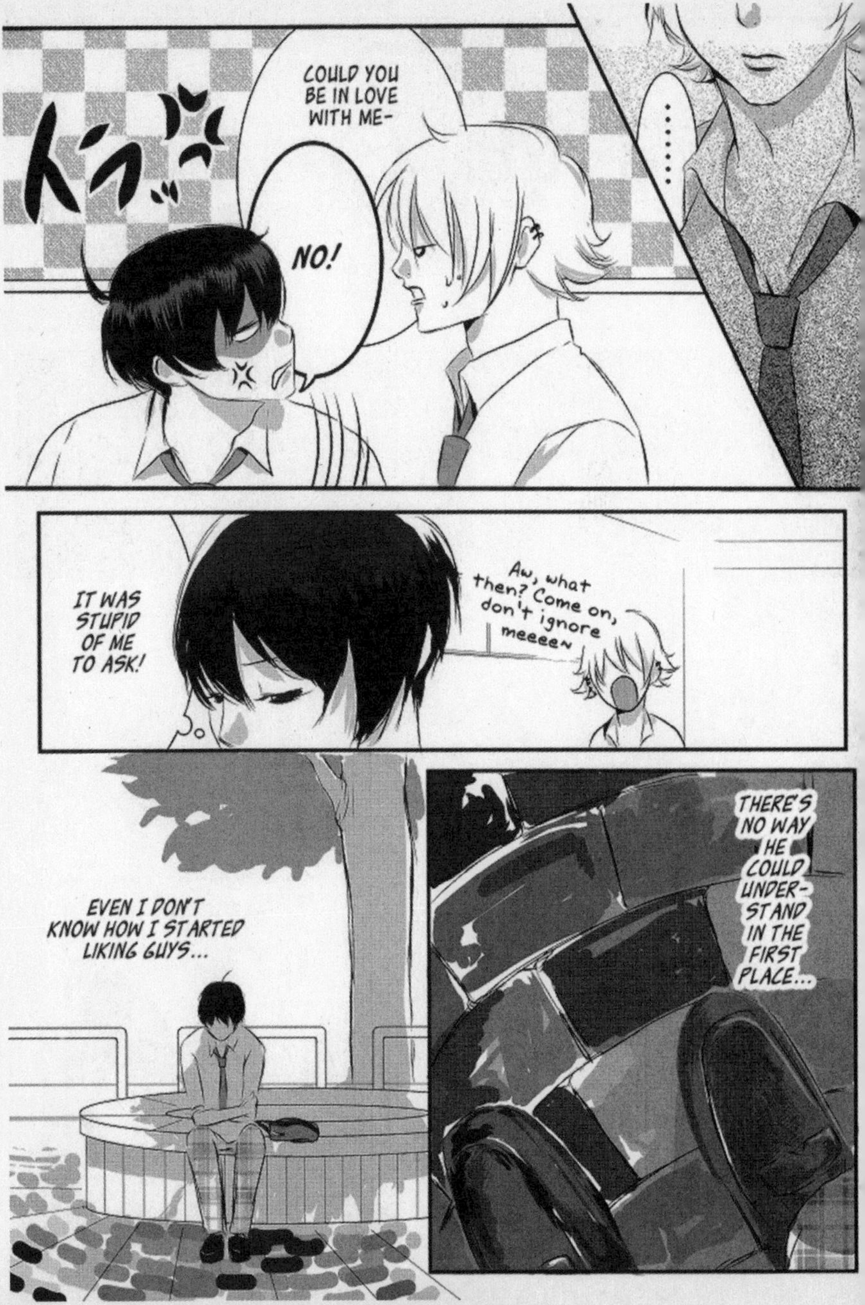
....
COULD YOU BE IN LOVE WITH ME-
NO!
Aw, what then? Come on, don't ignore meeeee~
IT WAS STUPID OF ME TO ASK!
THERE'S NO WAY HE COULD UNDER-STAND IN THE FIRST PLACE...
EVEN I DON'T KNOW HOW I STARTED LIKING GUYS...

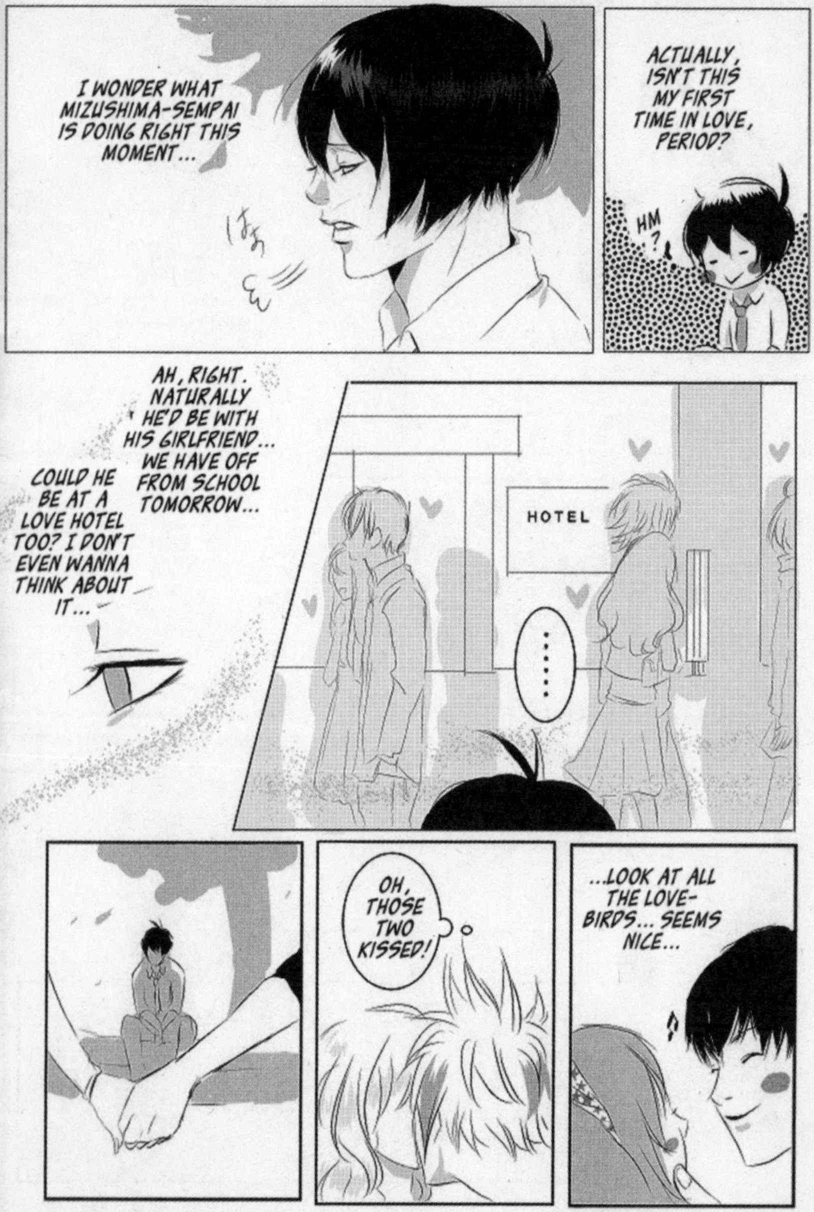
ACTUALLY, ISN'T THIS MY FIRST TIME IN LOVE, PERIOD?
HM ?
I WONDER WHAT MIZUSHIMA-SEMPAI IS DOING RIGHT THIS MOMENT...
HOTEL
......
AH, RIGHT. NATURALLY HE'D BE WITH HIS GIRLFRIEND... WE HAVE OFF FROM SCHOOL TOMORROW...
COULD HE BE AT A LOVE HOTEL TOO? I DON'T EVEN WANNA THINK ABOUT IT...
...LOOK AT ALL THE LOVE-BIRDS... SEEMS NICE...
OH, THOSE TWO KISSED!

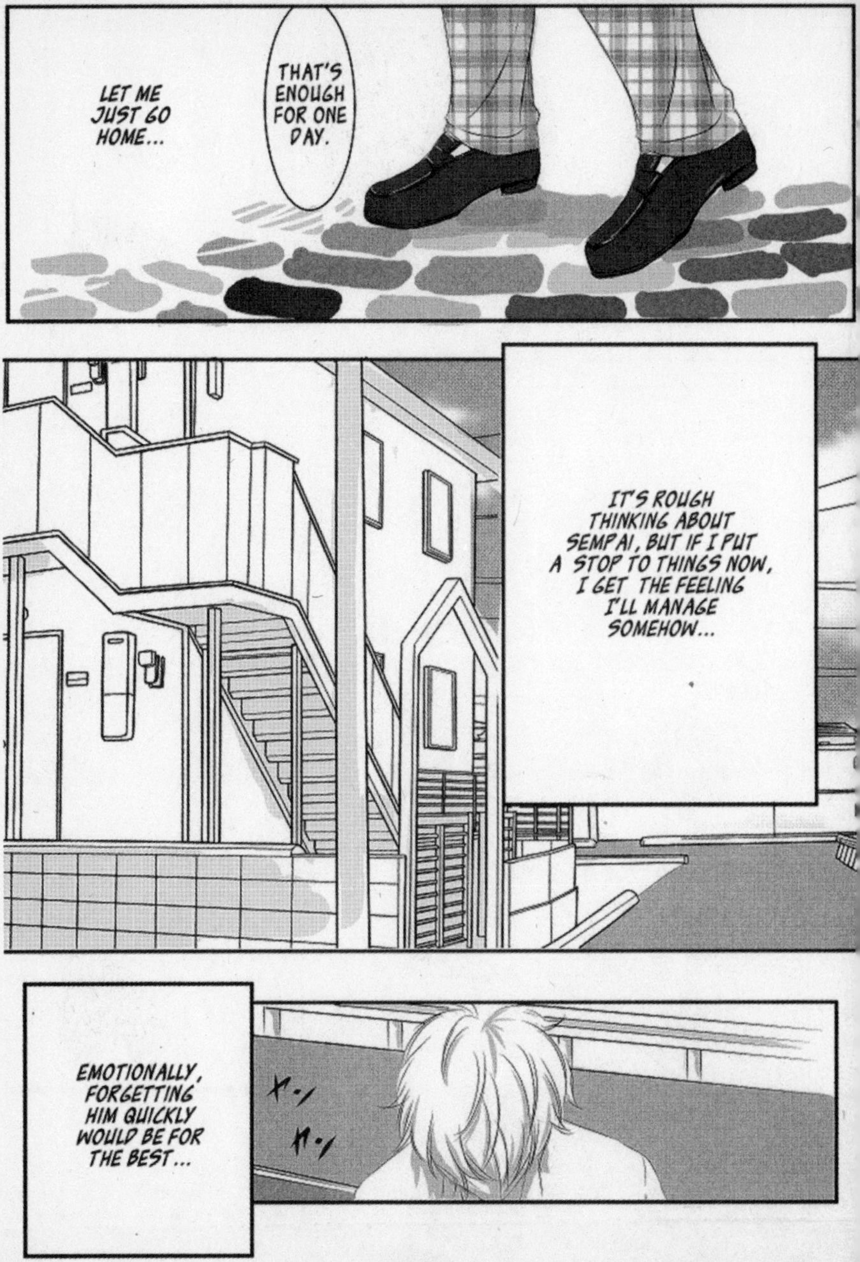
THAT'S ENOUGH FOR ONE DAY.
LET ME JUST GO HOME...
IT'S ROUGH THINKING ABOUT SEMPAI, BUT IF I PUT A STOP TO THINGS NOW, I GET THE FEELING I'LL MANAGE SOMEHOW...
EMOTIONALLY, FORGETTING HIM QUICKLY WOULD BE FOR THE BEST...

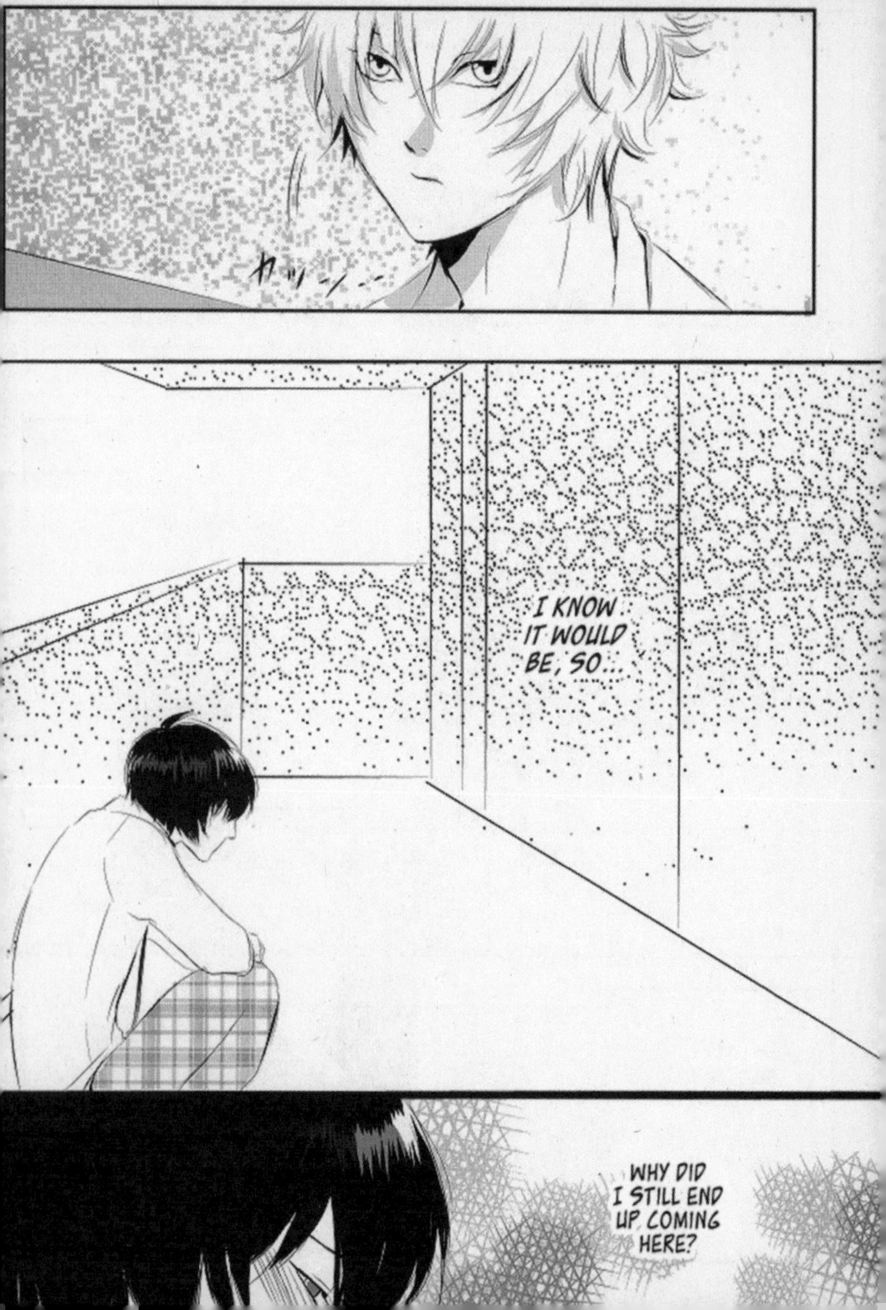
I KNOW IT WOULD BE, SO...
WHY DID I STILL END UP COMING HERE?

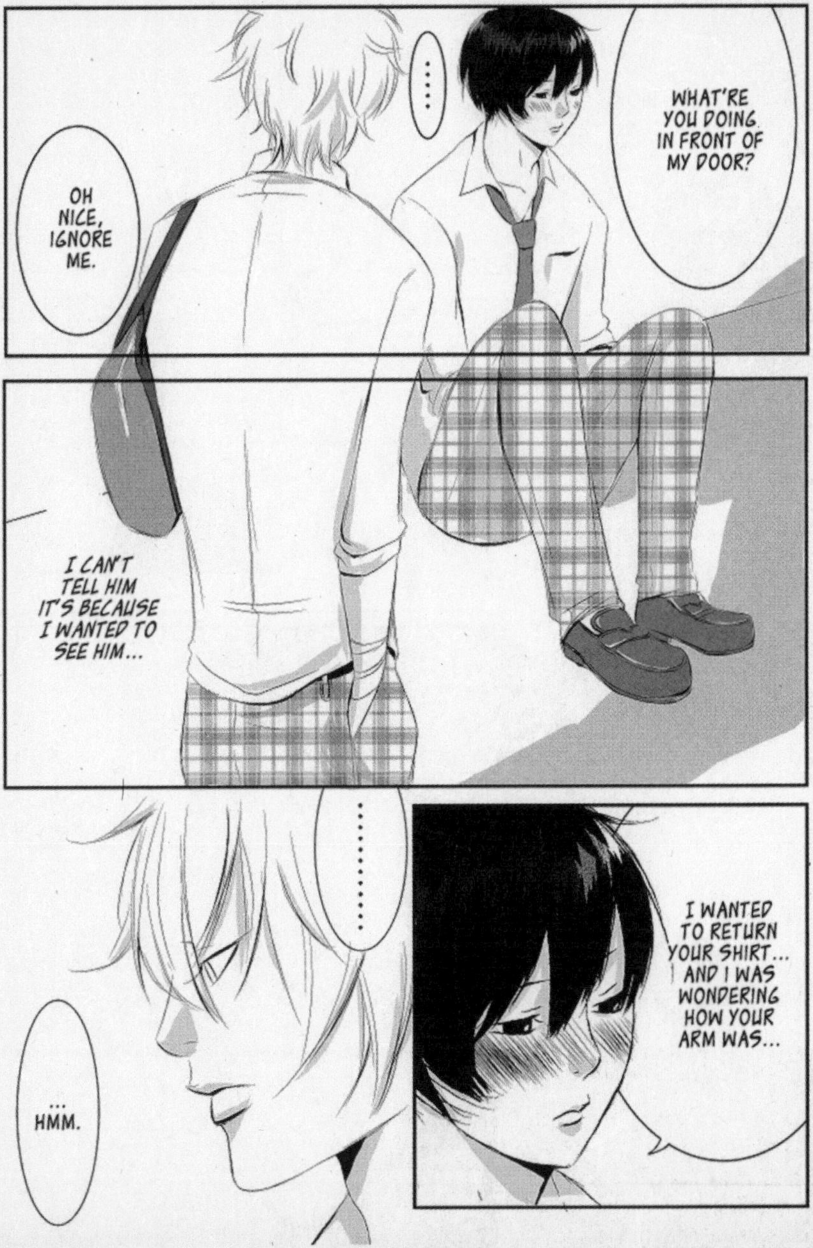
WHAT'RE YOU DOING IN FRONT OF MY DOOR?
......
OH NICE, IGNORE ME.
I CAN'T TELL HIM IT'S BECAUSE I WANTED TO SEE HIM...
I WANTED TO RETURN YOUR SHIRT... AND I WAS WONDERING HOW YOUR ARM WAS...
....
... HMM.

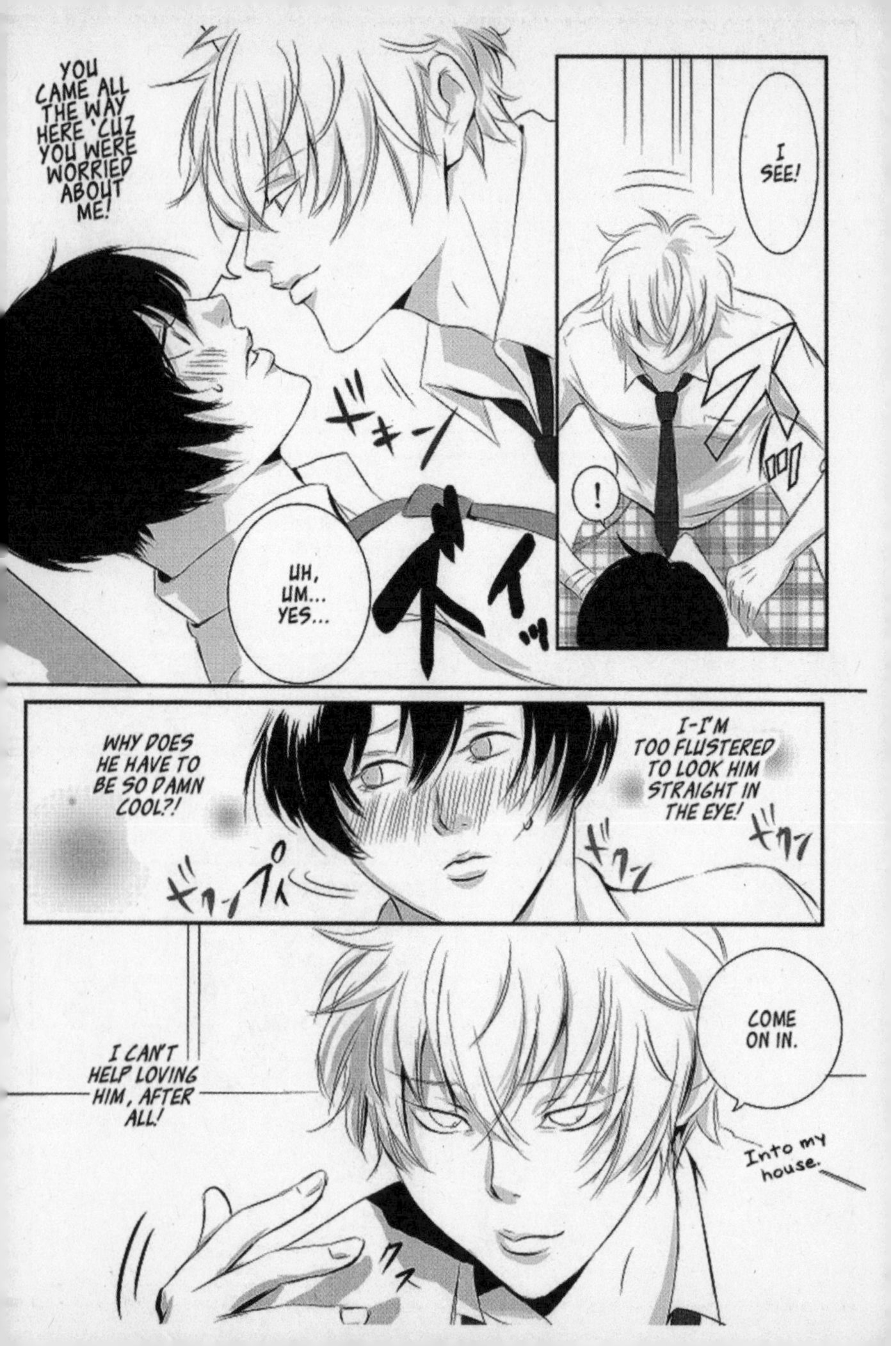
I SEE!
!
YOU CAME ALL THE WAY HERE 'CUZ YOU WERE WORRIED ABOUT ME!
UH, UM... YES...
I-I'M TOO FLUSTERED TO LOOK HIM STRAIGHT IN THE EYE!
WHY DOES HE HAVE TO BE SO DAMN COOL?!
COME ON IN.
Into my house.
I CAN'T HELP LOVING HIM, AFTER ALL!

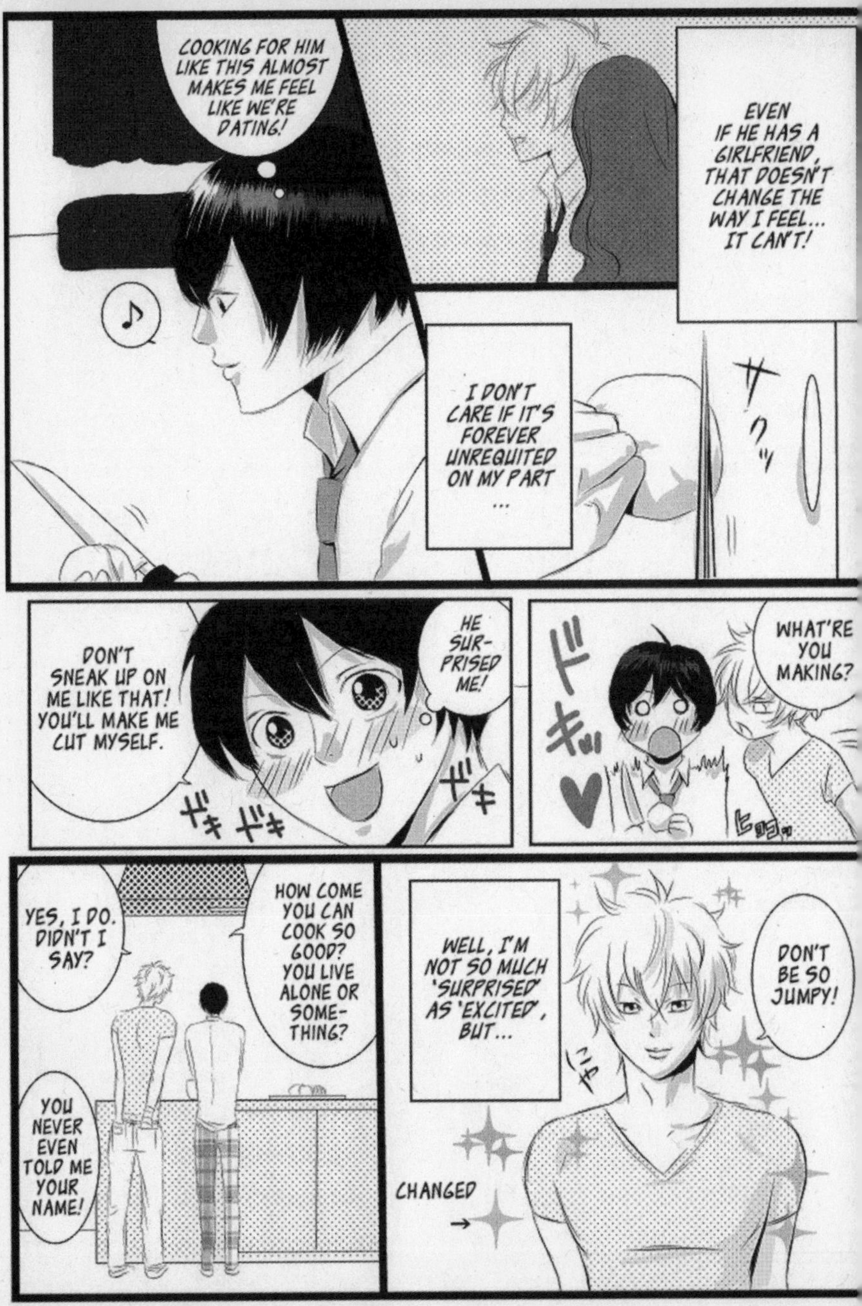
EVEN IF HE HAS A GIRLFRIEND, THAT DOESN'T CHANGE THE WAY I FEEL... IT CAN'T!
I DON'T CARE IF IT'S FOREVER UNREQUITED ON MY PART ...
COOKING FOR HIM LIKE THIS ALMOST MAKES ME FEEL LIKE WE'RE DATING!
♪
WHAT'RE YOU MAKING?
HE SUR-PRISED ME!
DON'T SNEAK UP ON ME LIKE THAT! YOU'LL MAKE ME CUT MYSELF.
DON'T BE SO JUMPY!
WELL, I'M NOT SO MUCH 'SURPRISED' AS 'EXCITED', BUT...
CHANGED →
HOW COME YOU CAN COOK SO GOOD? YOU LIVE ALONE OR SOME-THING?
YES, I DO. DIDN'T I SAY?
YOU NEVER EVEN TOLD ME YOUR NAME!

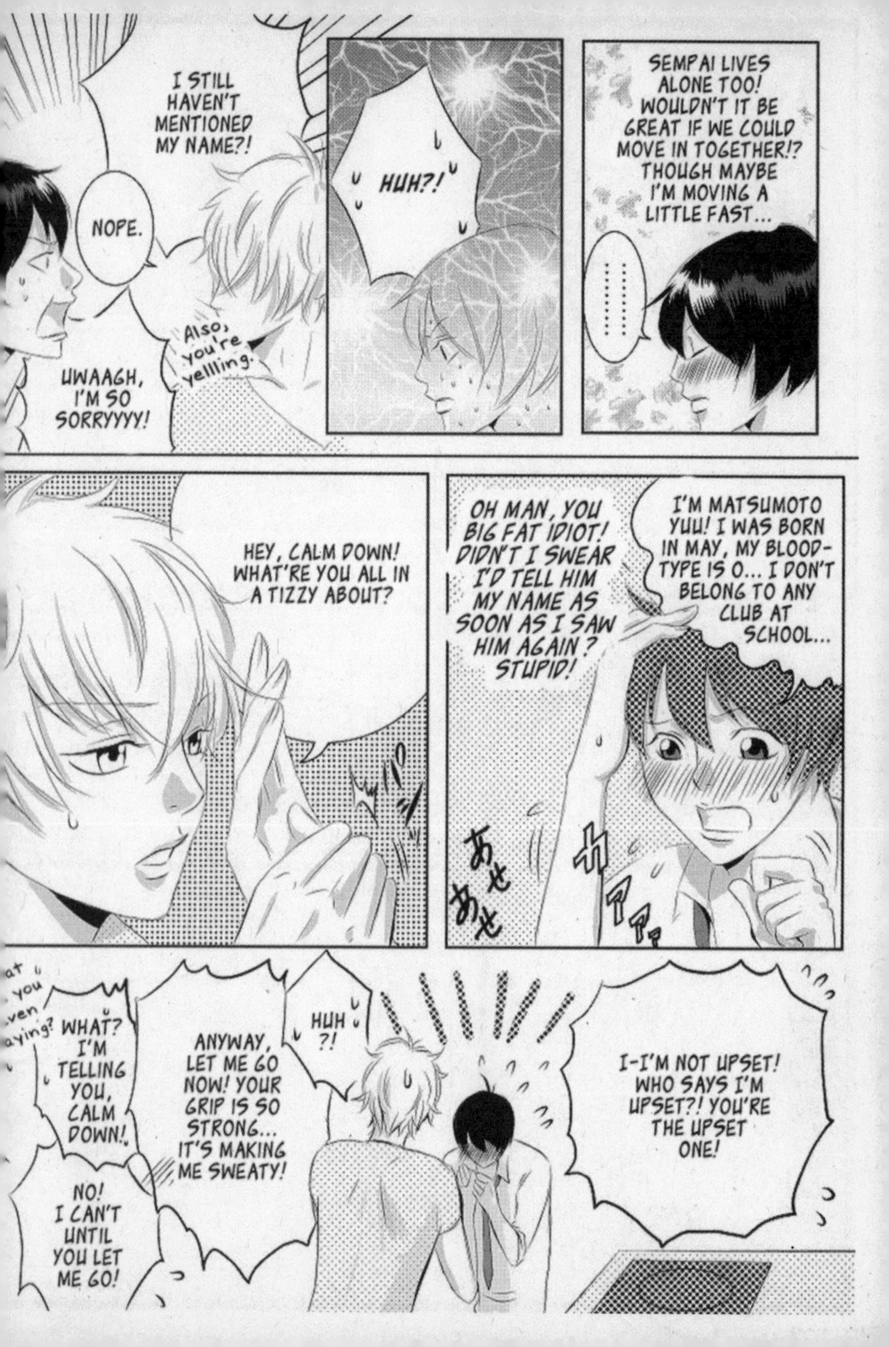
SEMPAI LIVES ALONE TOO! WOULDN'T IT BE GREAT IF WE COULD MOVE IN TOGETHER!? THOUGH MAYBE I'M MOVING A LITTLE FAST...
......
HUH?!
I STILL HAVEN'T MENTIONED MY NAME?!
NOPE.
Also, you're yellling.
UWAAGH, I'M SO SORRYYYY!
I'M MATSUMOTO YUU! I WAS BORN IN MAY, MY BLOOD-TYPE IS O... I DON'T BELONG TO ANY CLUB AT SCHOOL...
OH MAN, YOU BIG FAT IDIOT! DIDN'T I SWEAR I'D TELL HIM MY NAME AS SOON AS I SAW HIM AGAIN? STUPID!
カァァ
あせあせ
HEY, CALM DOWN! WHAT'RE YOU ALL IN A TIZZY ABOUT?
I-I'M NOT UPSET! WHO SAYS I'M UPSET?! YOU'RE THE UPSET ONE!
HUH ?!
ANYWAY, LET ME GO NOW! YOUR GRIP IS SO STRONG... IT'S MAKING ME SWEATY!
WHAT? I'M TELLING YOU, CALM DOWN!
NO! I CAN'T UNTIL YOU LET ME GO!

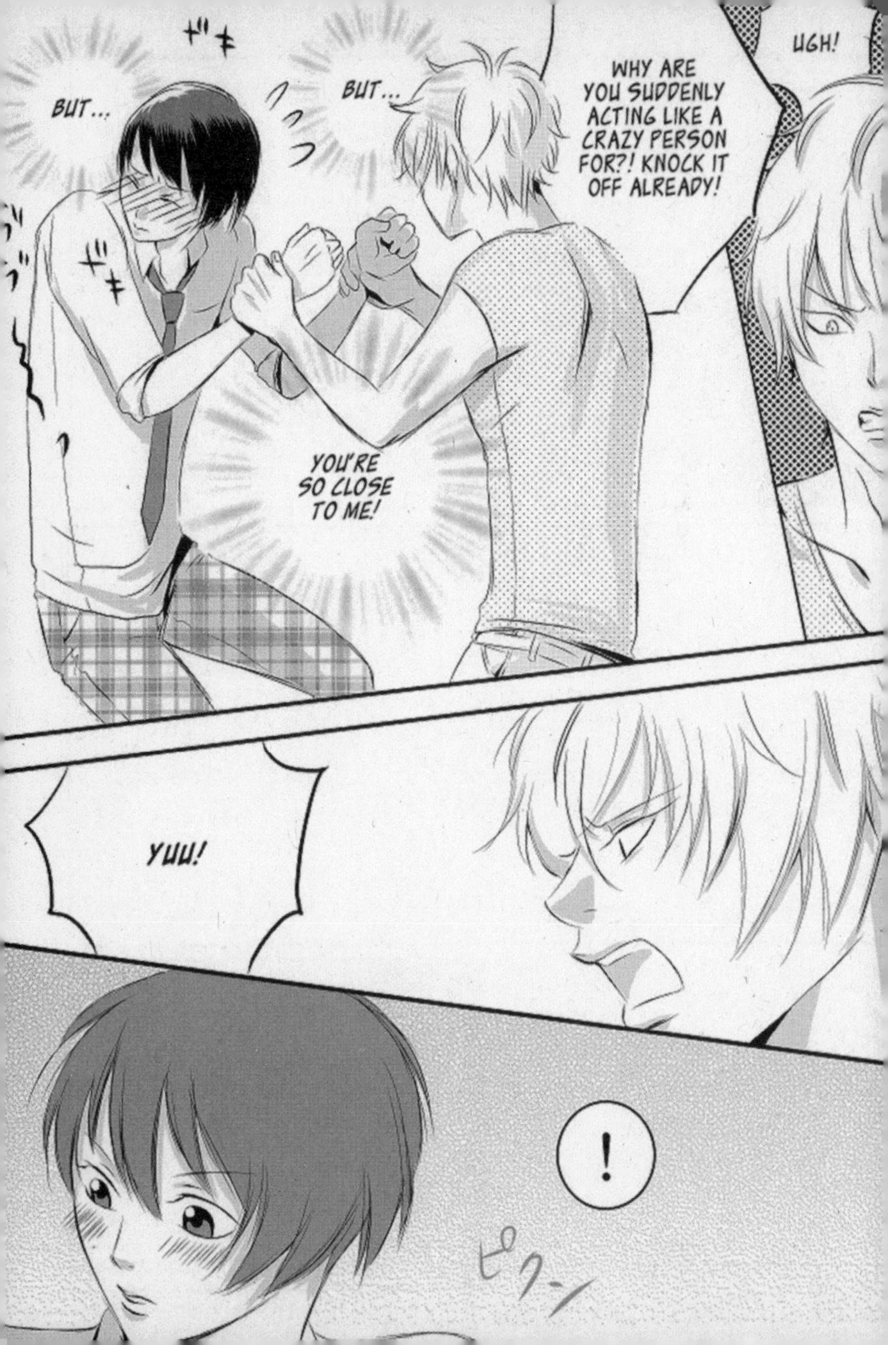
UGH!
WHY ARE YOU SUDDENLY ACTING LIKE A CRAZY PERSON FOR?! KNOCK IT OFF ALREADY!
BUT...
ドキ
BUT...
ドキ
YOU'RE SO CLOSE TO ME!
YUU!
!

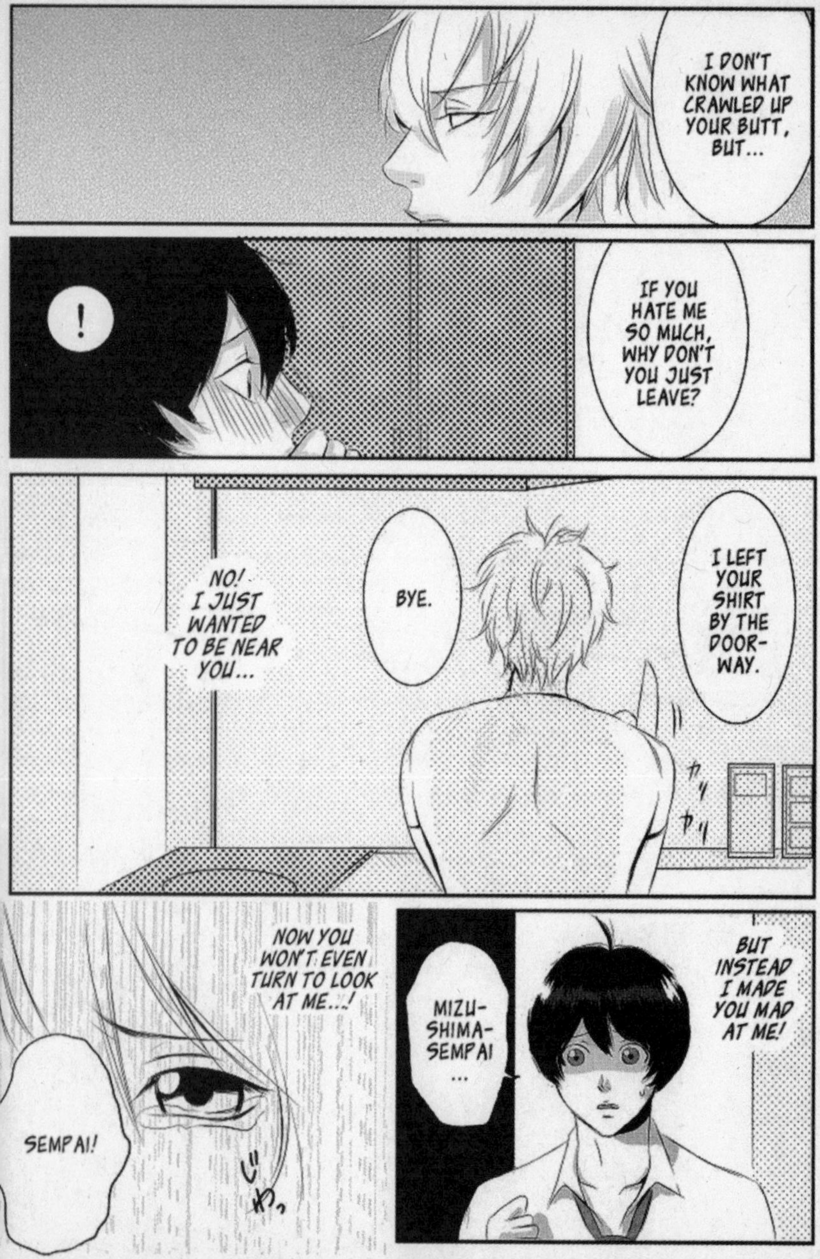

I DON'T KNOW WHAT CRAWLED UP YOUR BUTT, BUT...
IF YOU HATE ME SO MUCH, WHY DON'T YOU JUST LEAVE?
!
I LEFT YOUR SHIRT BY THE DOOR-WAY.
カリ カリ
BYE.
NO! I JUST WANTED TO BE NEAR YOU...
BUT INSTEAD I MADE YOU MAD AT ME!
MIZU-SHIMA-SEMPAI ...
NOW YOU WON'T EVEN TURN TO LOOK AT ME...!
SEMPAI!
じわっ

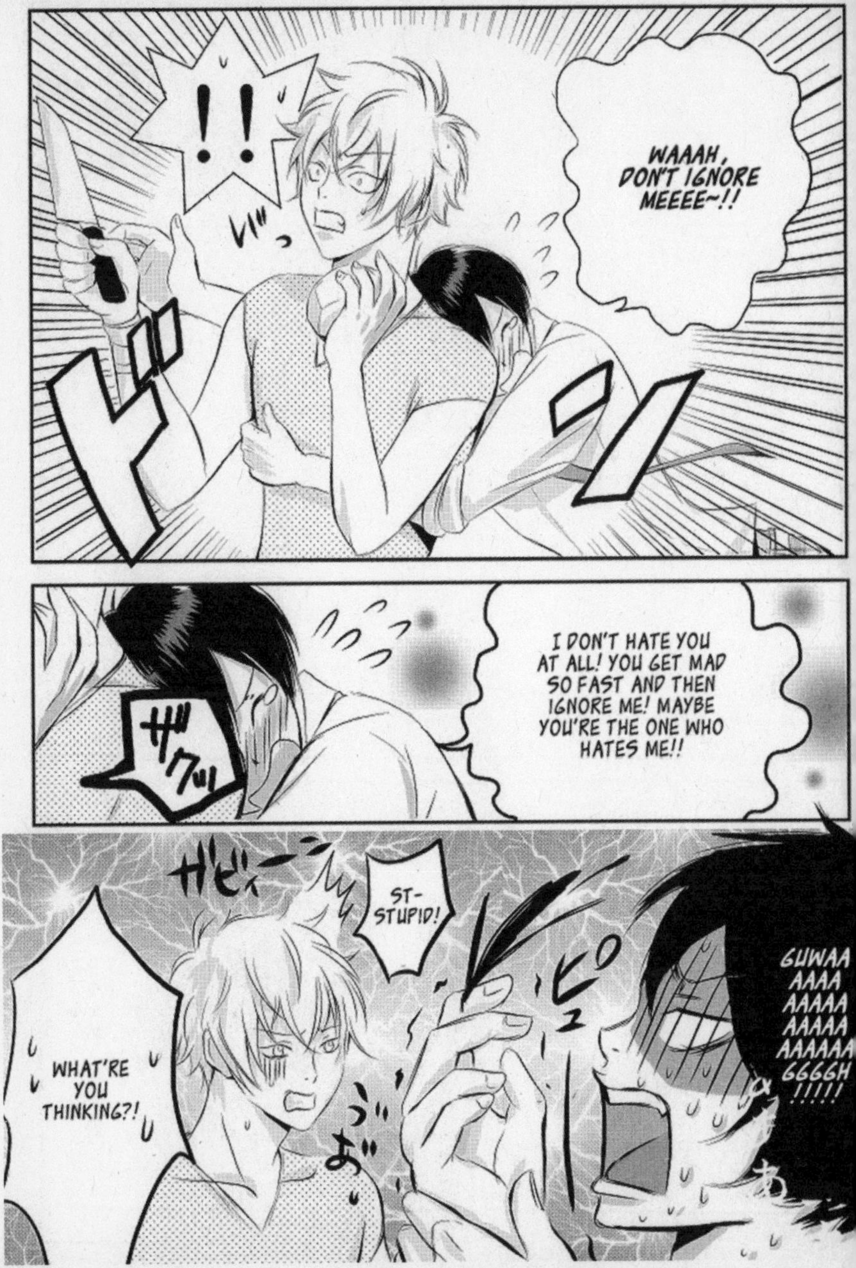
WAAAH, DON'T IGNORE MEEEE~!!
!!
I DON'T HATE YOU AT ALL! YOU GET MAD SO FAST AND THEN IGNORE ME! MAYBE YOU'RE THE ONE WHO HATES ME!!
GUWAA AAAA AAAAA AAAAA AAAAAA GGGGH !!!!!
ST-STUPID!
WHAT'RE YOU THINKING?!

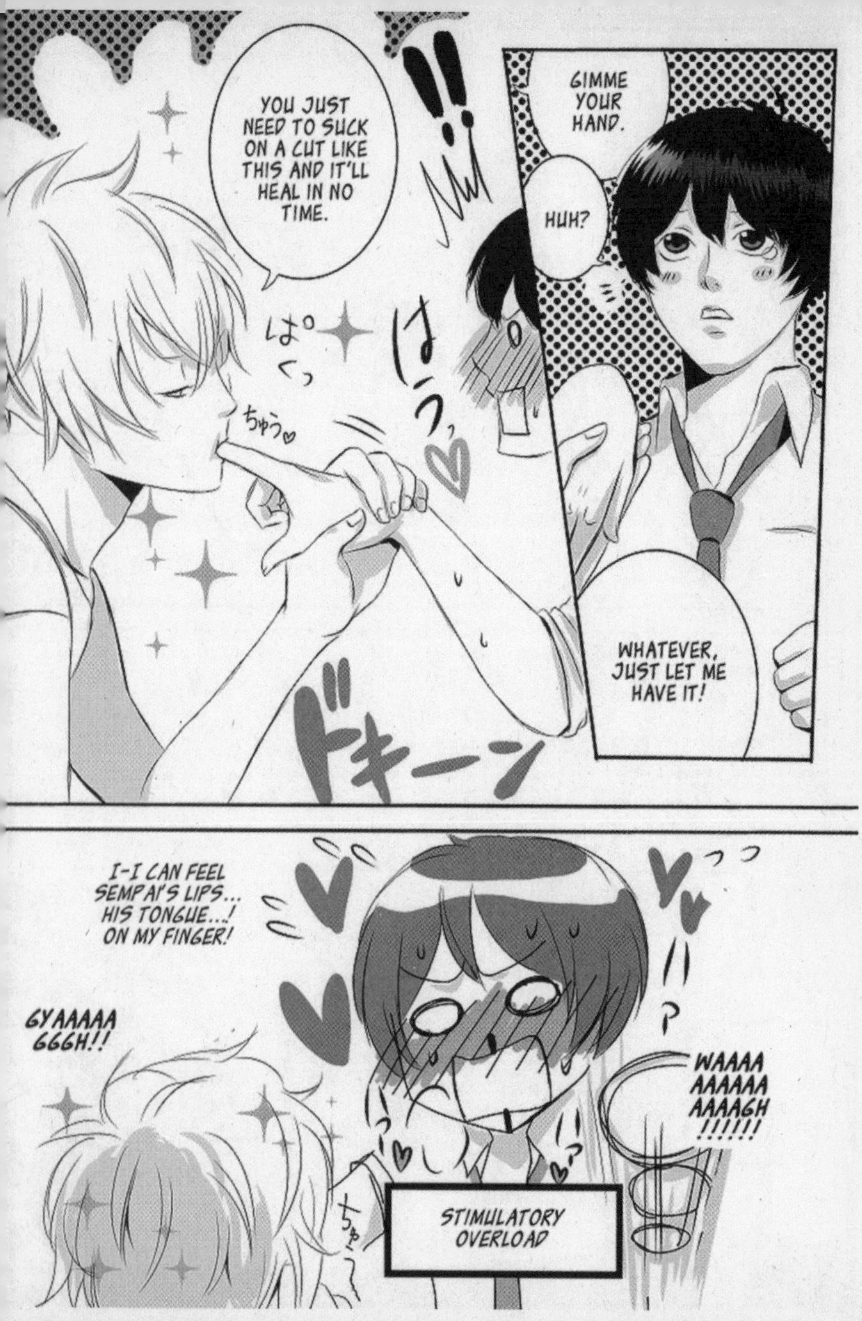
GIMME YOUR HAND.
HUH?
WHATEVER, JUST LET ME HAVE IT!
YOU JUST NEED TO SUCK ON A CUT LIKE THIS AND IT'LL HEAL IN NO TIME.
ぱくっ
ちゅう♡
はうっ
ドキーン
I-I CAN FEEL SEMPAI'S LIPS... HIS TONGUE...! ON MY FINGER!
WAAAA AAAAAA AAAAGH !!!!!!
GYAAAAA GGGH!!
STIMULATORY OVERLOAD

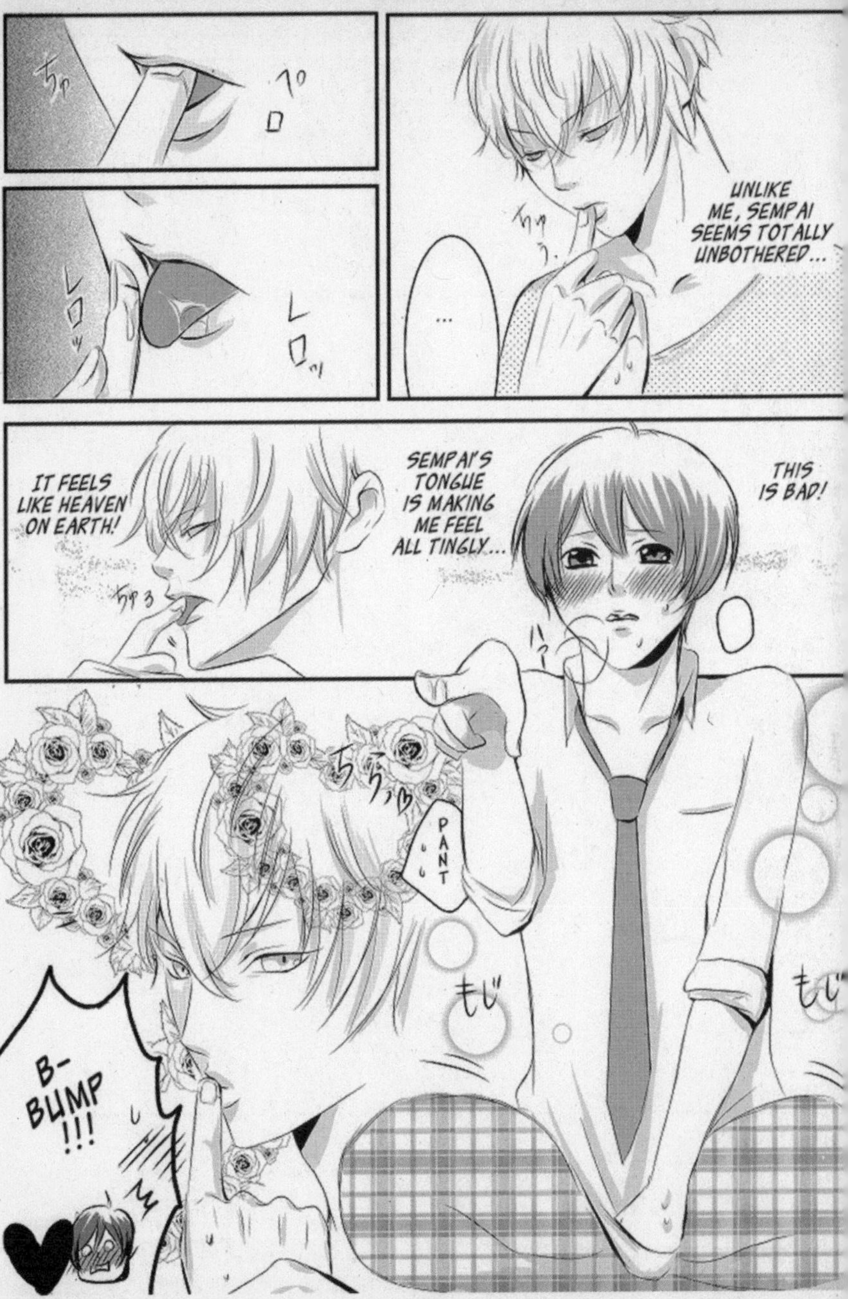
...
UNLIKE ME, SEMPAI SEEMS TOTALLY UNBOTHERED...
THIS IS BAD!
SEMPAI'S TONGUE IS MAKING ME FEEL ALL TINGLY...
IT FEELS LIKE HEAVEN ON EARTH!
PANT
B-BUMP!!!

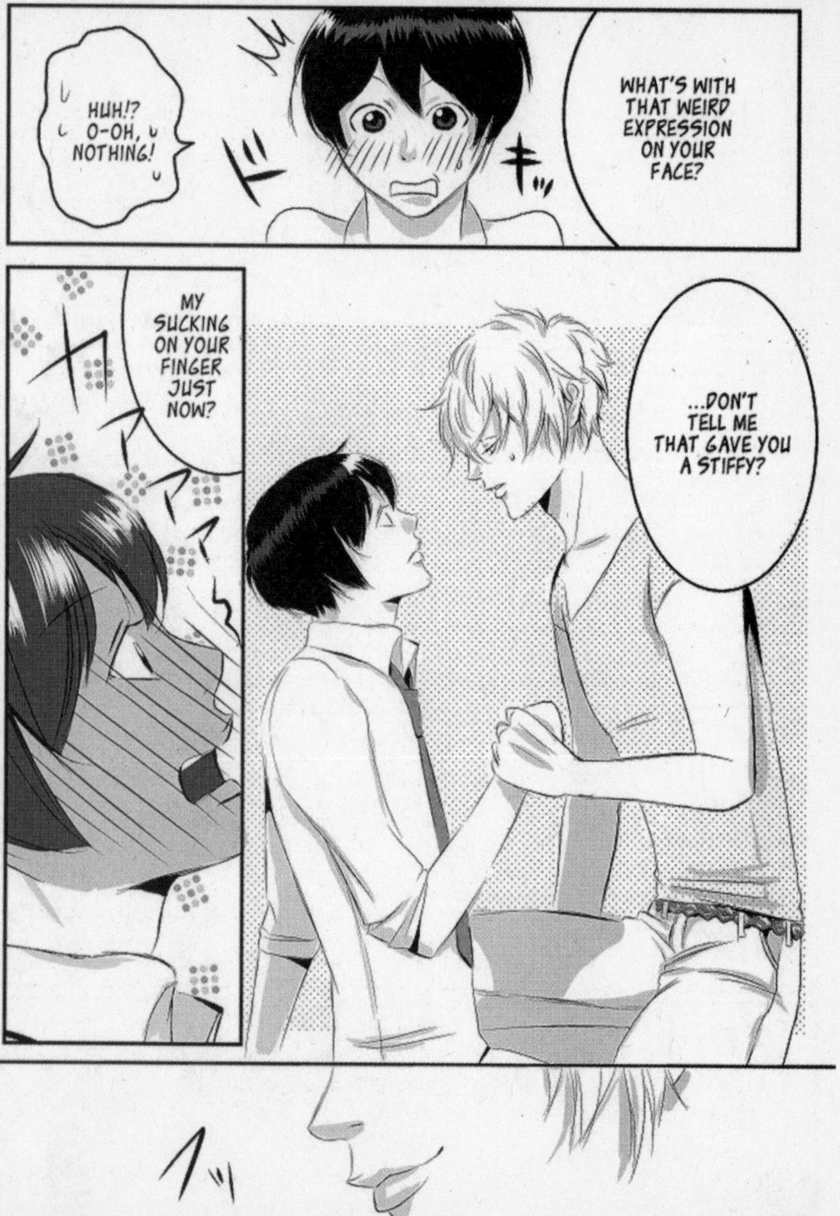
WHAT'S WITH THAT WEIRD EXPRESSION ON YOUR FACE?
HUH!? O-OH, NOTHING!
...DON'T TELL ME THAT GAVE YOU A STIFFY?
MY SUCKING ON YOUR FINGER JUST NOW?

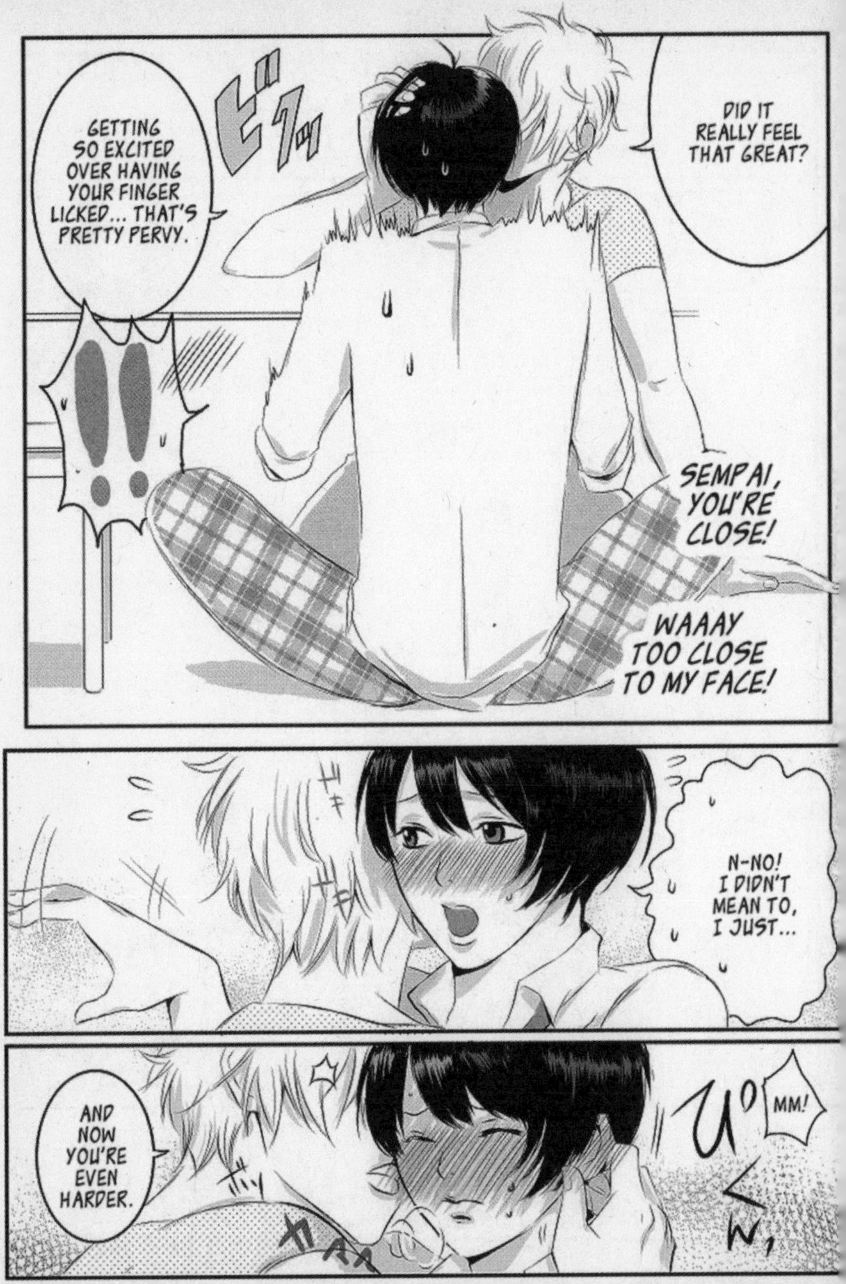
DID IT REALLY FEEL THAT GREAT?
GETTING SO EXCITED OVER HAVING YOUR FINGER LICKED... THAT'S PRETTY PERVY.
SEMPAI, YOU'RE CLOSE!
WAAAY TOO CLOSE TO MY FACE!
N-NO! I DIDN'T MEAN TO, I JUST...
MM!
AND NOW YOU'RE EVEN HARDER.

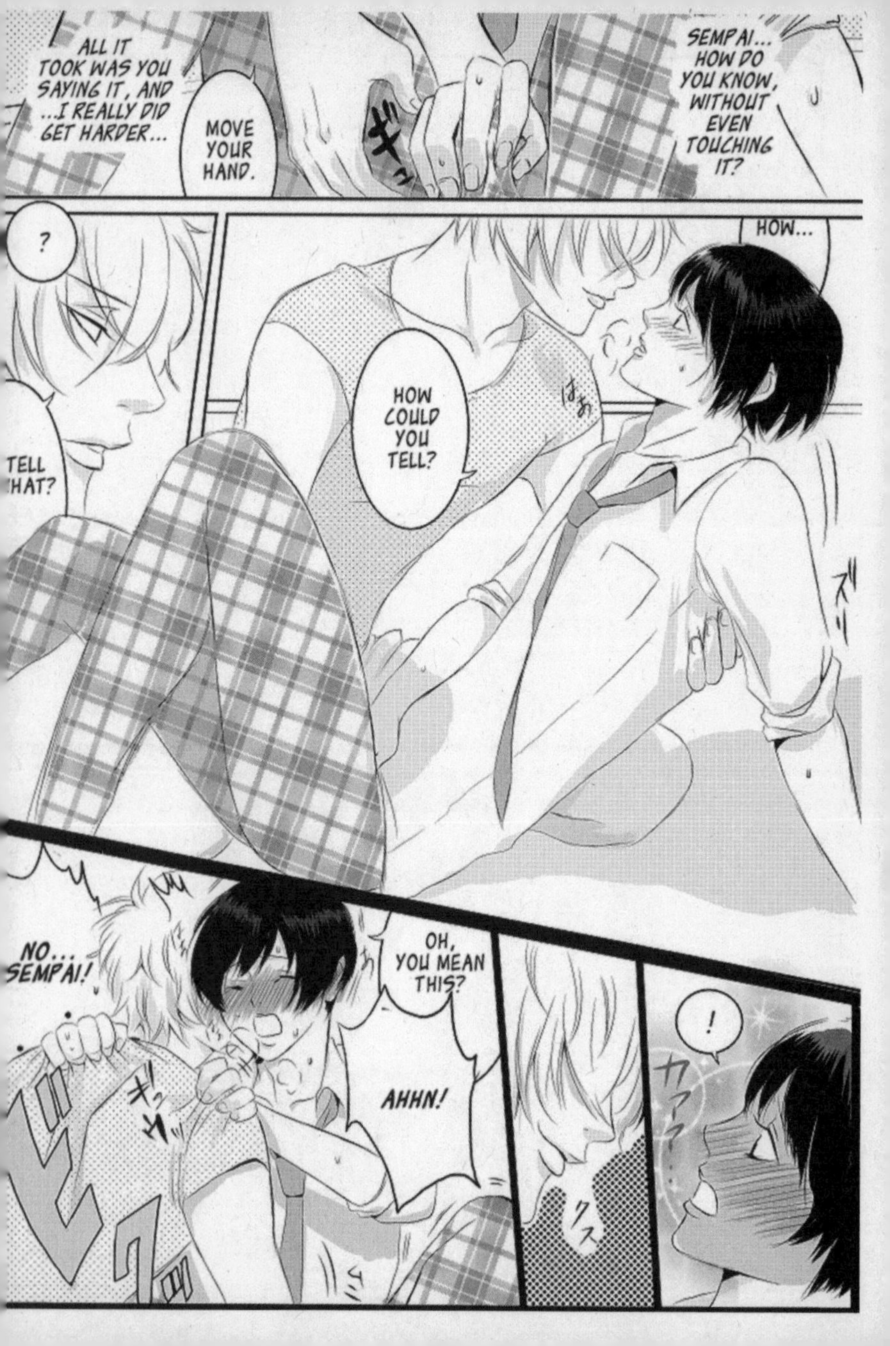
SEMPAI... HOW DO YOU KNOW, WITHOUT EVEN TOUCHING IT?
MOVE YOUR HAND.
ALL IT TOOK WAS YOU SAYING IT, AND ...I REALLY DID GET HARDER...
HOW...
HOW COULD YOU TELL?
はぁ
?
TELL HAT?
!
OH, YOU MEAN THIS?
AHHN!
NO... SEMPAI!

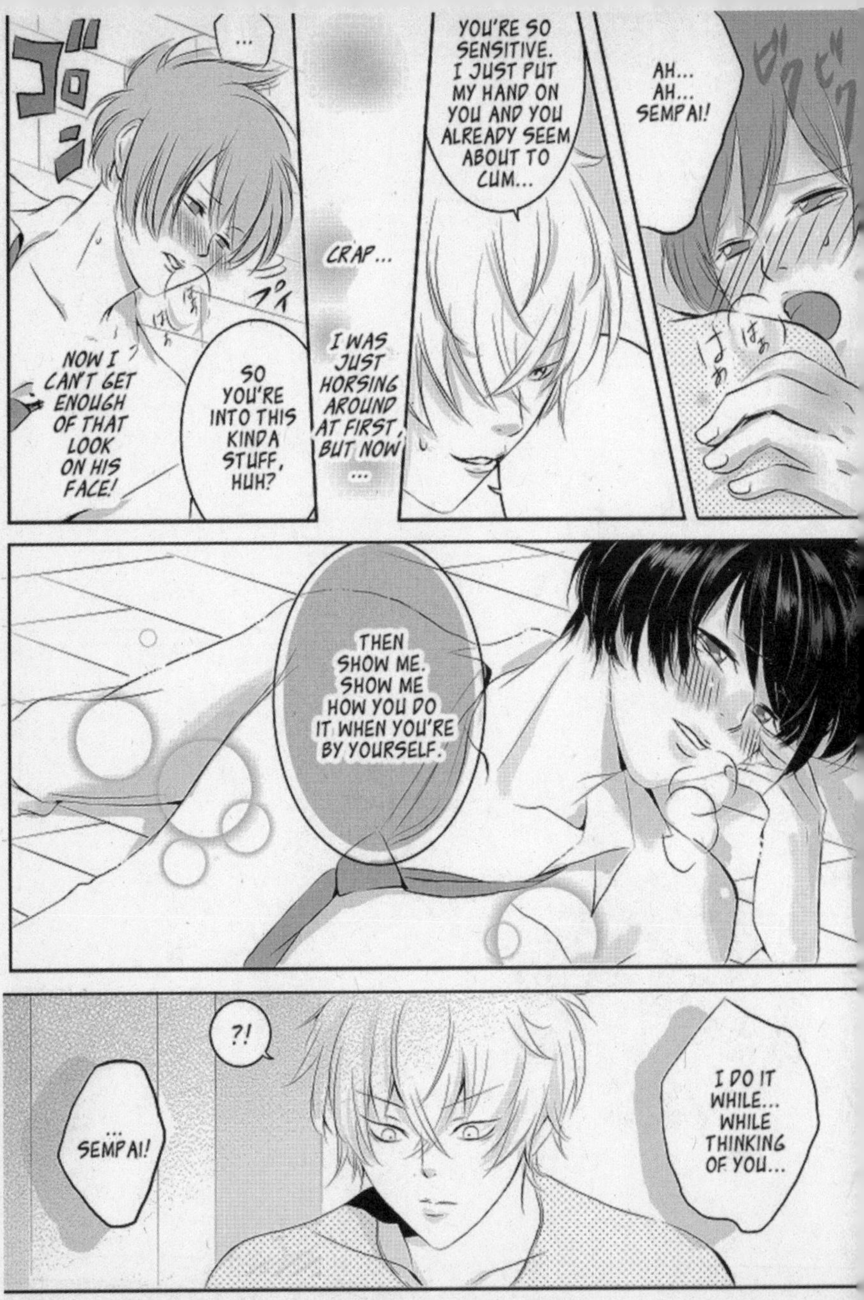
ビクビク
AH... AH... SEMPAI!
YOU'RE SO SENSITIVE. I JUST PUT MY HAND ON YOU AND YOU ALREADY SEEM ABOUT TO CUM...
CRAP...
I WAS JUST HORSING AROUND AT FIRST, BUT NOW ...
ゴロン
...
プイ
SO YOU'RE INTO THIS KINDA STUFF, HUH?
NOW I CAN'T GET ENOUGH OF THAT LOOK ON HIS FACE!
THEN SHOW ME. SHOW ME HOW YOU DO IT WHEN YOU'RE BY YOURSELF.
I DO IT WHILE... WHILE THINKING OF YOU...
?!
... SEMPAI!

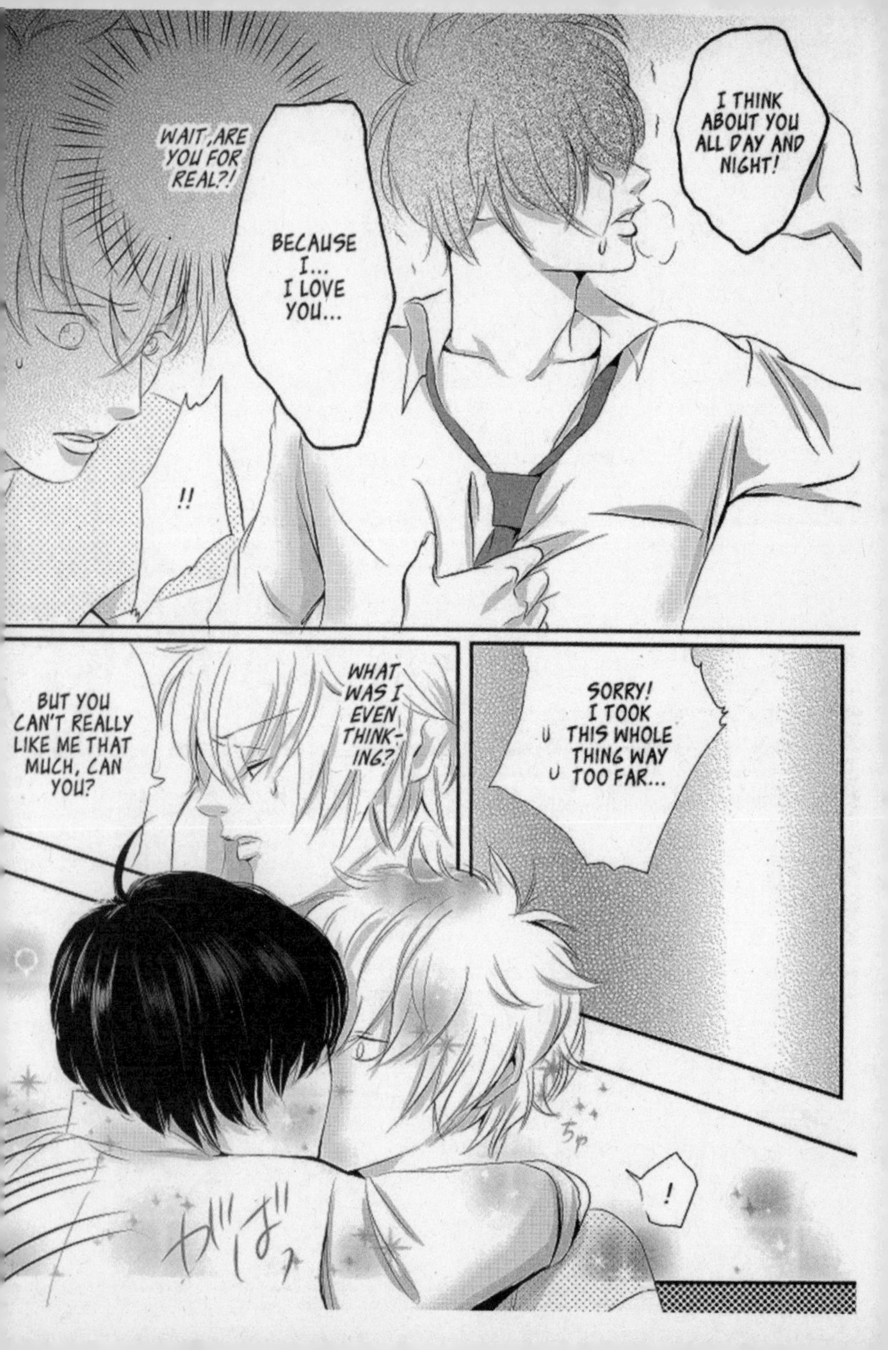
I THINK ABOUT YOU ALL DAY AND NIGHT!
BECAUSE I... I LOVE YOU...
WAIT, ARE YOU FOR REAL?!
!!
SORRY! I TOOK THIS WHOLE THING WAY TOO FAR...
WHAT WAS I EVEN THINKING?
BUT YOU CAN'T REALLY LIKE ME THAT MUCH, CAN YOU?
!
ちゅ
がばっ

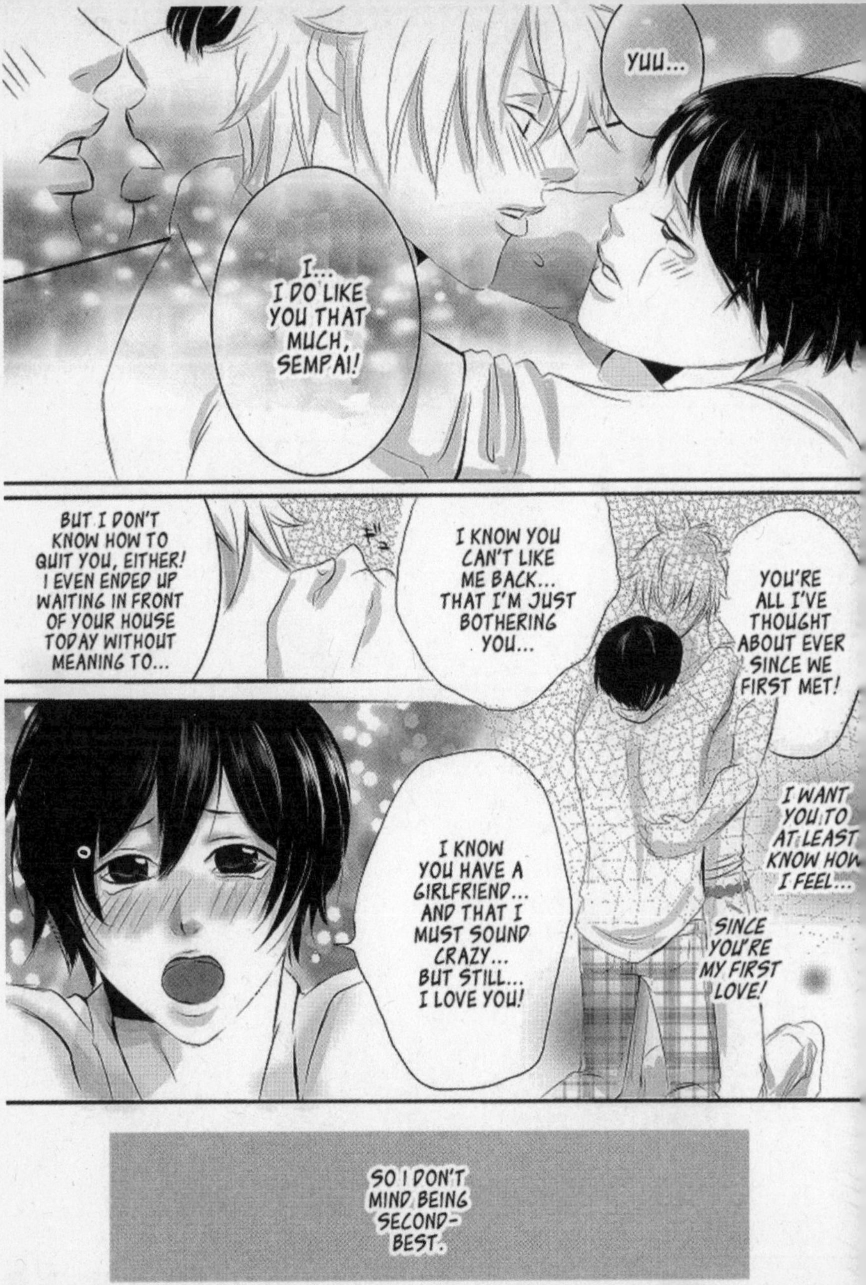
YUU...
I... I DO LIKE YOU THAT MUCH, SEMPAI!
YOU'RE ALL I'VE THOUGHT ABOUT EVER SINCE WE FIRST MET!
I WANT YOU TO AT LEAST KNOW HOW I FEEL...
SINCE YOU'RE MY FIRST LOVE!
I KNOW YOU CAN'T LIKE ME BACK... THAT I'M JUST BOTHERING YOU...
BUT I DON'T KNOW HOW TO QUIT YOU, EITHER! I EVEN ENDED UP WAITING IN FRONT OF YOUR HOUSE TODAY WITHOUT MEANING TO...
I KNOW YOU HAVE A GIRLFRIEND... AND THAT I MUST SOUND CRAZY... BUT STILL... I LOVE YOU!
SO I DON'T MIND BEING SECOND-BEST.

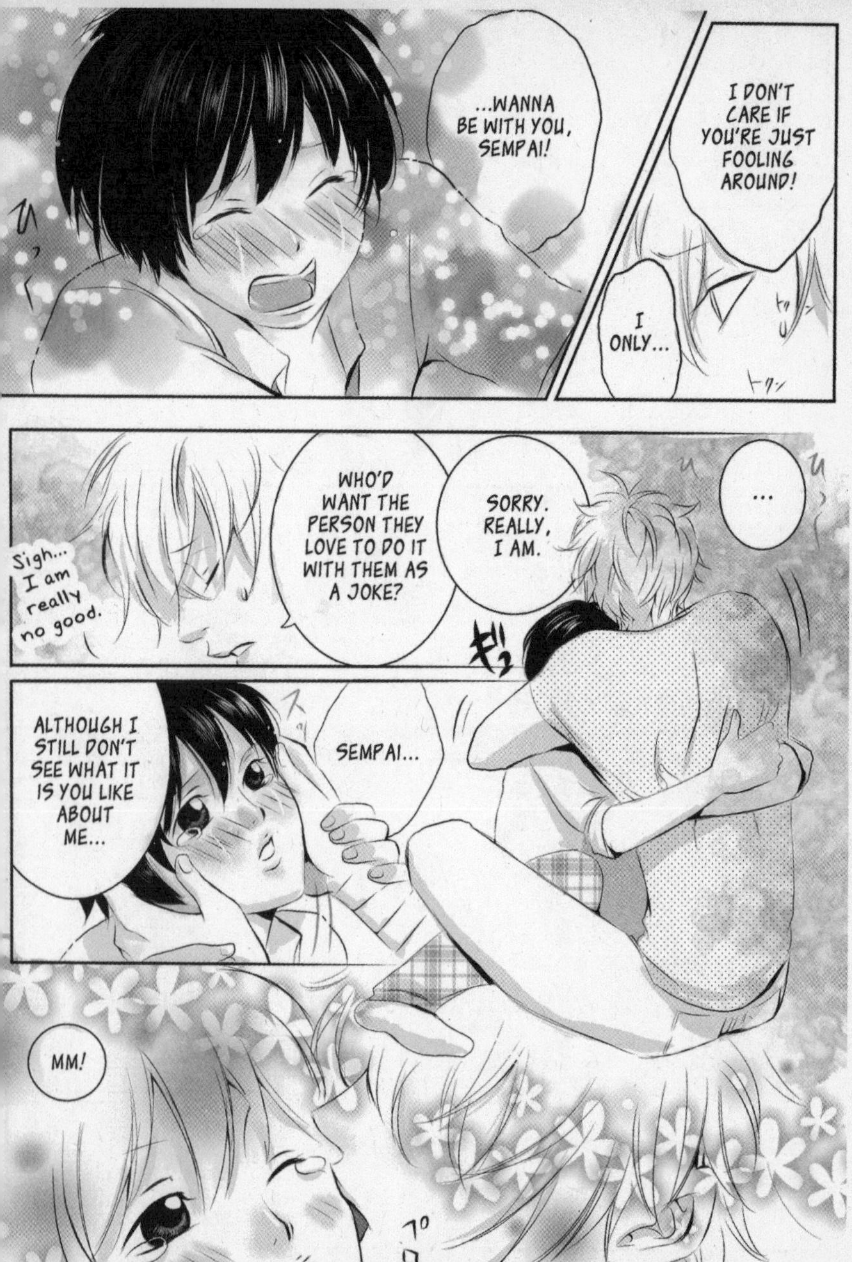
I DON'T CARE IF YOU'RE JUST FOOLING AROUND!
I ONLY...
...WANNA BE WITH YOU, SEMPAI!
...
SORRY. REALLY, I AM.
WHO'D WANT THE PERSON THEY LOVE TO DO IT WITH THEM AS A JOKE?
Sigh... I am really no good.
SEMPAI...
ALTHOUGH I STILL DON'T SEE WHAT IT IS YOU LIKE ABOUT ME...
MM!

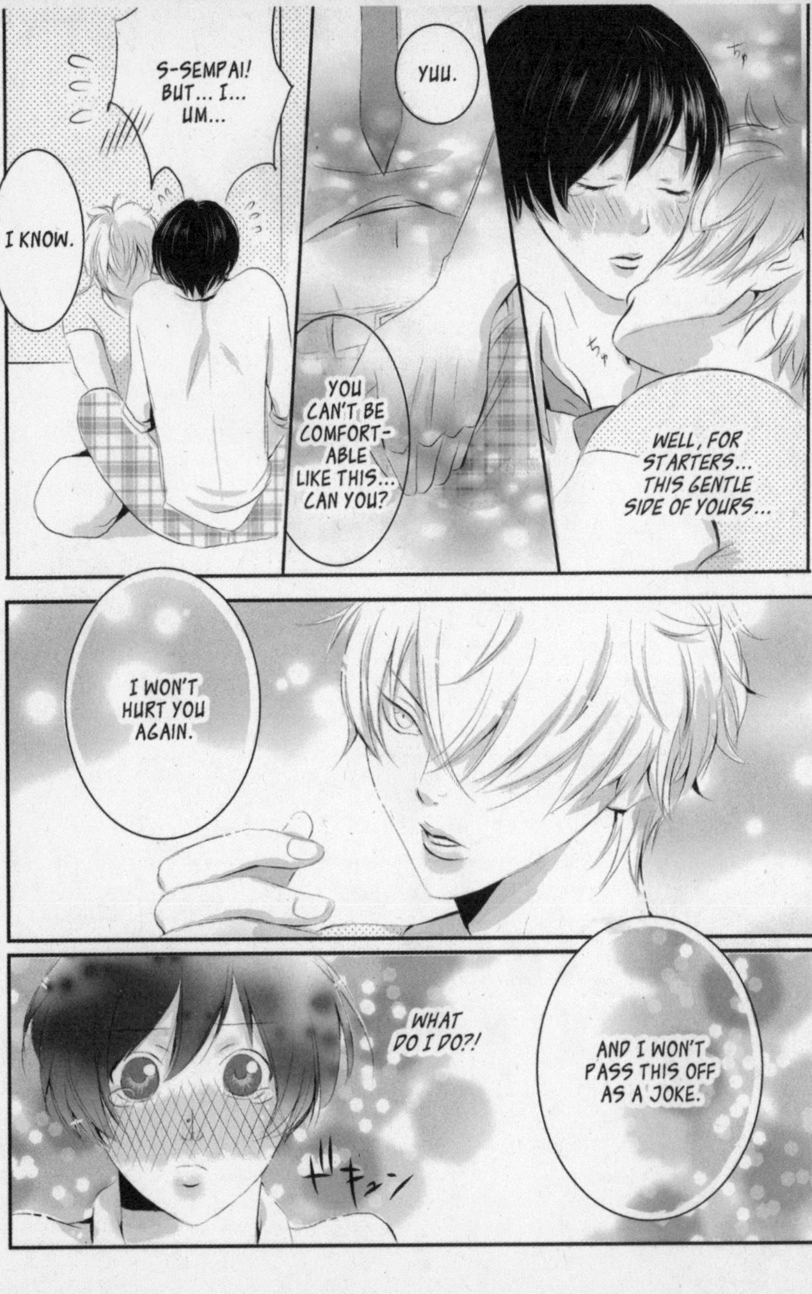
WELL, FOR STARTERS... THIS GENTLE SIDE OF YOURS...
YUU.
YOU CAN'T BE COMFORT-ABLE LIKE THIS... CAN YOU?
S-SEMPAI! BUT... I... UM...
I KNOW.
I WON'T HURT YOU AGAIN.
AND I WON'T PASS THIS OFF AS A JOKE.
WHAT DO I DO?!

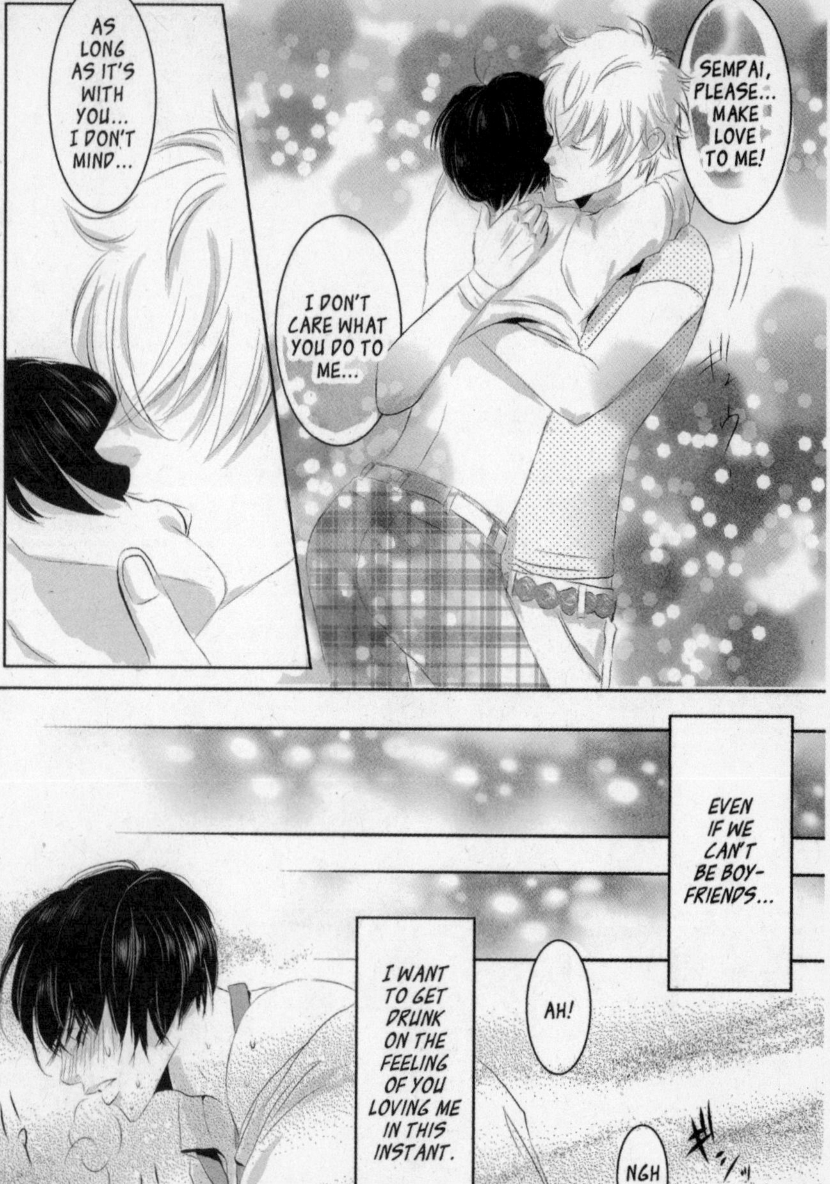
SEMPAI, PLEASE... MAKE LOVE TO ME!
I DON'T CARE WHAT YOU DO TO ME...
AS LONG AS IT'S WITH YOU... I DON'T MIND...
EVEN IF WE CAN'T BE BOY-FRIENDS...
AH!
I WANT TO GET DRUNK ON THE FEELING OF YOU LOVING ME IN THIS INSTANT.
NGH!

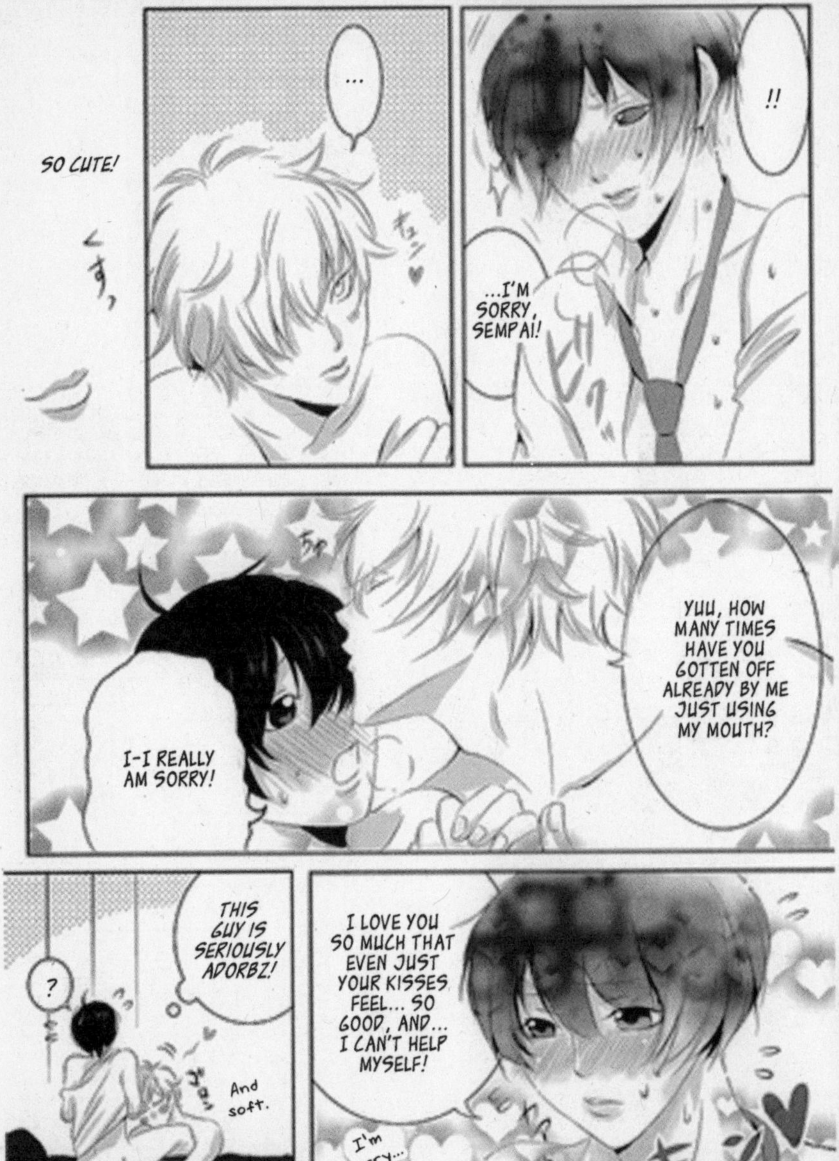
!!
...I'M SORRY, SEMPAI!
...
SO CUTE!
くすっ
YUU, HOW MANY TIMES HAVE YOU GOTTEN OFF ALREADY BY ME JUST USING MY MOUTH?
I-I REALLY AM SORRY!
I LOVE YOU SO MUCH THAT EVEN JUST YOUR KISSES FEEL... SO GOOD, AND... I CAN'T HELP MYSELF!
I'm sorry...
THIS GUY IS SERIOUSLY ADORBZ!
?
And soft.

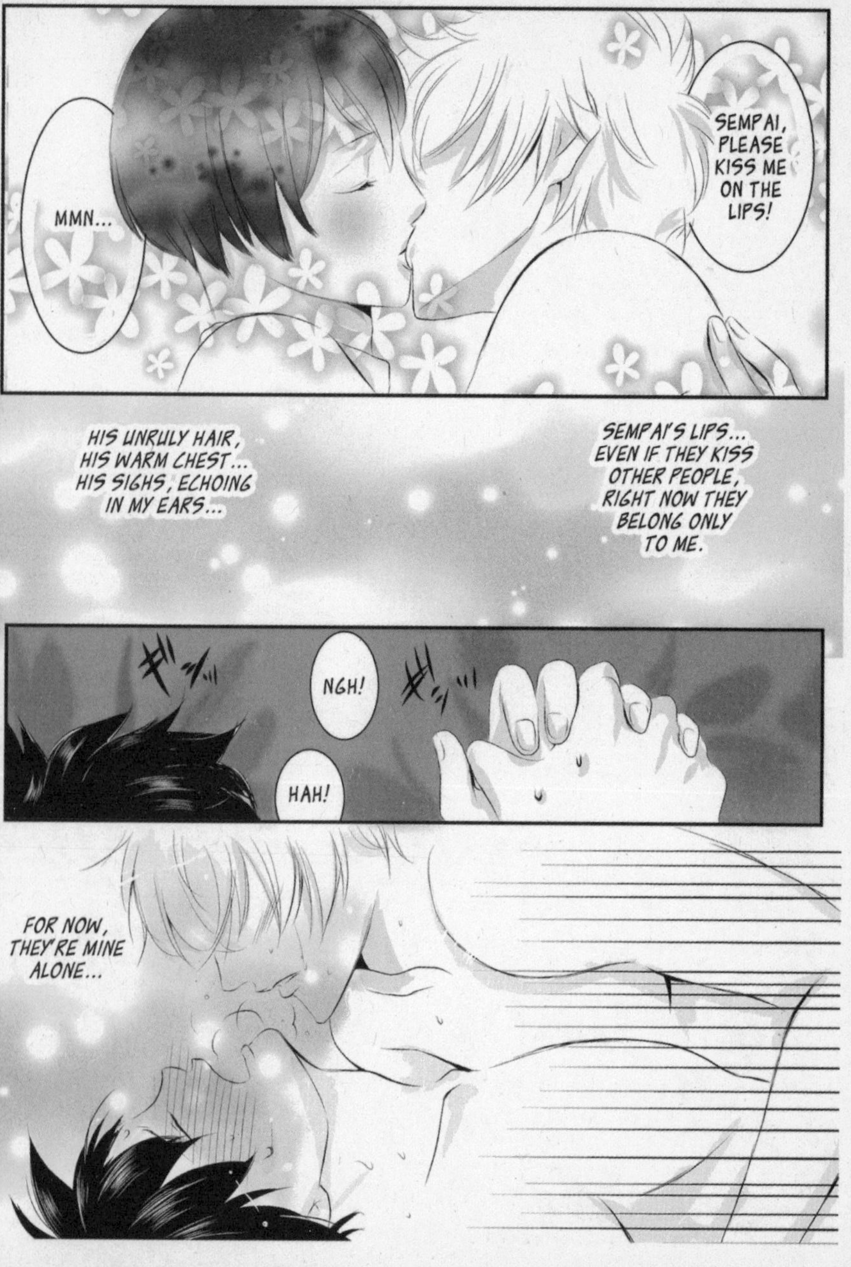
SEMPAI, PLEASE KISS ME ON THE LIPS!
MMN...
SEMPAI'S LIPS... EVEN IF THEY KISS OTHER PEOPLE, RIGHT NOW THEY BELONG ONLY TO ME.
HIS UNRULY HAIR, HIS WARM CHEST... HIS SIGHS, ECHOING IN MY EARS...
NGH!
HAH!
FOR NOW, THEY'RE MINE ALONE...

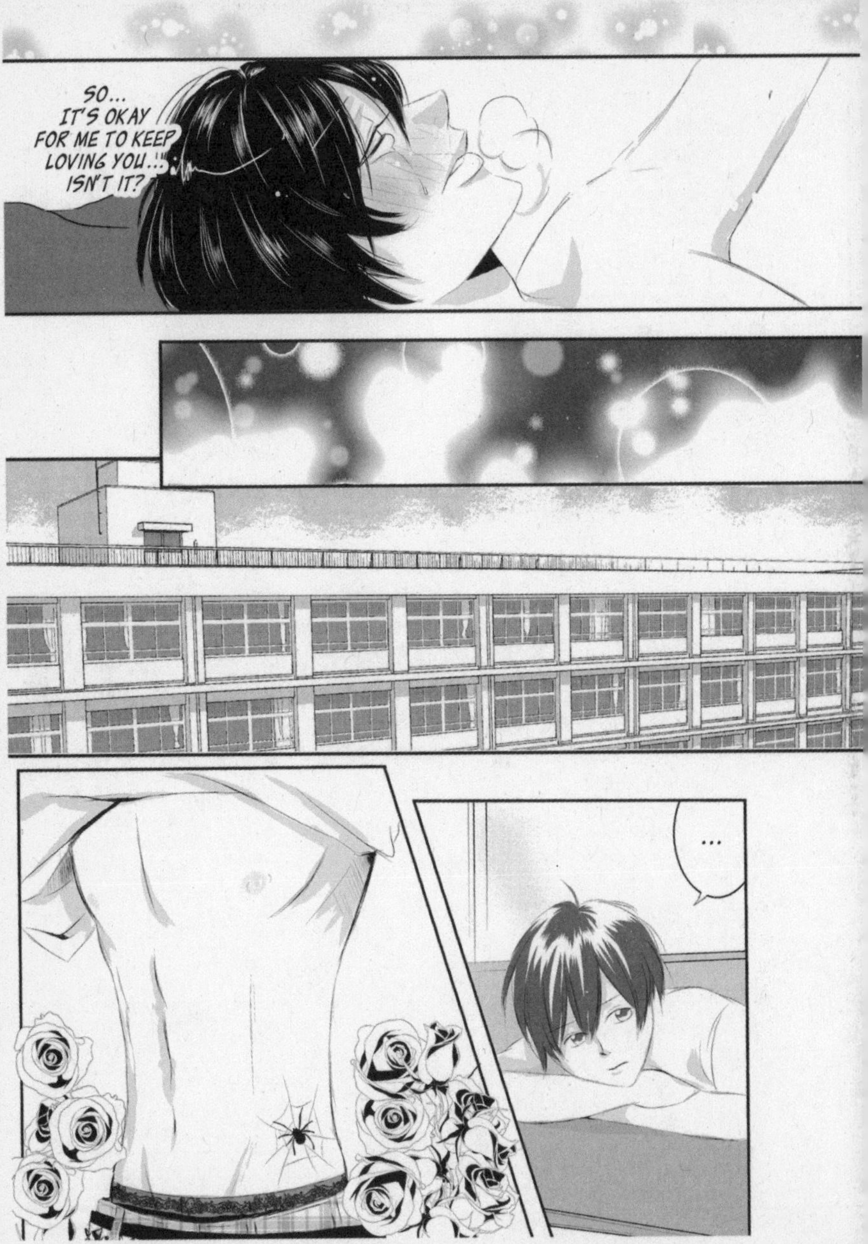
SO... IT'S OKAY FOR ME TO KEEP LOVING YOU... ISN'T IT?
...

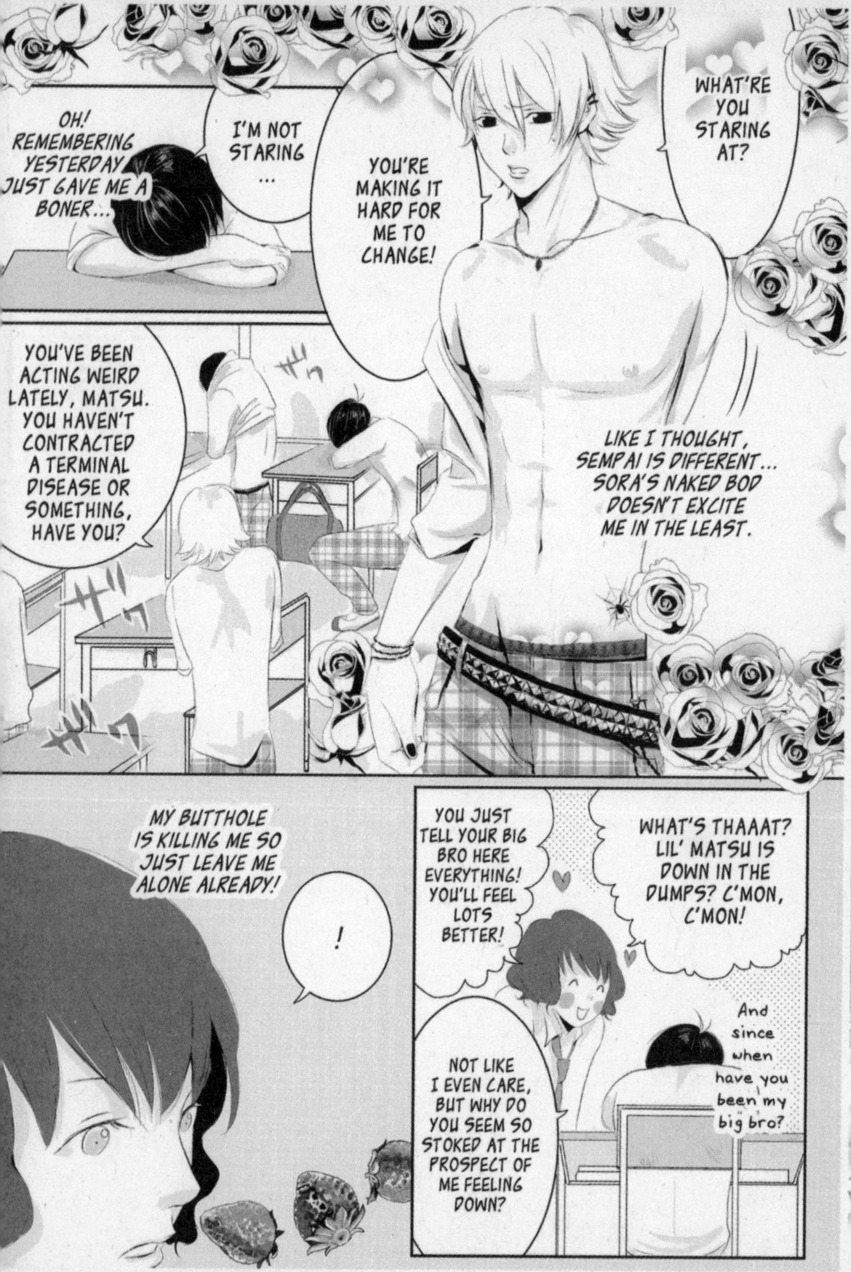
WHAT'RE YOU STARING AT?
YOU'RE MAKING IT HARD FOR ME TO CHANGE!
LIKE I THOUGHT, SEMPAI IS DIFFERENT... SORA'S NAKED BOD DOESN'T EXCITE ME IN THE LEAST.
I'M NOT STARING ...
OH! REMEMBERING YESTERDAY JUST GAVE ME A BONER...
YOU'VE BEEN ACTING WEIRD LATELY, MATSU. YOU HAVEN'T CONTRACTED A TERMINAL DISEASE OR SOMETHING, HAVE YOU?
WHAT'S THAAAT? LIL' MATSU IS DOWN IN THE DUMPS? C'MON, C'MON!
YOU JUST TELL YOUR BIG BRO HERE EVERYTHING! YOU'LL FEEL LOTS BETTER!
And since when have you been my big bro?
NOT LIKE I EVEN CARE, BUT WHY DO YOU SEEM SO STOKED AT THE PROSPECT OF ME FEELING DOWN?
MY BUTTHOLE IS KILLING ME SO JUST LEAVE ME ALONE ALREADY!
!

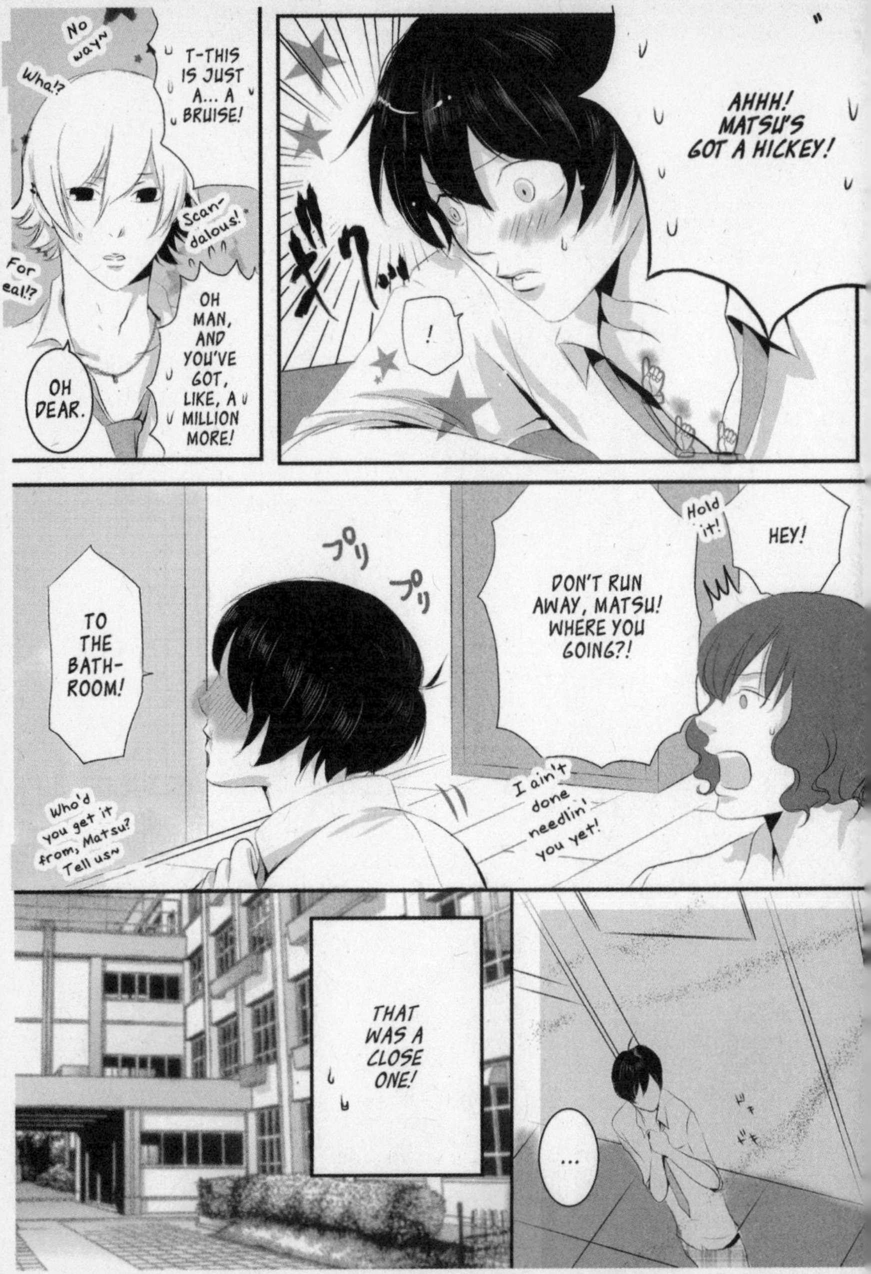
AHHH! MATSU'S GOT A HICKEY!
!
T-THIS IS JUST A... A BRUISE!
No way~
Wha!?
Scan-dalous!
For eal!?
OH MAN, AND YOU'VE GOT, LIKE, A MILLION MORE!
OH DEAR.
HEY!
Hold it!
DON'T RUN AWAY, MATSU! WHERE YOU GOING?!
I ain't done needlin' you yet!
プリ
プリ
TO THE BATH-ROOM!
Who'd you get it from, Matsu? Tell us~
...
ドキ
ドキ
THAT WAS A CLOSE ONE!

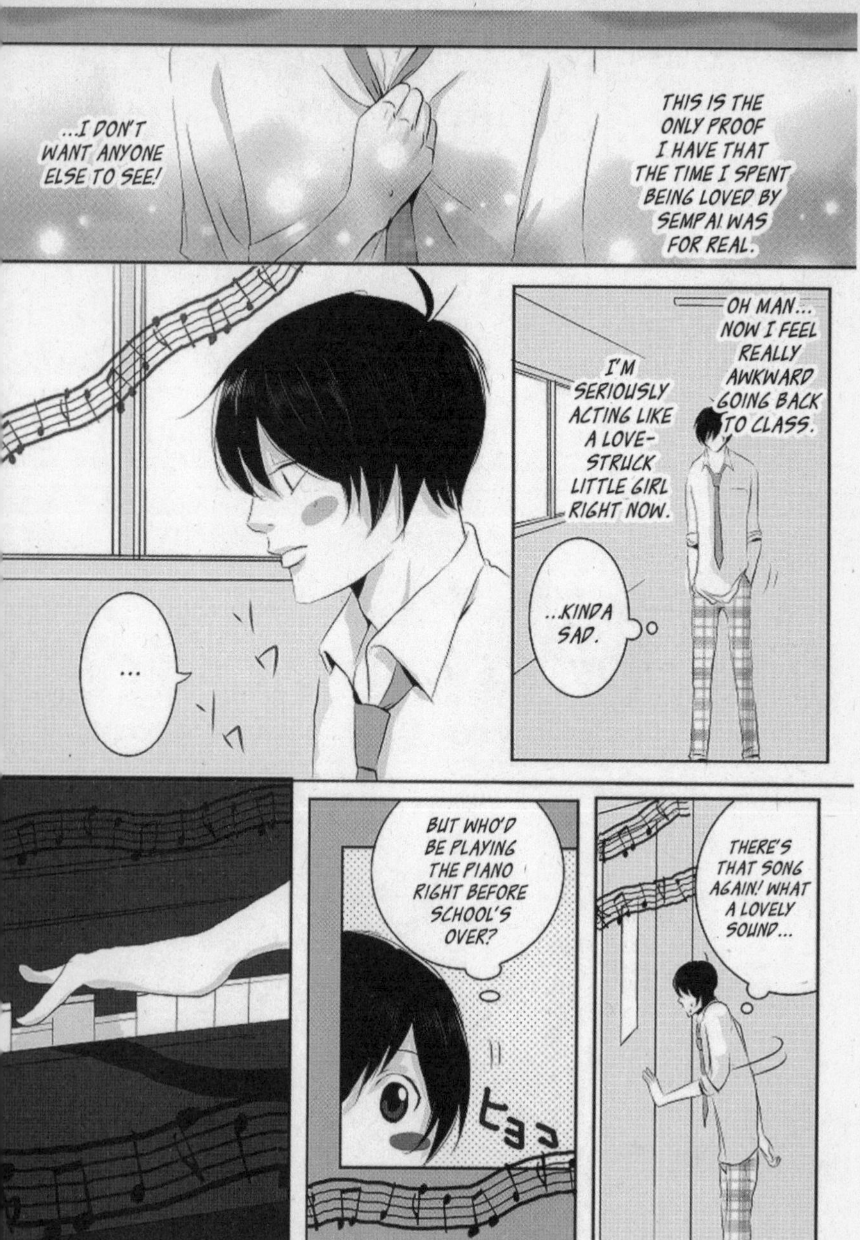
THIS IS THE ONLY PROOF I HAVE THAT THE TIME I SPENT BEING LOVED BY SEMPAI WAS FOR REAL.
...I DON'T WANT ANYONE ELSE TO SEE!
OH MAN... NOW I FEEL REALLY AWKWARD GOING BACK TO CLASS.
I'M SERIOUSLY ACTING LIKE A LOVE-STRUCK LITTLE GIRL RIGHT NOW.
...KINDA SAD.
...
THERE'S THAT SONG AGAIN! WHAT A LOVELY SOUND...
BUT WHO'D BE PLAYING THE PIANO RIGHT BEFORE SCHOOL'S OVER?
ヒョコ

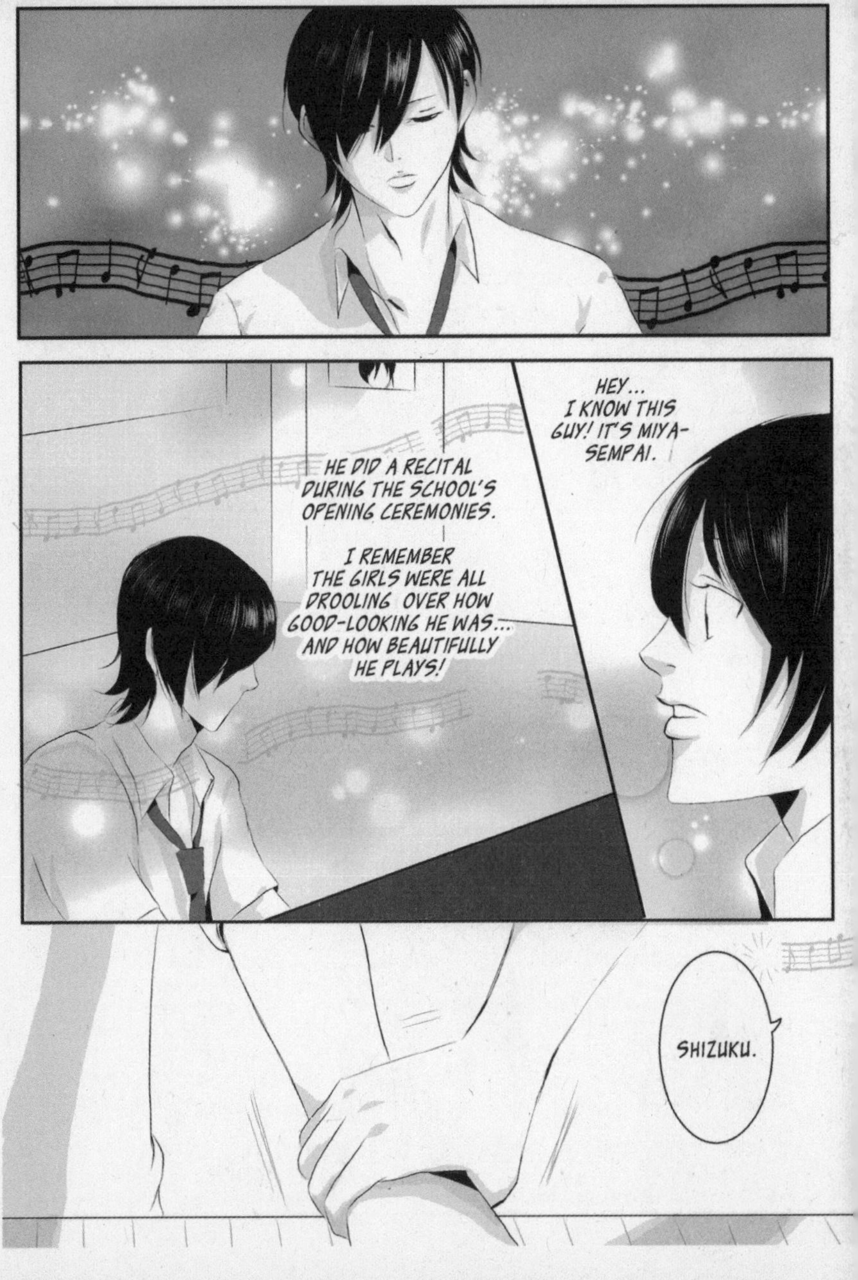
HEY... I KNOW THIS GUY! IT'S MIYA-SEMPAI.
HE DID A RECITAL DURING THE SCHOOL'S OPENING CEREMONIES.
I REMEMBER THE GIRLS WERE ALL DROOLING OVER HOW GOOD-LOOKING HE WAS... AND HOW BEAUTIFULLY HE PLAYS!
SHIZUKU.

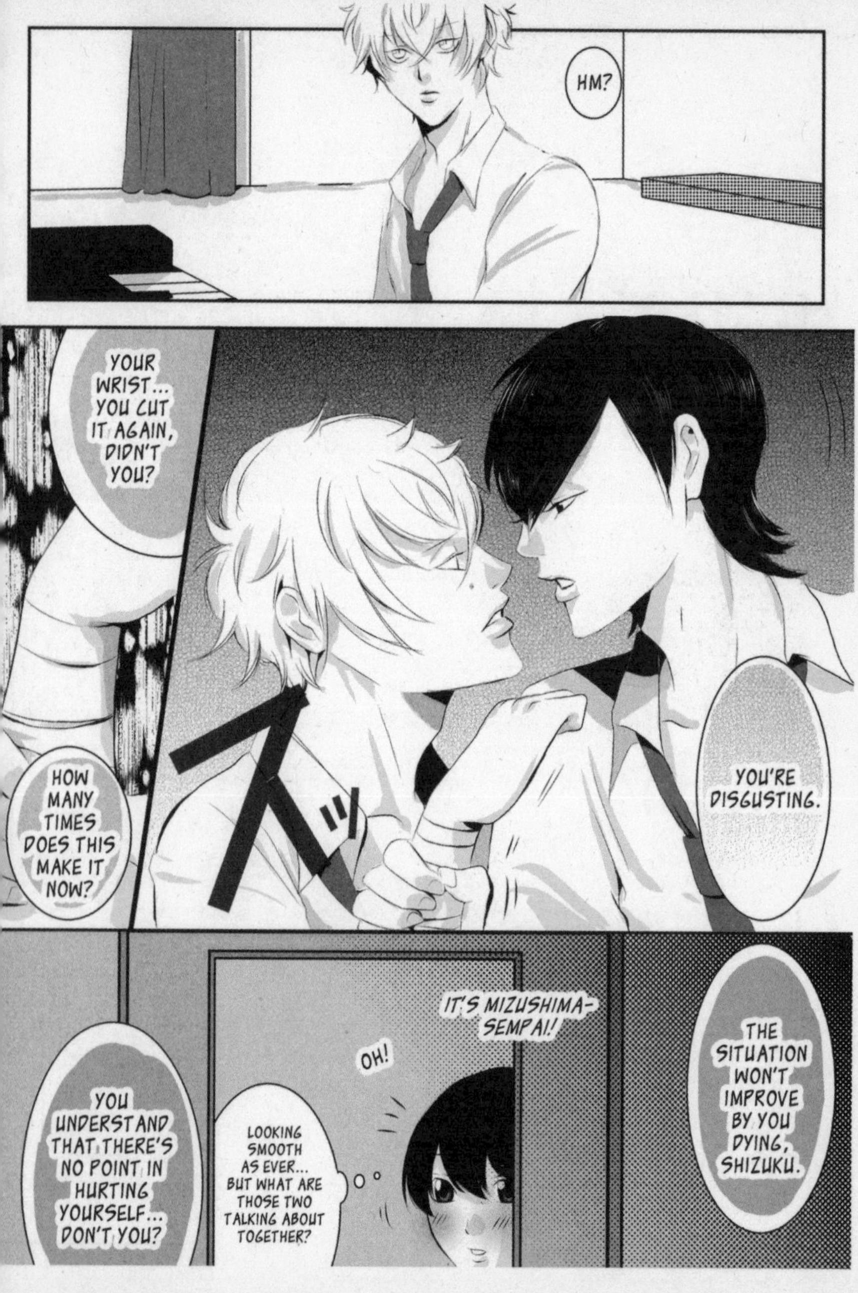
HM?
YOUR WRIST... YOU CUT IT AGAIN, DIDN'T YOU?
YOU'RE DISGUSTING.
HOW MANY TIMES DOES THIS MAKE IT NOW?
THE SITUATION WON'T IMPROVE BY YOU DYING, SHIZUKU.
IT'S MIZUSHIMA-SEMPAI!
OH!
LOOKING SMOOTH AS EVER... BUT WHAT ARE THOSE TWO TALKING ABOUT TOGETHER?
YOU UNDERSTAND THAT THERE'S NO POINT IN HURTING YOURSELF... DON'T YOU?

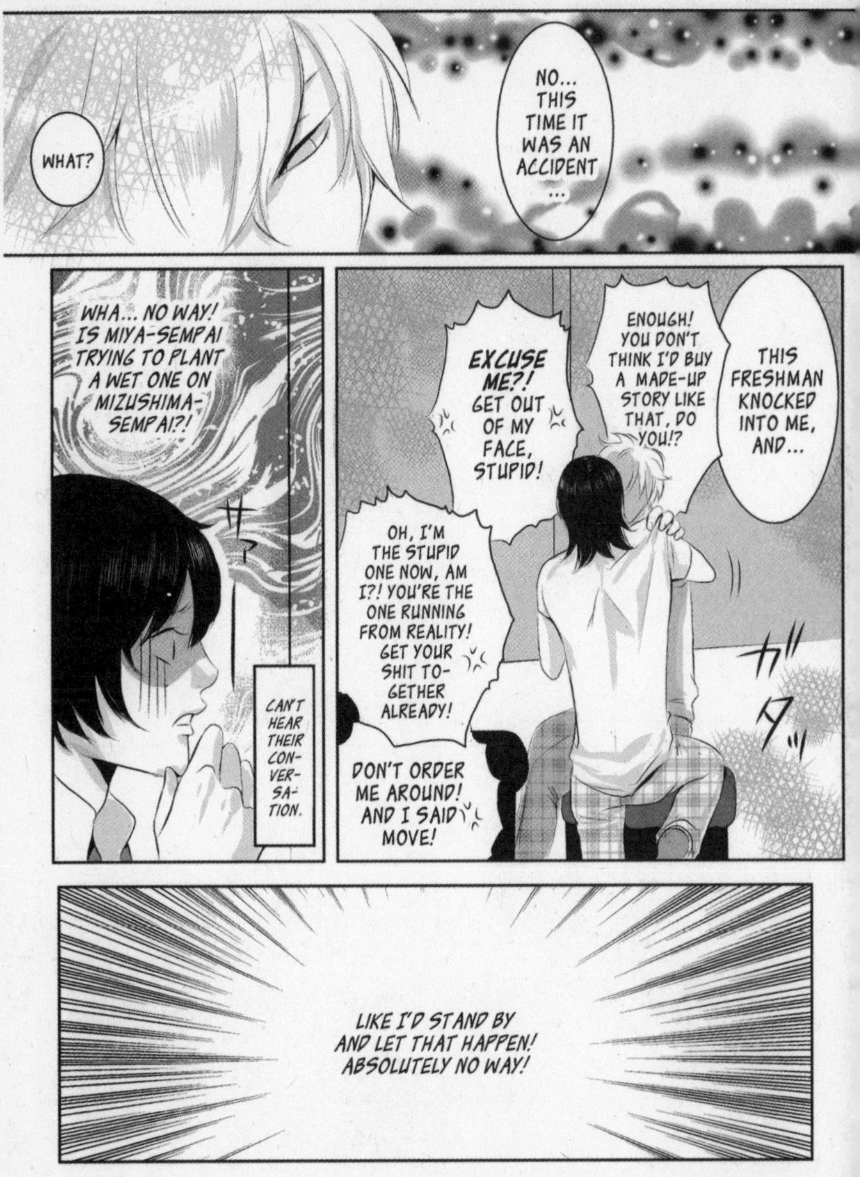
NO... THIS TIME IT WAS AN ACCIDENT...
WHAT?
THIS FRESHMAN KNOCKED INTO ME, AND...
ENOUGH! YOU DON'T THINK I'D BUY A MADE-UP STORY LIKE THAT, DO YOU!?
EXCUSE ME?! GET OUT OF MY FACE, STUPID!
OH, I'M THE STUPID ONE NOW, AM I?! YOU'RE THE ONE RUNNING FROM REALITY! GET YOUR SHIT TOGETHER ALREADY!
DON'T ORDER ME AROUND! AND I SAID MOVE!
WHA... NO WAY! IS MIYA-SEMPAI TRYING TO PLANT A WET ONE ON MIZUSHIMA-SEMPAI?!
CAN'T HEAR THEIR CONVERSATION.
LIKE I'D STAND BY AND LET THAT HAPPEN! ABSOLUTELY NO WAY!

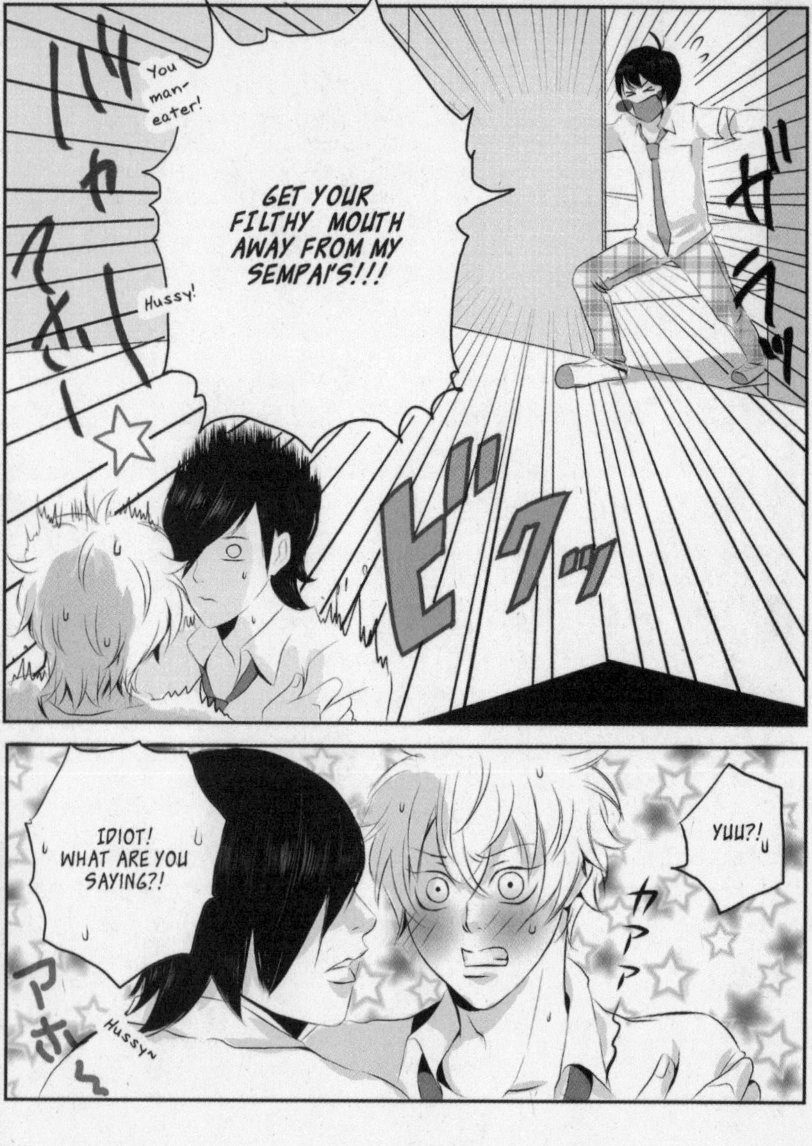
GET YOUR FILTHY MOUTH AWAY FROM MY SEMPAI'S!!!
You man-eater!
Hussy!
ビクッ
YUU?!
IDIOT! WHAT ARE YOU SAYING?!
Hussy~

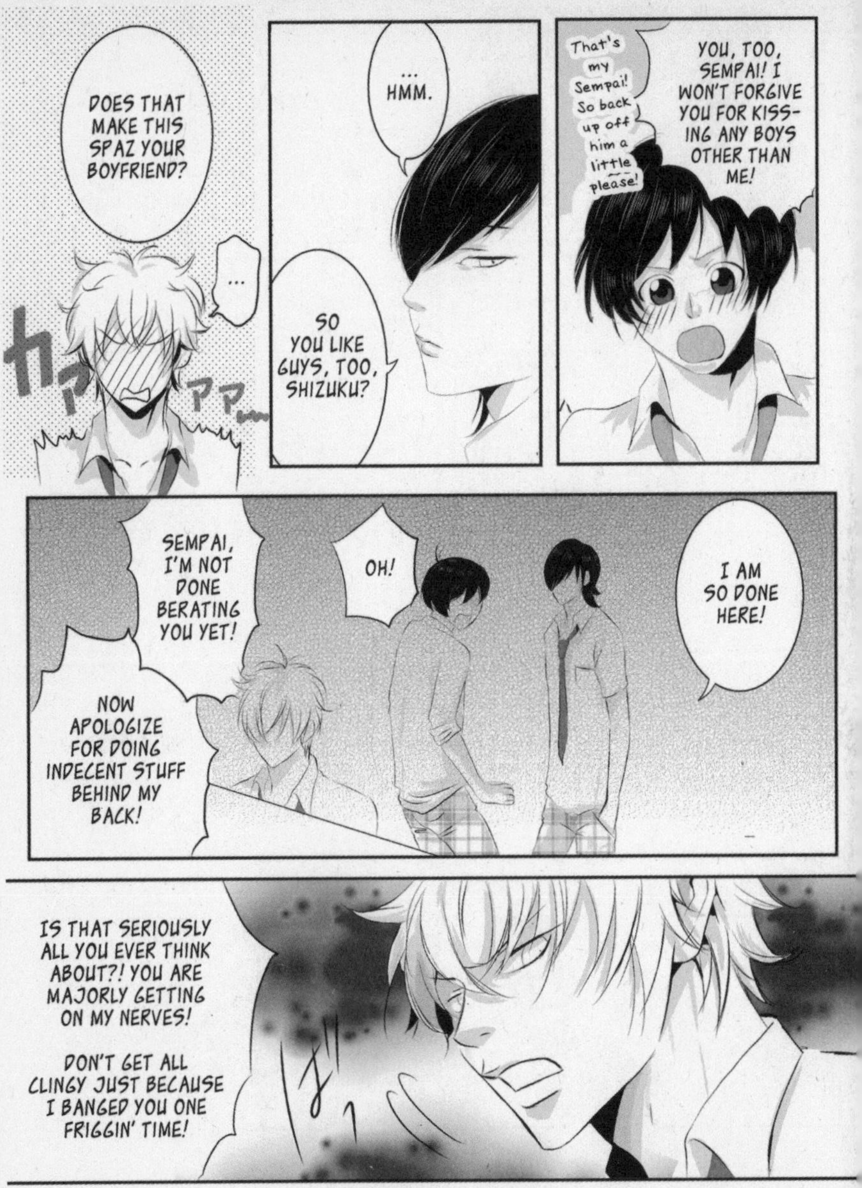
YOU, TOO, SEMPAI! I WON'T FORGIVE YOU FOR KISS-ING ANY BOYS OTHER THAN ME!
That's my Sempai! So back up off him a little please!
... HMM.
SO YOU LIKE GUYS, TOO, SHIZUKU?
DOES THAT MAKE THIS SPAZ YOUR BOYFRIEND?
...
I AM SO DONE HERE!
OH!
SEMPAI, I'M NOT DONE BERATING YOU YET!
NOW APOLOGIZE FOR DOING INDECENT STUFF BEHIND MY BACK!
IS THAT SERIOUSLY ALL YOU EVER THINK ABOUT?! YOU ARE MAJORLY GETTING ON MY NERVES!
DON'T GET ALL CLINGY JUST BECAUSE I BANGED YOU ONE FRIGGIN' TIME!

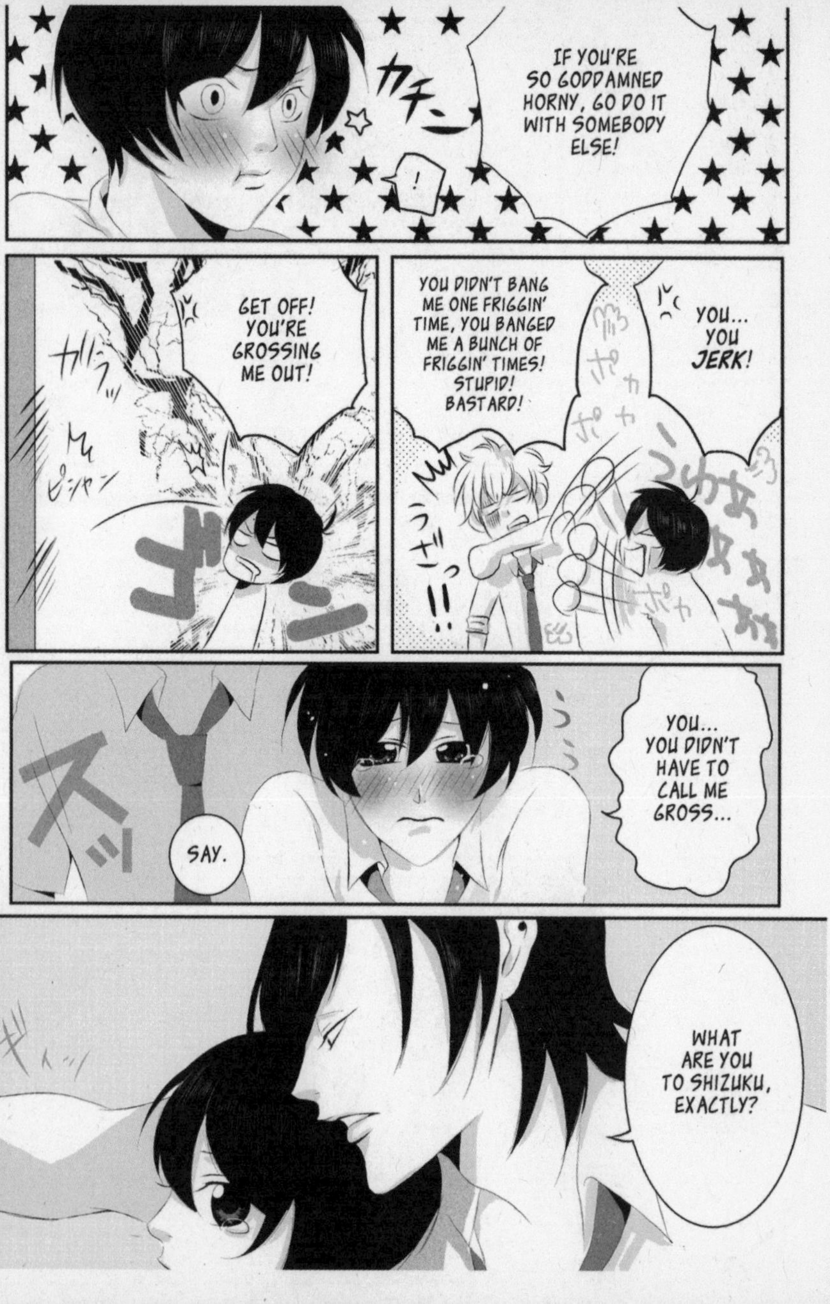
IF YOU'RE SO GODDAMNED HORNY, GO DO IT WITH SOMEBODY ELSE!
!
YOU... YOU JERK!
YOU DIDN'T BANG ME ONE FRIGGIN' TIME, YOU BANGED ME A BUNCH OF FRIGGIN' TIMES! STUPID! BASTARD!
GET OFF! YOU'RE GROSSING ME OUT!
YOU... YOU DIDN'T HAVE TO CALL ME GROSS...
SAY.
WHAT ARE YOU TO SHIZUKU, EXACTLY?

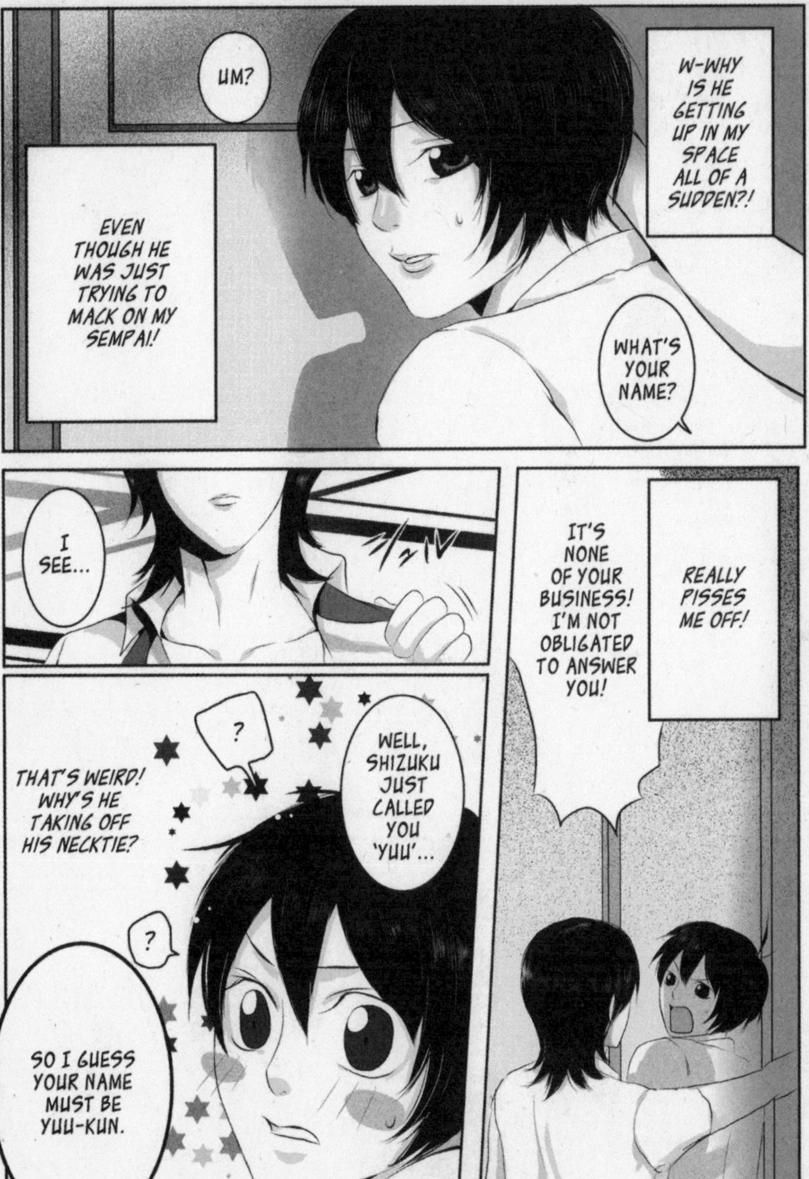

W-WHY IS HE GETTING UP IN MY SPACE ALL OF A SUDDEN?!
UM?
WHAT'S YOUR NAME?
EVEN THOUGH HE WAS JUST TRYING TO MACK ON MY SEMPAI!
REALLY PISSES ME OFF!
IT'S NONE OF YOUR BUSINESS! I'M NOT OBLIGATED TO ANSWER YOU!
I SEE...
WELL, SHIZUKU JUST CALLED YOU 'YUU'...
?
THAT'S WEIRD! WHY'S HE TAKING OFF HIS NECKTIE?
?
SO I GUESS YOUR NAME MUST BE YUU-KUN.

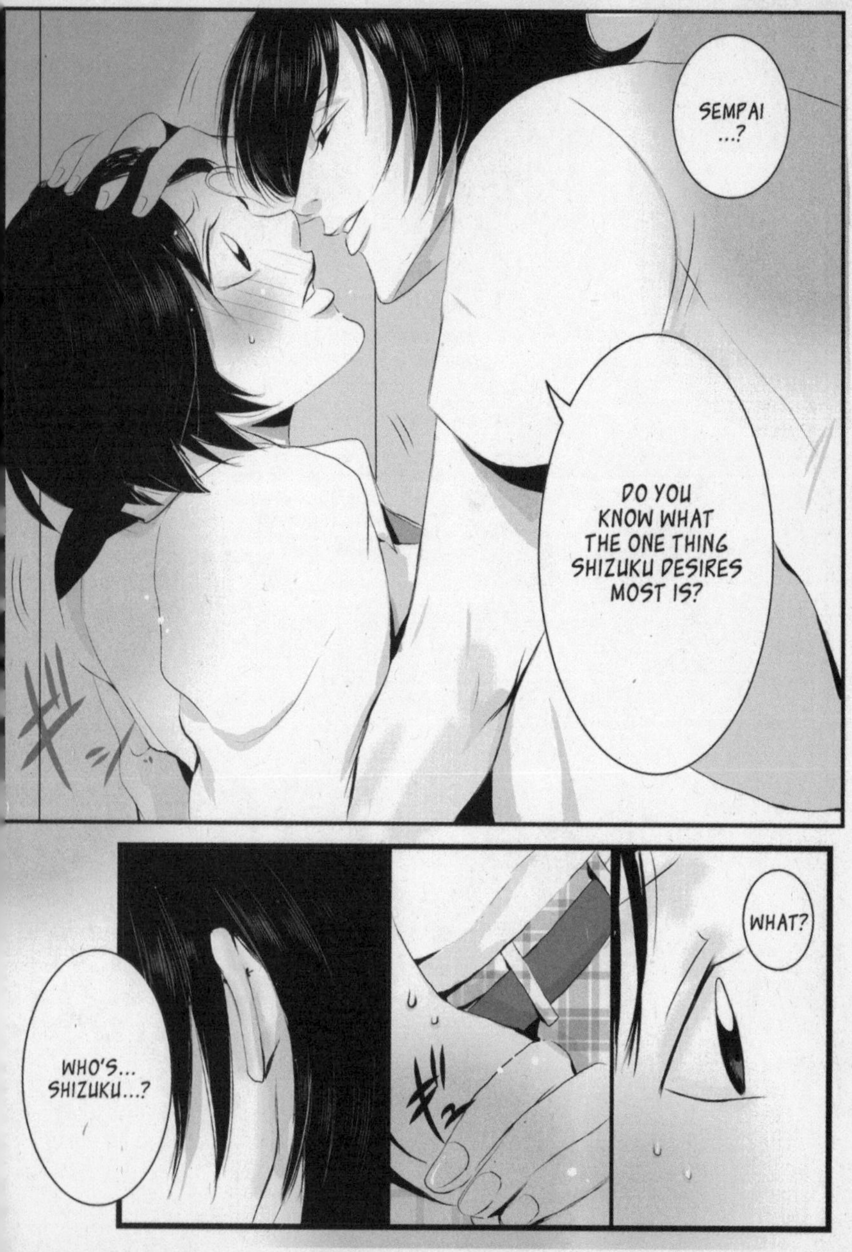
SEMPAI ...?
DO YOU KNOW WHAT THE ONE THING SHIZUKU DESIRES MOST IS?
WHAT?
WHO'S... SHIZUKU...?

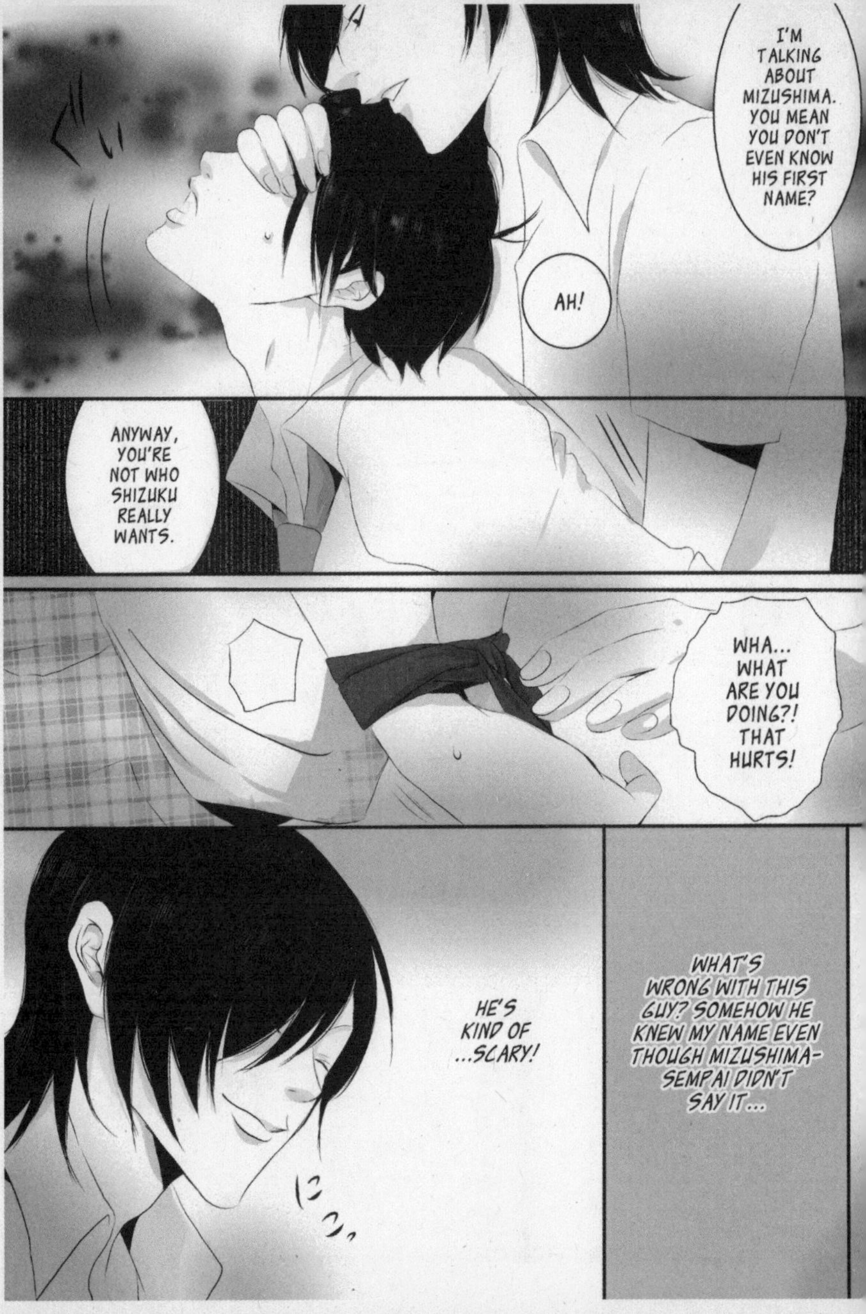
I'M TALKING ABOUT MIZUSHIMA. YOU MEAN YOU DON'T EVEN KNOW HIS FIRST NAME?
AH!
ANYWAY, YOU'RE NOT WHO SHIZUKU REALLY WANTS.
WHA... WHAT ARE YOU DOING?! THAT HURTS!
WHAT'S WRONG WITH THIS GUY? SOMEHOW HE KNEW MY NAME EVEN THOUGH MIZUSHIMA-SEMPAI DIDN'T SAY IT...
HE'S KIND OF ...SCARY!

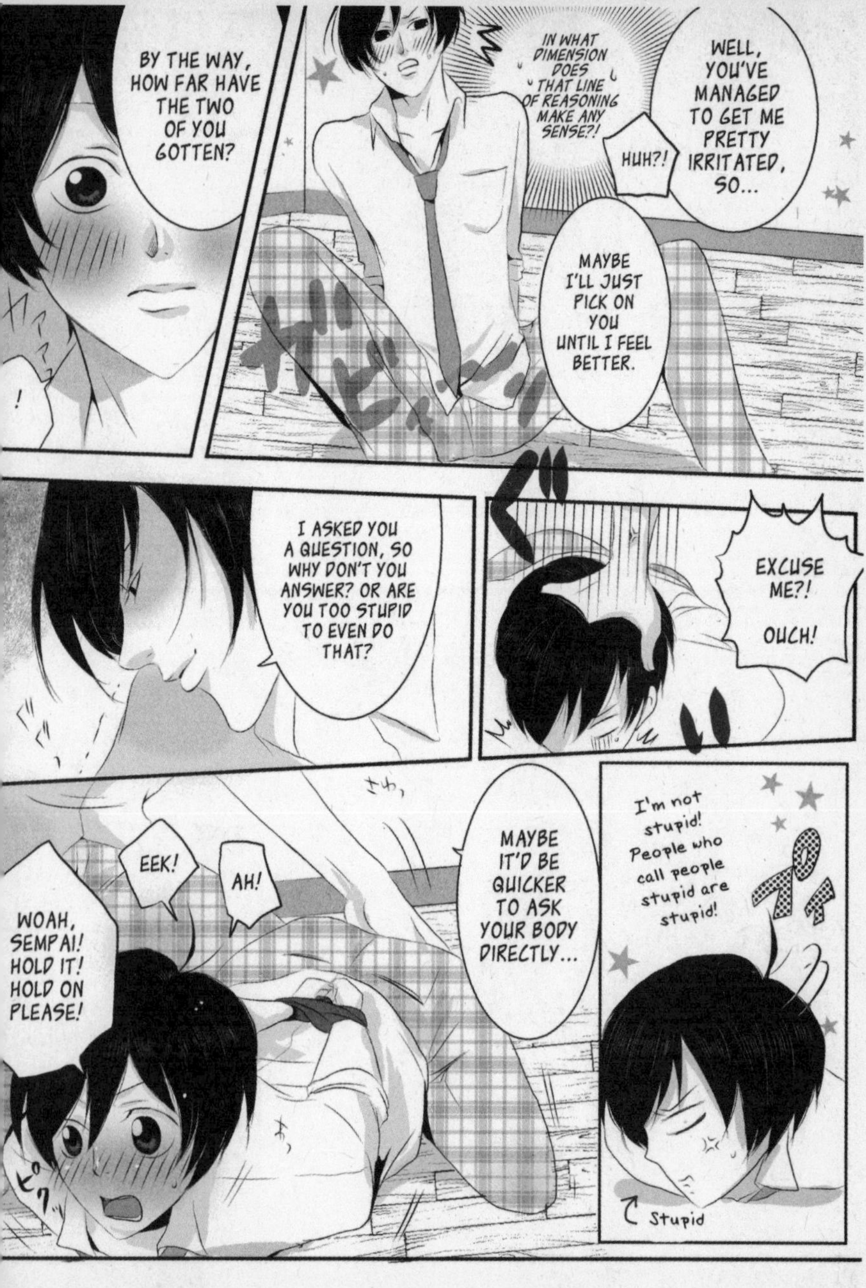
WELL, YOU'VE MANAGED TO GET ME PRETTY IRRITATED, SO...
HUH?!
IN WHAT DIMENSION DOES THAT LINE OF REASONING MAKE ANY SENSE?!
MAYBE I'LL JUST PICK ON YOU UNTIL I FEEL BETTER.
BY THE WAY, HOW FAR HAVE THE TWO OF YOU GOTTEN?
EXCUSE ME?!
OUCH!
I ASKED YOU A QUESTION, SO WHY DON'T YOU ANSWER? OR ARE YOU TOO STUPID TO EVEN DO THAT?
I'm not stupid! People who call people stupid are stupid!
Stupid
MAYBE IT'D BE QUICKER TO ASK YOUR BODY DIRECTLY...
AH!
EEK!
WOAH, SEMPAI! HOLD IT! HOLD ON PLEASE!

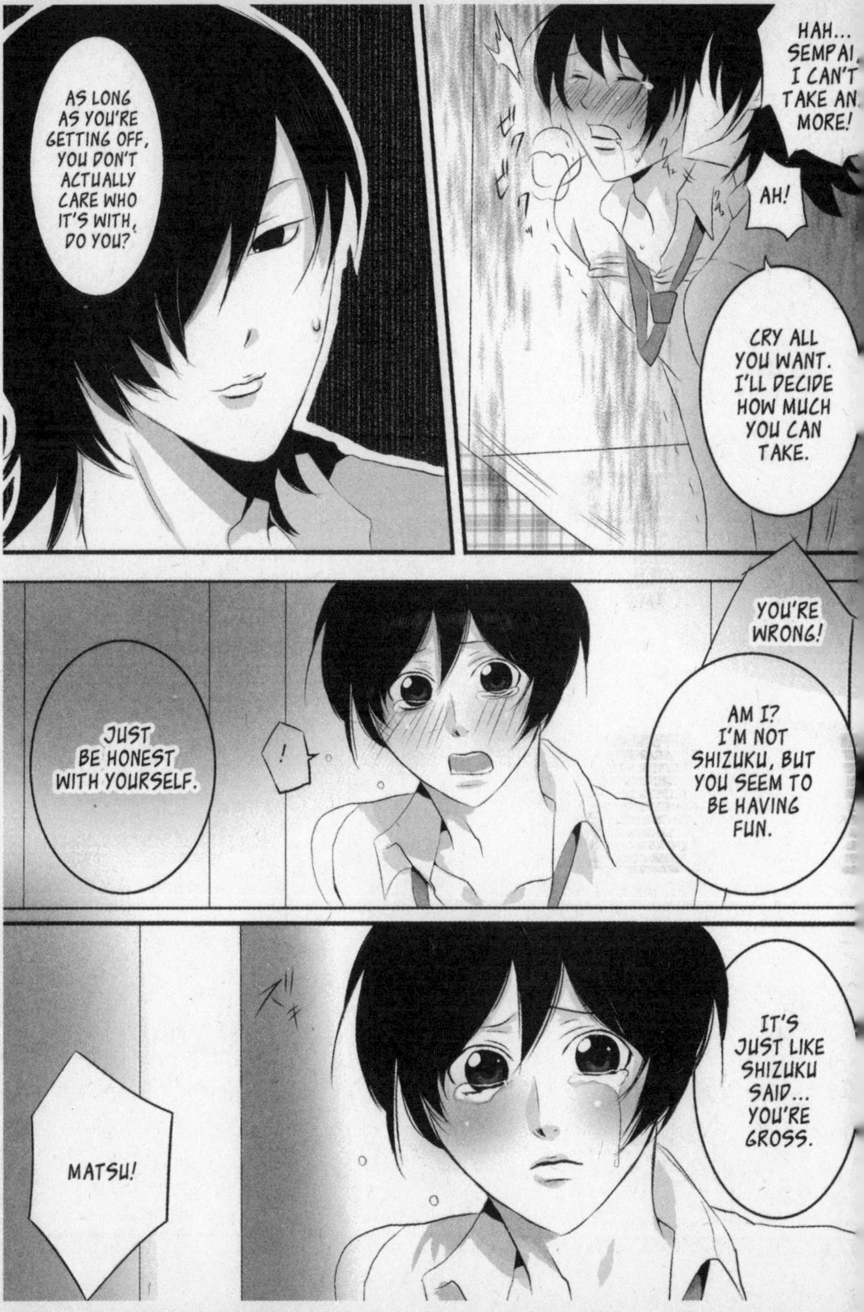
HAH... SEMPAI, I CAN'T TAKE AN MORE!
AH!
CRY ALL YOU WANT. I'LL DECIDE HOW MUCH YOU CAN TAKE.
AS LONG AS YOU'RE GETTING OFF, YOU DON'T ACTUALLY CARE WHO IT'S WITH, DO YOU?
YOU'RE WRONG!
AM I? I'M NOT SHIZUKU, BUT YOU SEEM TO BE HAVING FUN.
!
JUST BE HONEST WITH YOURSELF.
IT'S JUST LIKE SHIZUKU SAID... YOU'RE GROSS.
MATSU!

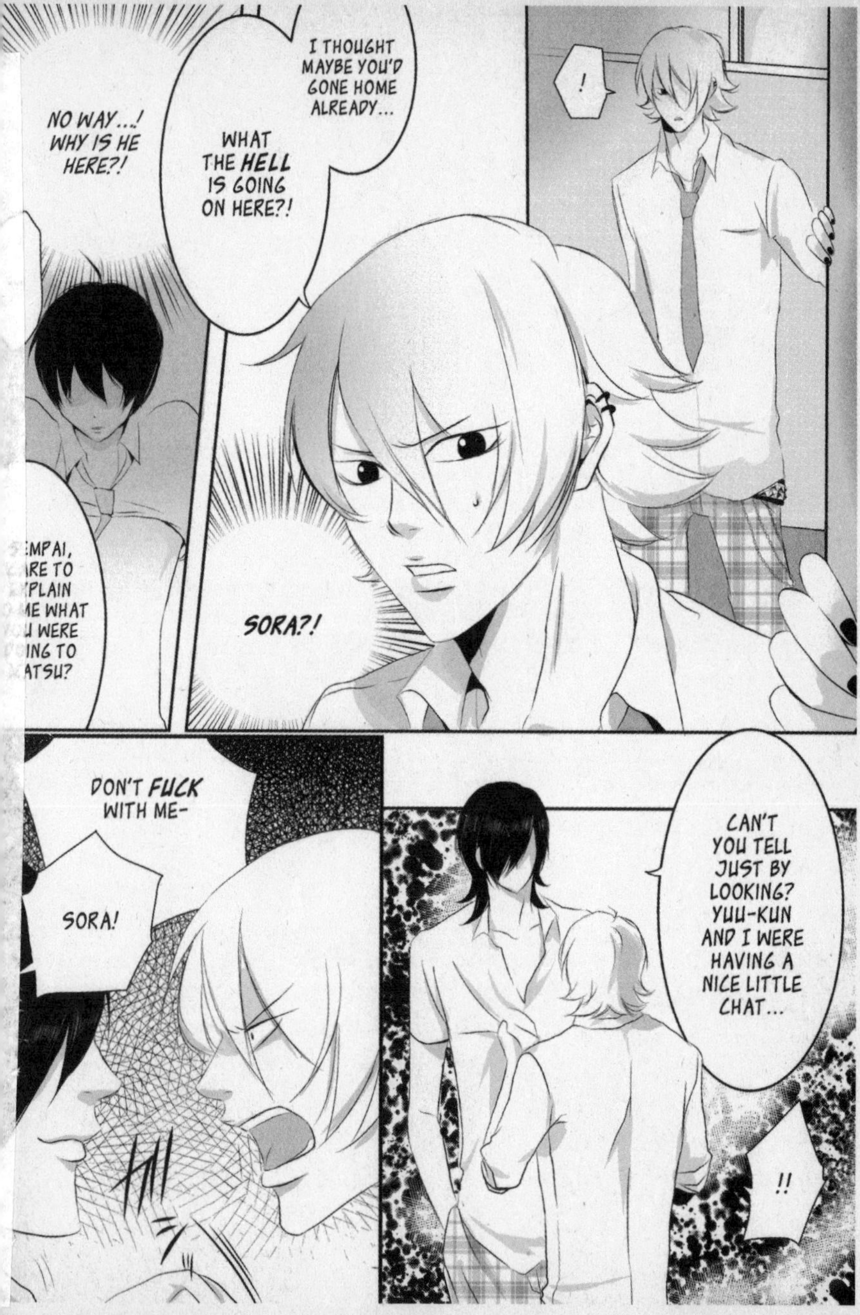
!
I THOUGHT MAYBE YOU'D GONE HOME ALREADY...
WHAT THE **HELL** IS GOING ON HERE?!
SORA?!
NO WAY...! WHY IS HE HERE?!
EMPAI, ARE TO XPLAIN O ME WHAT OU WERE OING TO ATSU?
CAN'T YOU TELL JUST BY LOOKING? YUU-KUN AND I WERE HAVING A NICE LITTLE CHAT...
!!
DON'T **FUCK** WITH ME-
SORA!

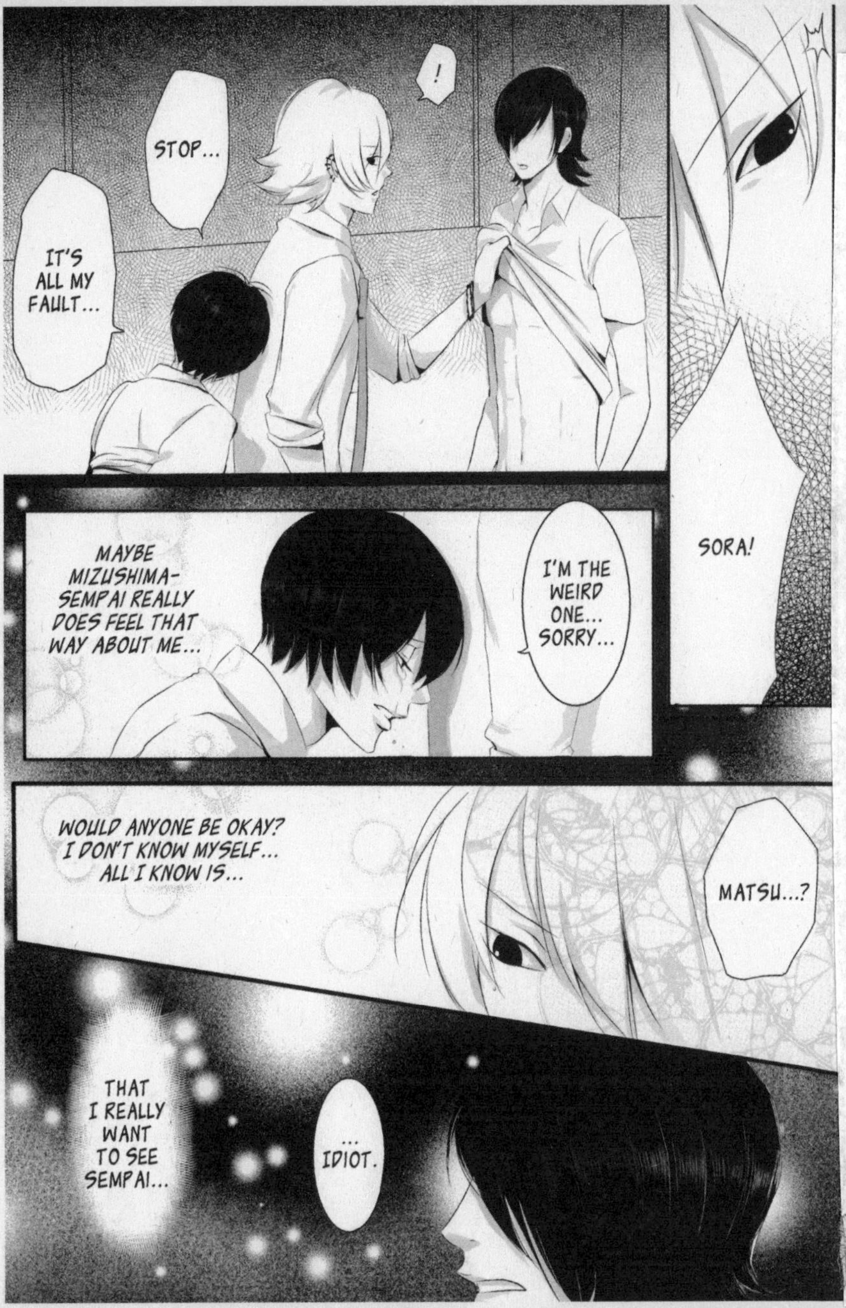
SORA!
!
STOP...
IT'S ALL MY FAULT...
I'M THE WEIRD ONE... SORRY...
MAYBE MIZUSHIMA-SEMPAI REALLY DOES FEEL THAT WAY ABOUT ME...
MATSU...?
WOULD ANYONE BE OKAY? I DON'T KNOW MYSELF... ALL I KNOW IS...
... IDIOT.
THAT I REALLY WANT TO SEE SEMPAI...

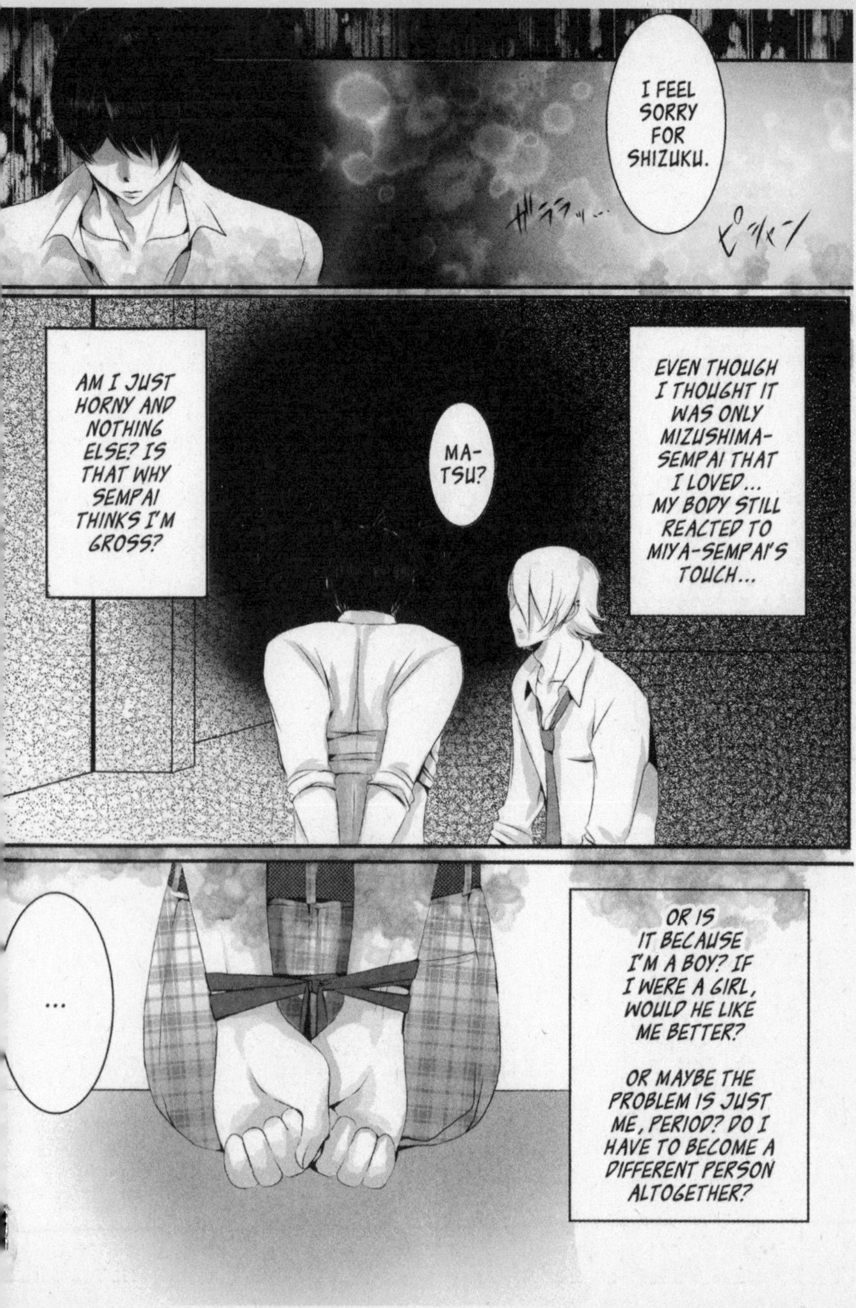
I FEEL SORRY FOR SHIZUKU.
EVEN THOUGH I THOUGHT IT WAS ONLY MIZUSHIMA-SEMPAI THAT I LOVED... MY BODY STILL REACTED TO MIYA-SEMPAI'S TOUCH...
MA-TSU?
AM I JUST HORNY AND NOTHING ELSE? IS THAT WHY SEMPAI THINKS I'M GROSS?
OR IS IT BECAUSE I'M A BOY? IF I WERE A GIRL, WOULD HE LIKE ME BETTER?
OR MAYBE THE PROBLEM IS JUST ME, PERIOD? DO I HAVE TO BECOME A DIFFERENT PERSON ALTOGETHER?
...

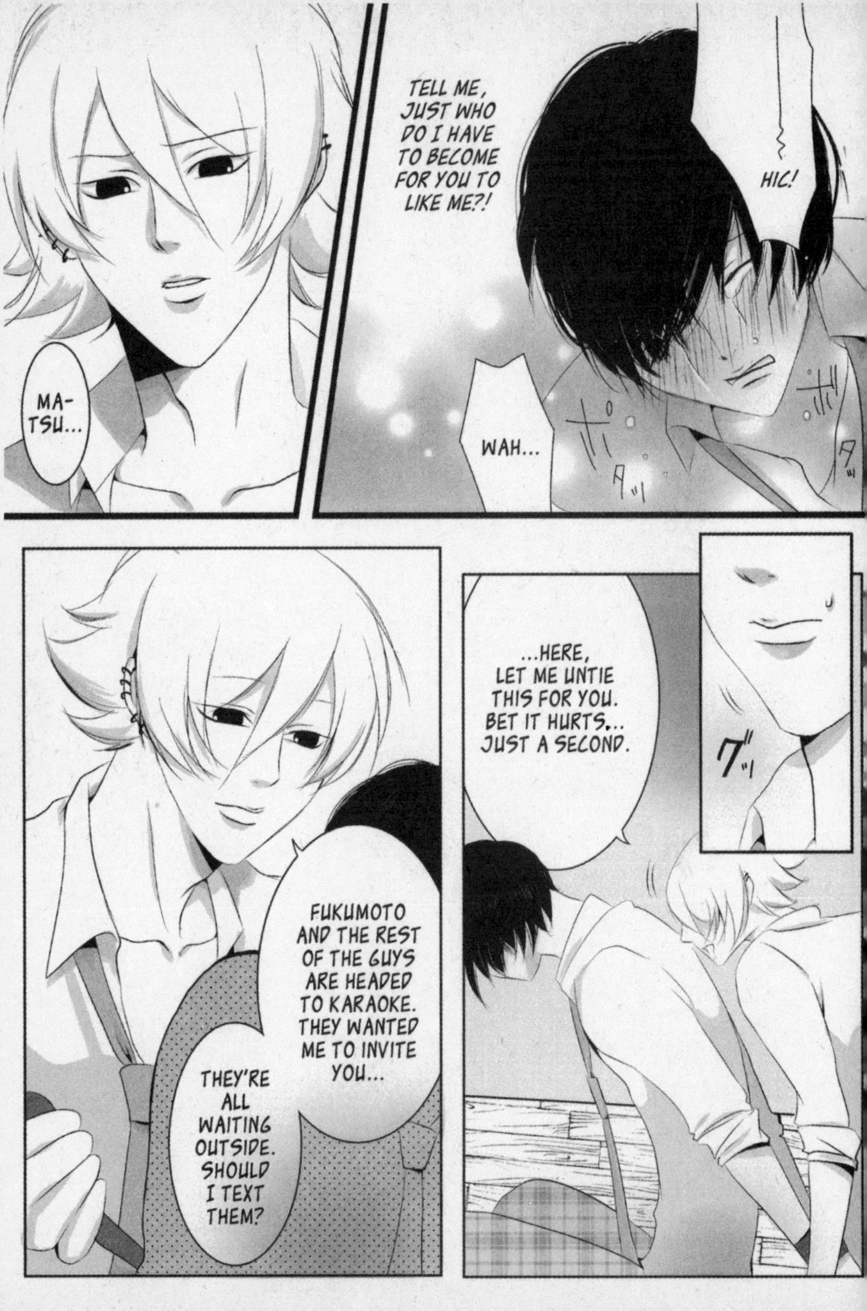
HIC!
TELL ME, JUST WHO DO I HAVE TO BECOME FOR YOU TO LIKE ME?!
WAH...
MA-TSU...
グッ
...HERE, LET ME UNTIE THIS FOR YOU. BET IT HURTS... JUST A SECOND.
FUKUMOTO AND THE REST OF THE GUYS ARE HEADED TO KARAOKE. THEY WANTED ME TO INVITE YOU...
THEY'RE ALL WAITING OUTSIDE. SHOULD I TEXT THEM?

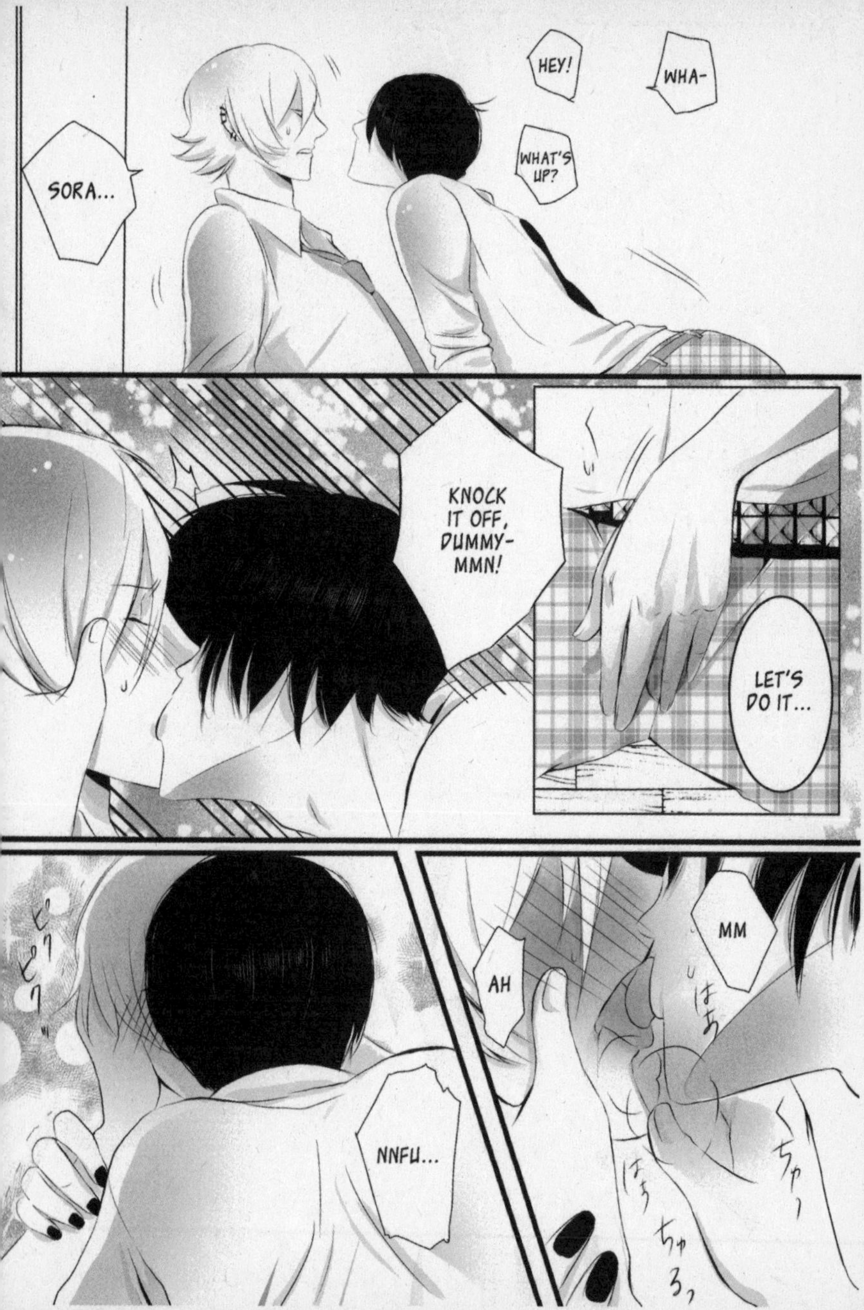
WHA-
HEY!
WHAT'S UP?
SORA...
LET'S DO IT...
KNOCK IT OFF, DUMMY-MMN!
MM
AH
NNFU...

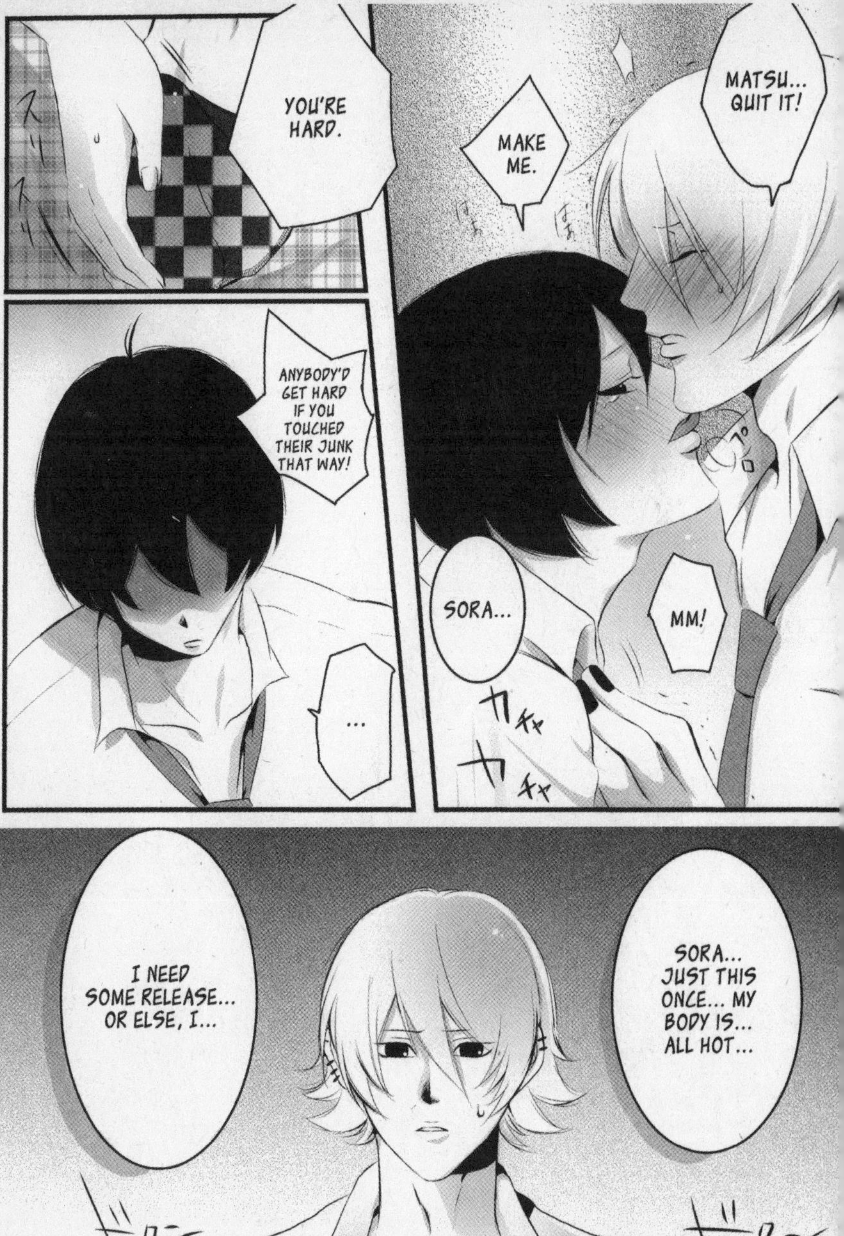
MATSU... QUIT IT!
MAKE ME.
MM!
SORA...
YOU'RE HARD.
ANYBODY'D GET HARD IF YOU TOUCHED THEIR JUNK THAT WAY!
...
SORA... JUST THIS ONCE... MY BODY IS... ALL HOT...
I NEED SOME RELEASE... OR ELSE, I...

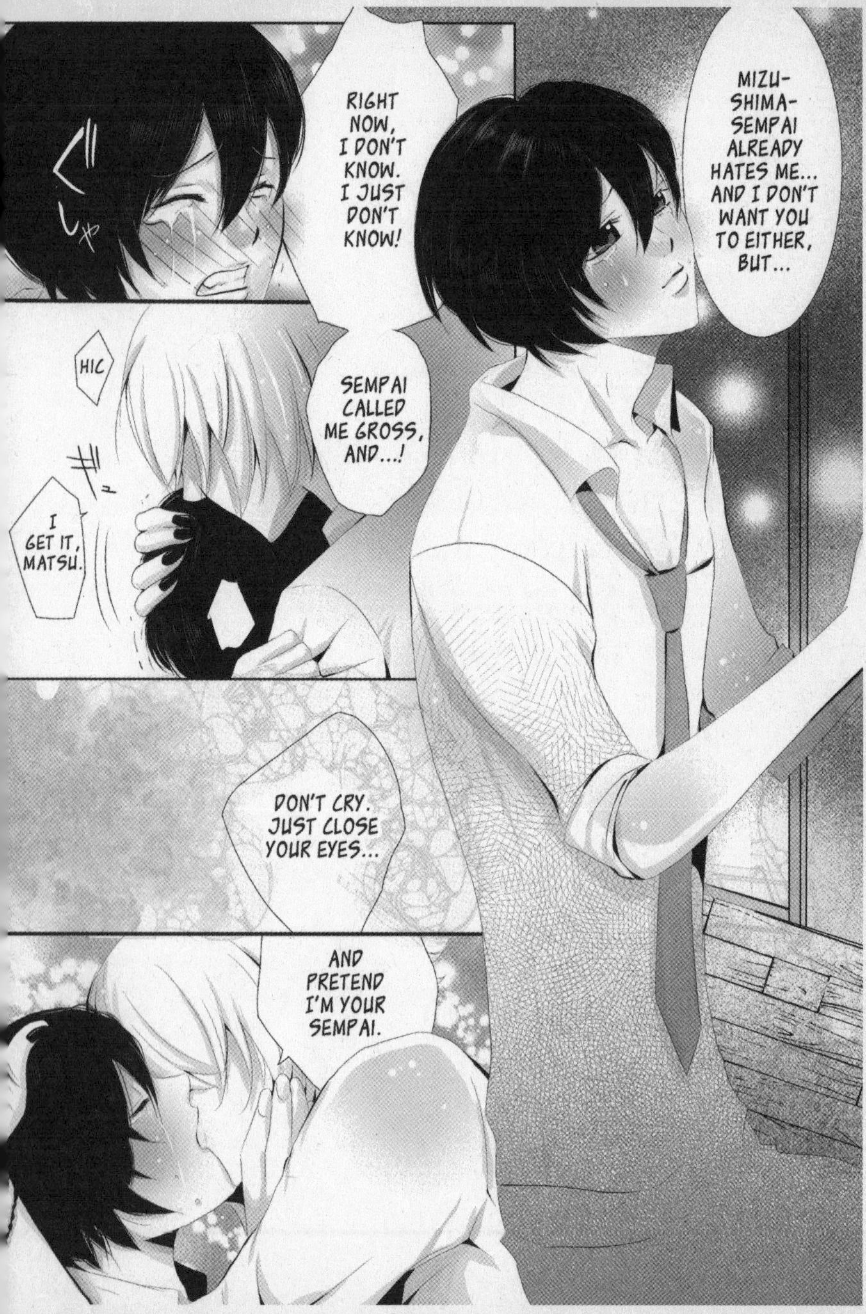
MIZU-SHIMA-SEMPAI ALREADY HATES ME... AND I DON'T WANT YOU TO EITHER, BUT...
RIGHT NOW, I DON'T KNOW. I JUST DON'T KNOW!
SEMPAI CALLED ME GROSS, AND...!
HIC
I GET IT, MATSU.
DON'T CRY. JUST CLOSE YOUR EYES...
AND PRETEND I'M YOUR SEMPAI.

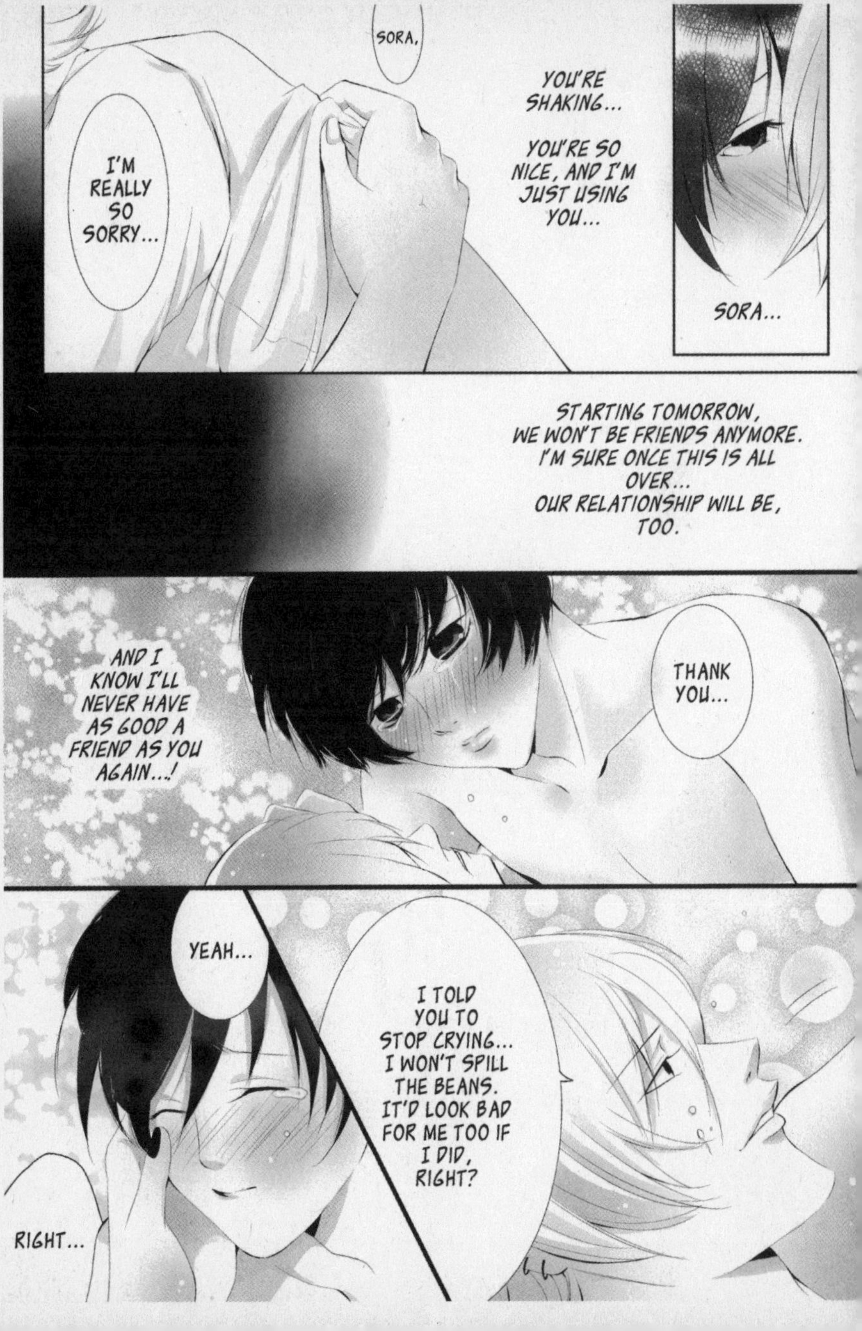
SORA...
SORA,
YOU'RE SHAKING...
YOU'RE SO NICE, AND I'M JUST USING YOU...
I'M REALLY SO SORRY...
STARTING TOMORROW, WE WON'T BE FRIENDS ANYMORE. I'M SURE ONCE THIS IS ALL OVER... OUR RELATIONSHIP WILL BE, TOO.
THANK YOU...
AND I KNOW I'LL NEVER HAVE AS GOOD A FRIEND AS YOU AGAIN...!
I TOLD YOU TO STOP CRYING... I WON'T SPILL THE BEANS. IT'D LOOK BAD FOR ME TOO IF I DID, RIGHT?
YEAH...
RIGHT...

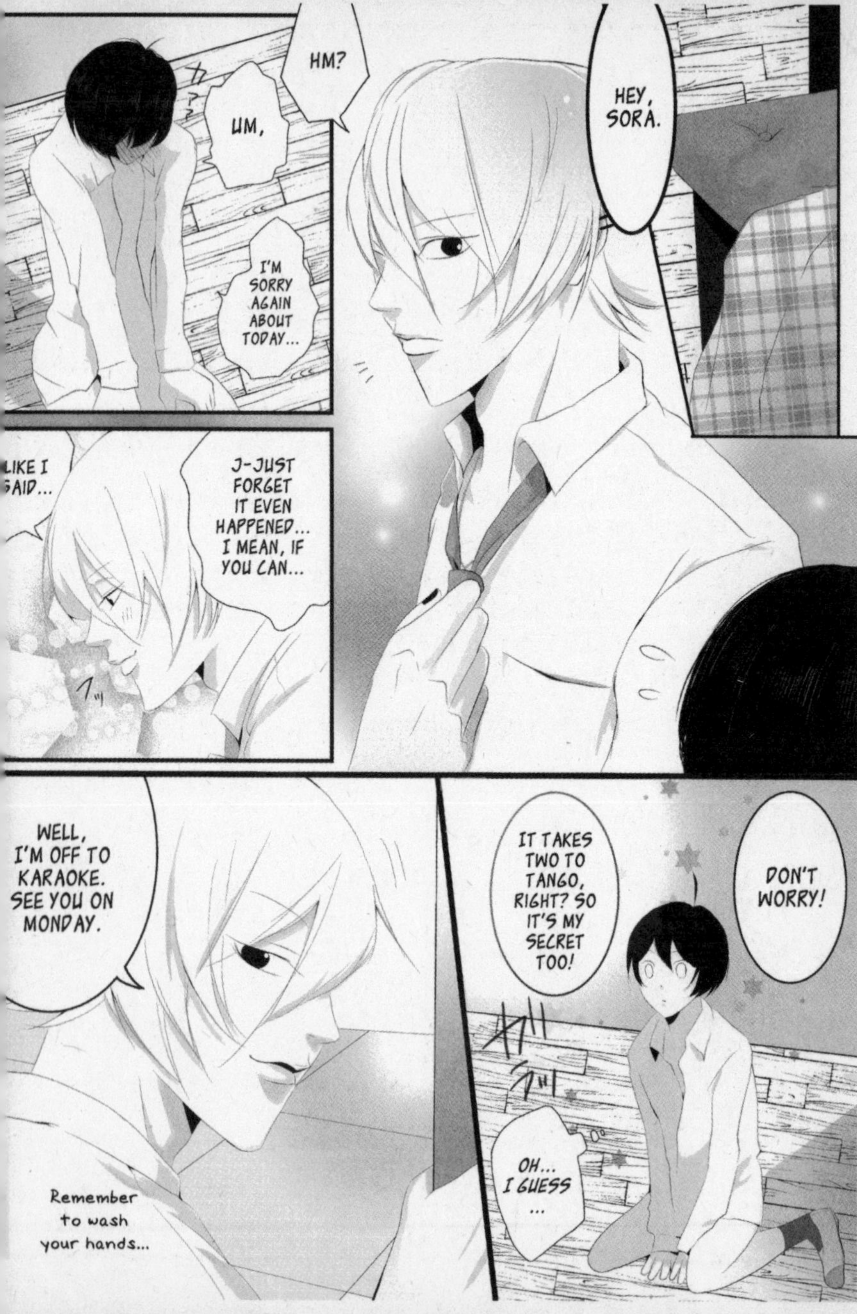
HEY, SORA.
HM?
UM,
I'M SORRY AGAIN ABOUT TODAY...
LIKE I SAID...
J-JUST FORGET IT EVEN HAPPENED... I MEAN, IF YOU CAN...
DON'T WORRY!
IT TAKES TWO TO TANGO, RIGHT? SO IT'S MY SECRET TOO!
OH... I GUESS ...
WELL, I'M OFF TO KARAOKE. SEE YOU ON MONDAY.
Remember to wash your hands...

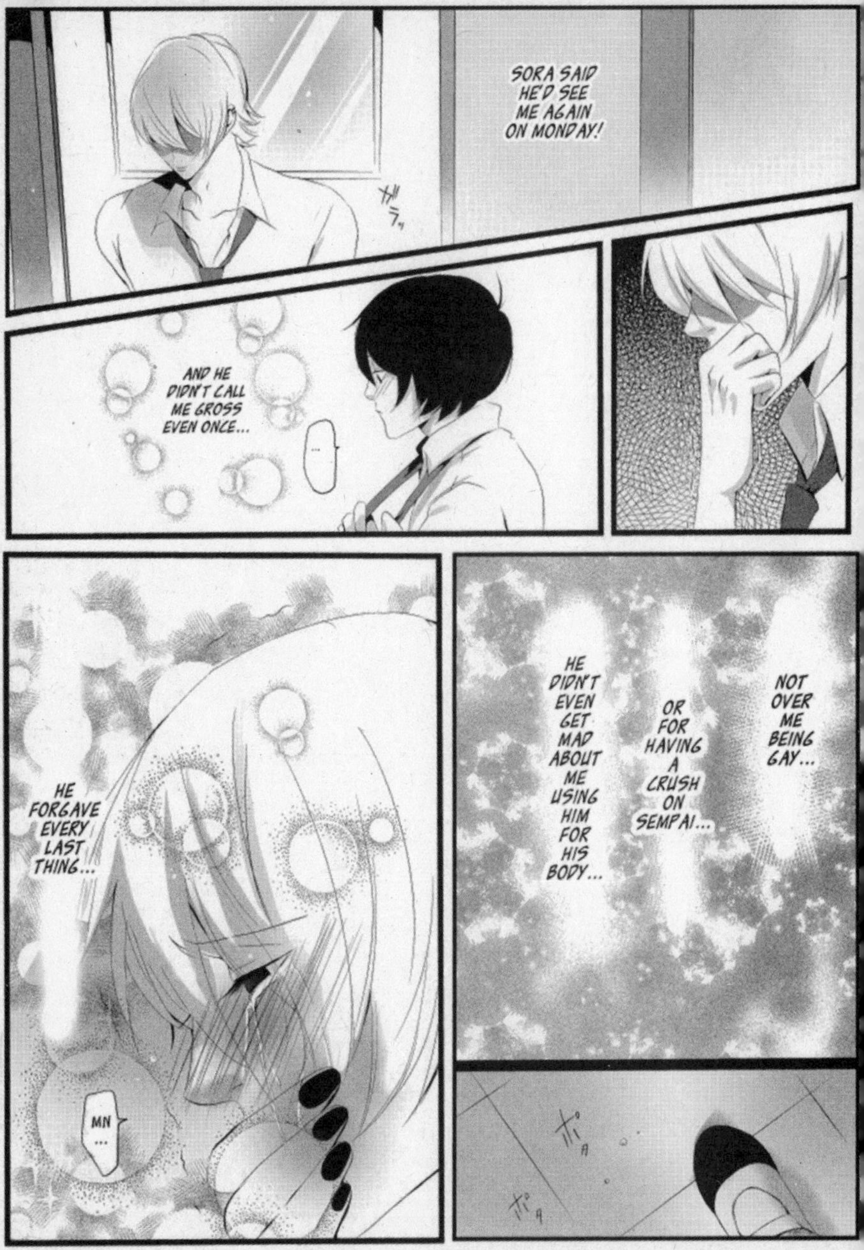
SORA SAID HE'D SEE ME AGAIN ON MONDAY!
ガラッ
AND HE DIDN'T CALL ME GROSS EVEN ONCE...
...
NOT OVER ME BEING GAY...
OR FOR HAVING A CRUSH ON SEMPAI...
HE DIDN'T EVEN GET MAD ABOUT ME USING HIM FOR HIS BODY...
ポタ
ポタ
HE FORGAVE EVERY LAST THING...
MN ...

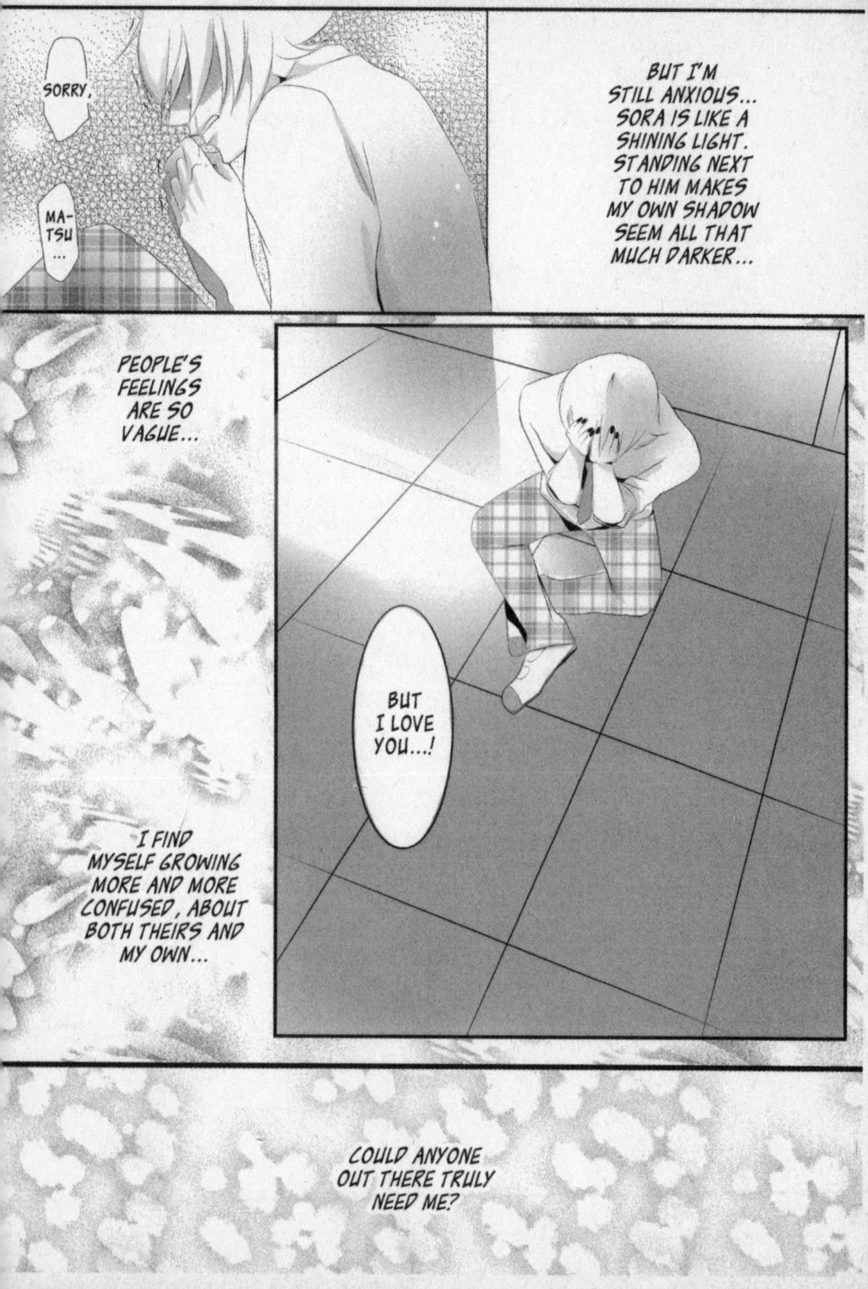
BUT I'M STILL ANXIOUS... SORA IS LIKE A SHINING LIGHT. STANDING NEXT TO HIM MAKES MY OWN SHADOW SEEM ALL THAT MUCH DARKER...
SORRY,
MA-TSU...
BUT I LOVE YOU...!
PEOPLE'S FEELINGS ARE SO VAGUE...
I FIND MYSELF GROWING MORE AND MORE CONFUSED, ABOUT BOTH THEIRS AND MY OWN...
COULD ANYONE OUT THERE TRULY NEED ME?

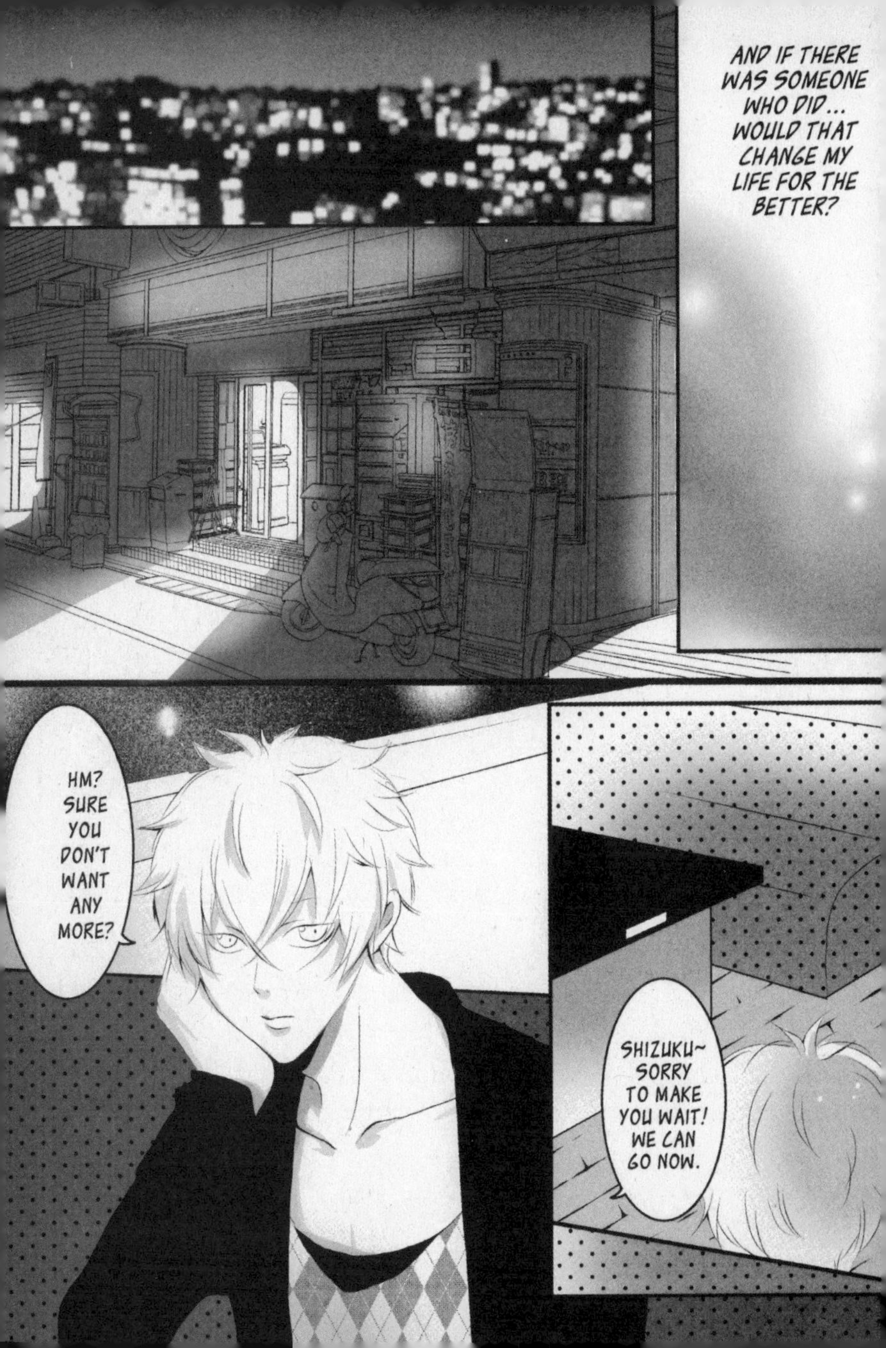
AND IF THERE WAS SOMEONE WHO DID... WOULD THAT CHANGE MY LIFE FOR THE BETTER?
SHIZUKU~ SORRY TO MAKE YOU WAIT! WE CAN GO NOW.
HM? SURE YOU DON'T WANT ANY MORE?

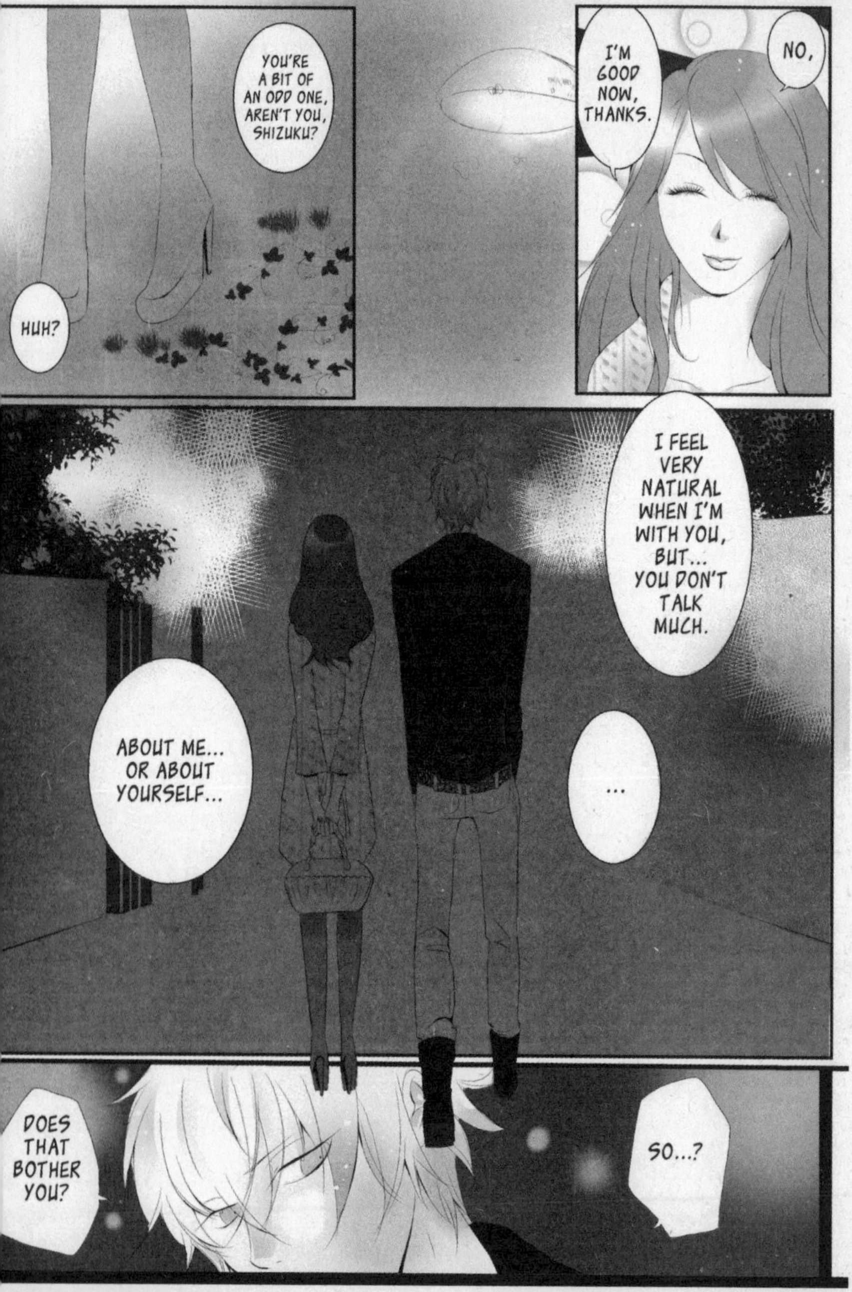
NO,
I'M GOOD NOW, THANKS.
YOU'RE A BIT OF AN ODD ONE, AREN'T YOU, SHIZUKU?
HUH?
I FEEL VERY NATURAL WHEN I'M WITH YOU, BUT... YOU DON'T TALK MUCH.
...
ABOUT ME... OR ABOUT YOURSELF...
SO...?
DOES THAT BOTHER YOU?

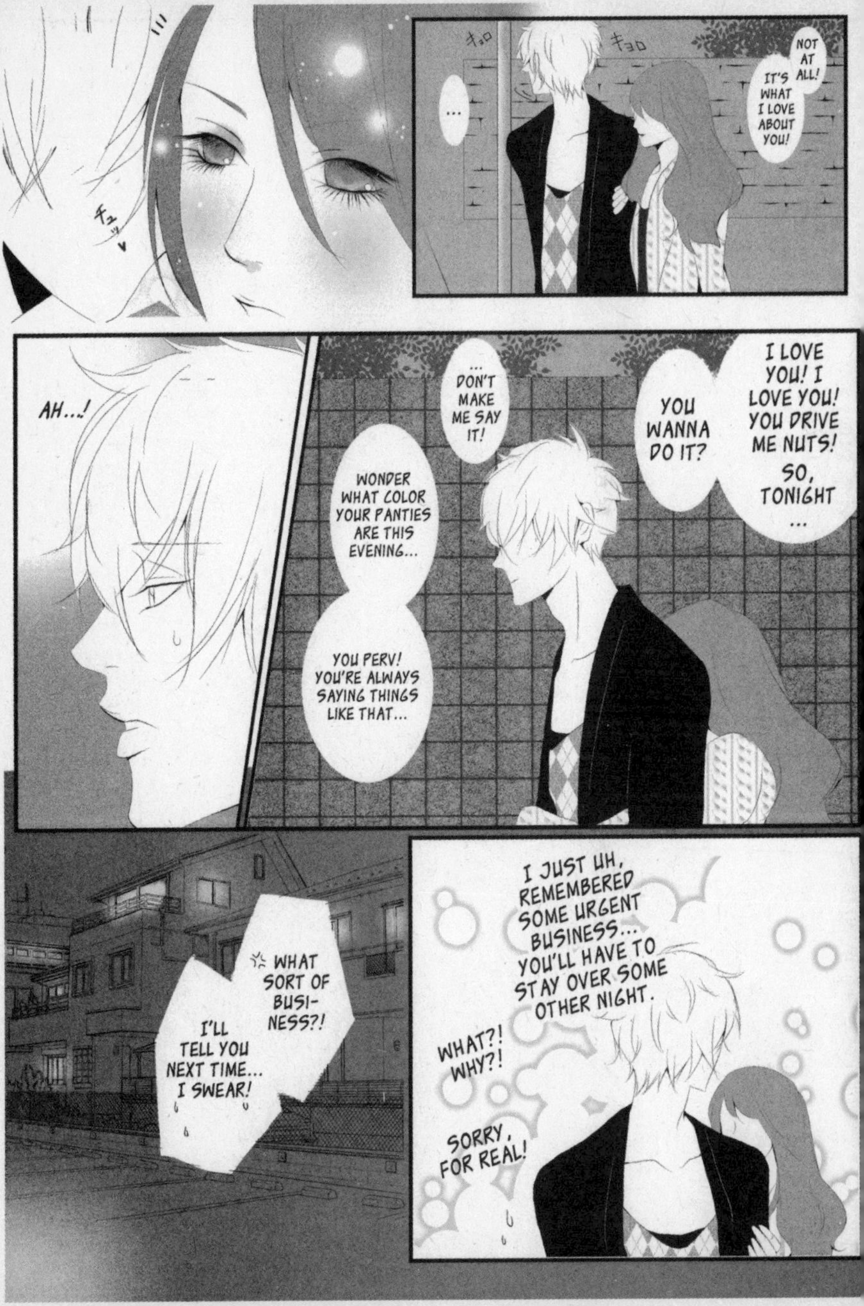
キョロ
キョロ
NOT AT ALL! IT'S WHAT I LOVE ABOUT YOU!
...
チュッ♥
I LOVE YOU! I LOVE YOU! YOU DRIVE ME NUTS! SO, TONIGHT ...
YOU WANNA DO IT?
... DON'T MAKE ME SAY IT!
WONDER WHAT COLOR YOUR PANTIES ARE THIS EVENING...
YOU PERV! YOU'RE ALWAYS SAYING THINGS LIKE THAT...
AH...!
I JUST UH, REMEMBERED SOME URGENT BUSINESS... YOU'LL HAVE TO STAY OVER SOME OTHER NIGHT.
WHAT?! WHY?!
SORRY, FOR REAL!
WHAT SORT OF BUSINESS?!
I'LL TELL YOU NEXT TIME... I SWEAR!

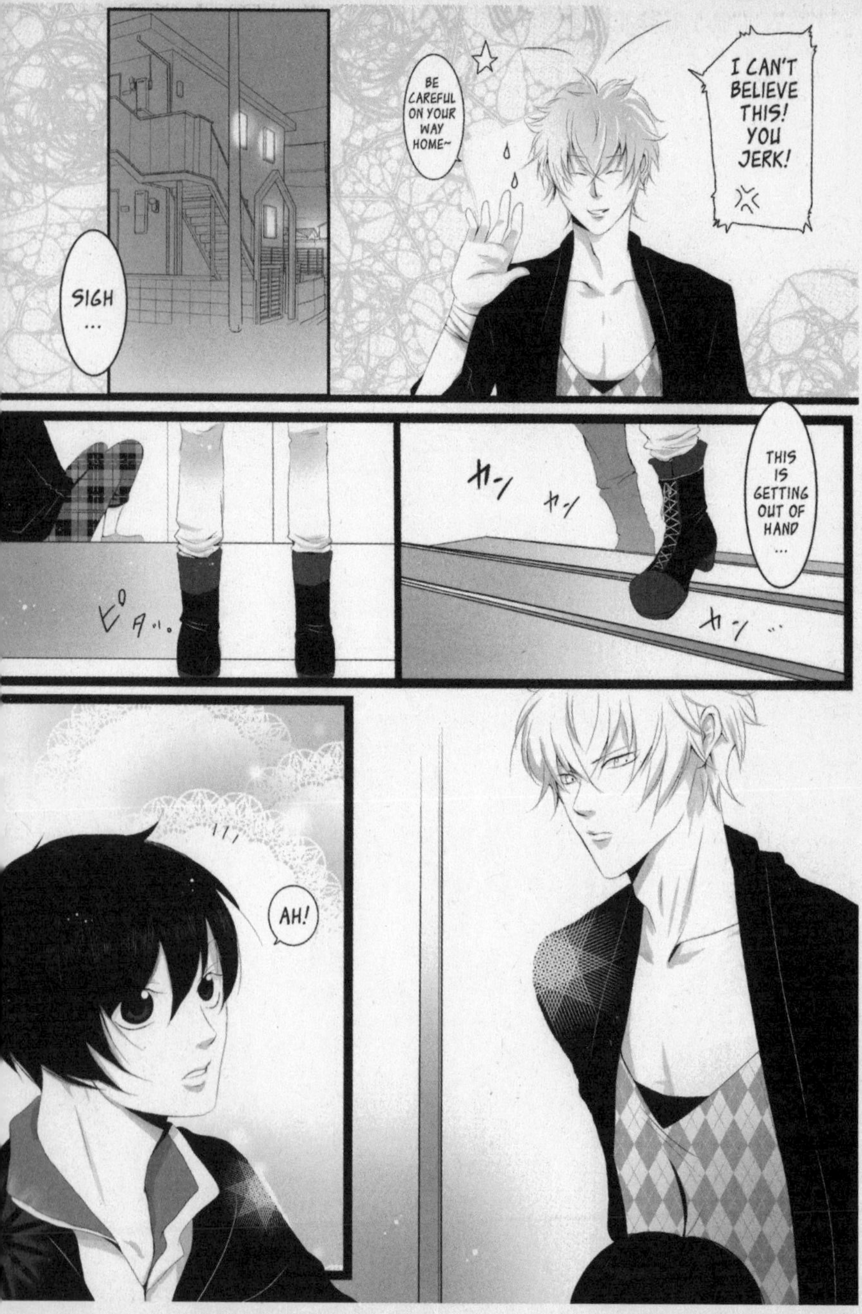
I CAN'T BELIEVE THIS! YOU JERK!
BE CAREFUL ON YOUR WAY HOME~
SIGH ...
THIS IS GETTING OUT OF HAND ...
AH!

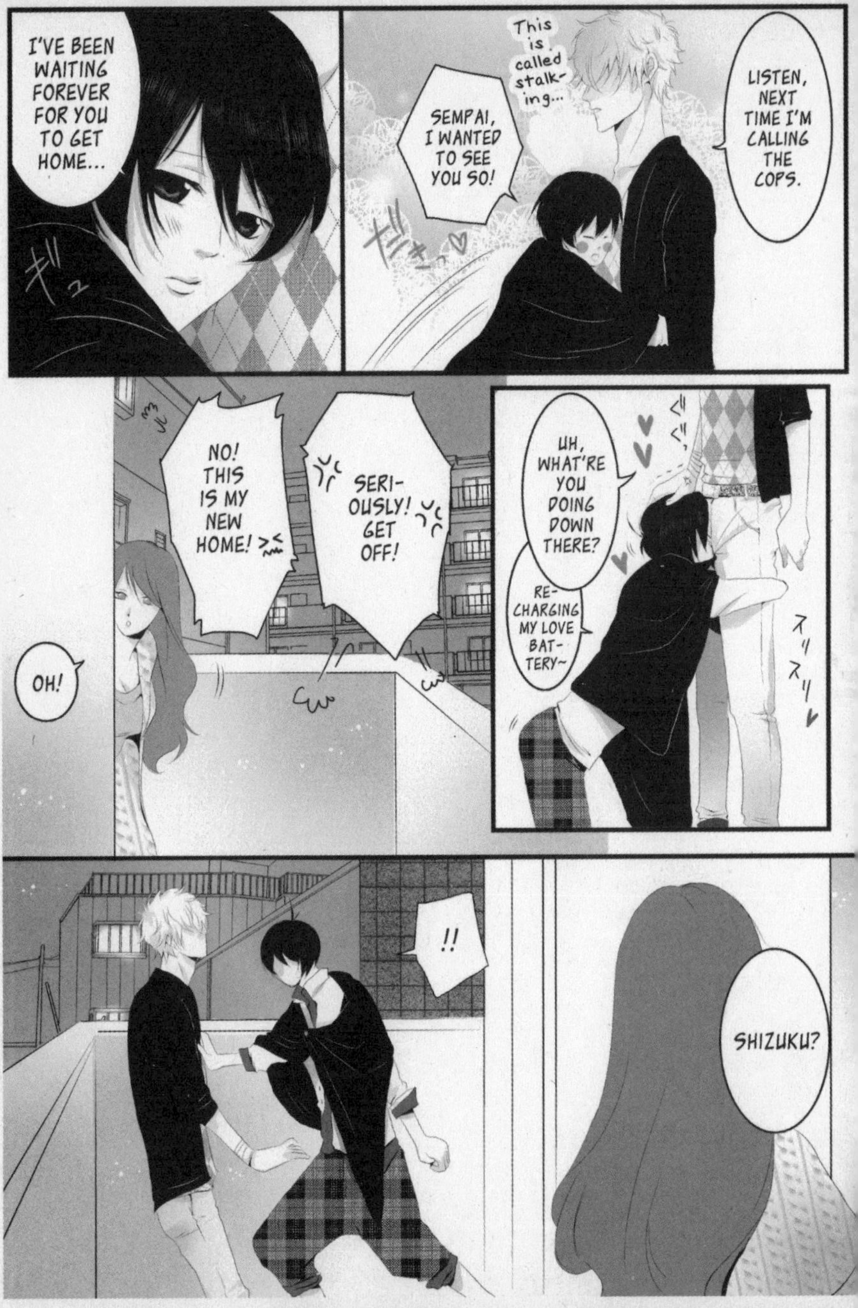
LISTEN, NEXT TIME I'M CALLING THE COPS.
This is called stalk-ing...
SEMPAI, I WANTED TO SEE YOU SO!
I'VE BEEN WAITING FOREVER FOR YOU TO GET HOME...
UH, WHAT'RE YOU DOING DOWN THERE?
RE-CHARGING MY LOVE BAT-TERY~
SERI-OUSLY! GET OFF!
NO! THIS IS MY NEW HOME!
OH!
SHIZUKU?
!!

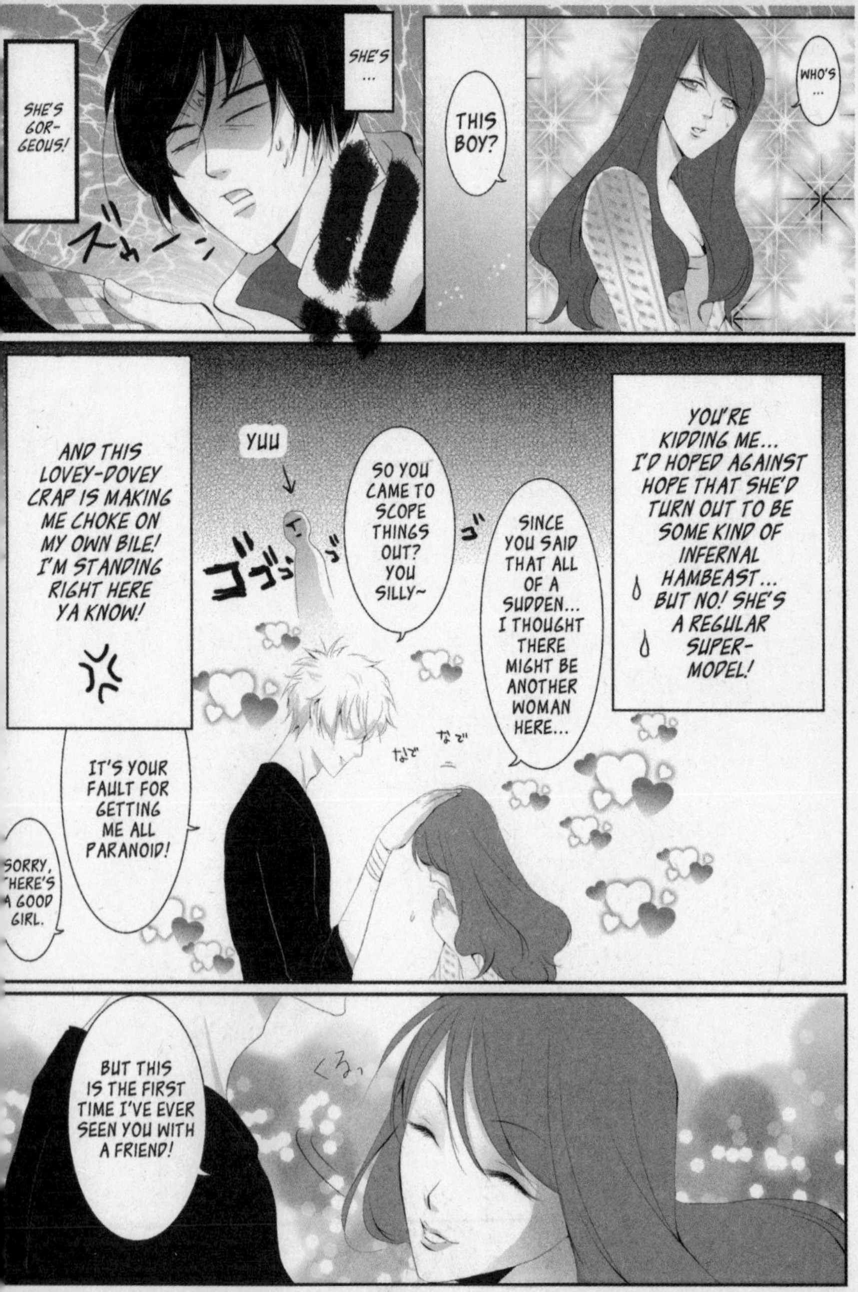
WHO'S ...
THIS BOY?
SHE'S ...
SHE'S GORGEOUS!
YOU'RE KIDDING ME... I'D HOPED AGAINST HOPE THAT SHE'D TURN OUT TO BE SOME KIND OF INFERNAL HAMBEAST... BUT NO! SHE'S A REGULAR SUPER-MODEL!
SINCE YOU SAID THAT ALL OF A SUDDEN... I THOUGHT THERE MIGHT BE ANOTHER WOMAN HERE...
SO YOU CAME TO SCOPE THINGS OUT? YOU SILLY~
YUU
AND THIS LOVEY-DOVEY CRAP IS MAKING ME CHOKE ON MY OWN BILE! I'M STANDING RIGHT HERE YA KNOW!
IT'S YOUR FAULT FOR GETTING ME ALL PARANOID!
なで なで
SORRY, THERE'S A GOOD GIRL.
BUT THIS IS THE FIRST TIME I'VE EVER SEEN YOU WITH A FRIEND!
くるっ

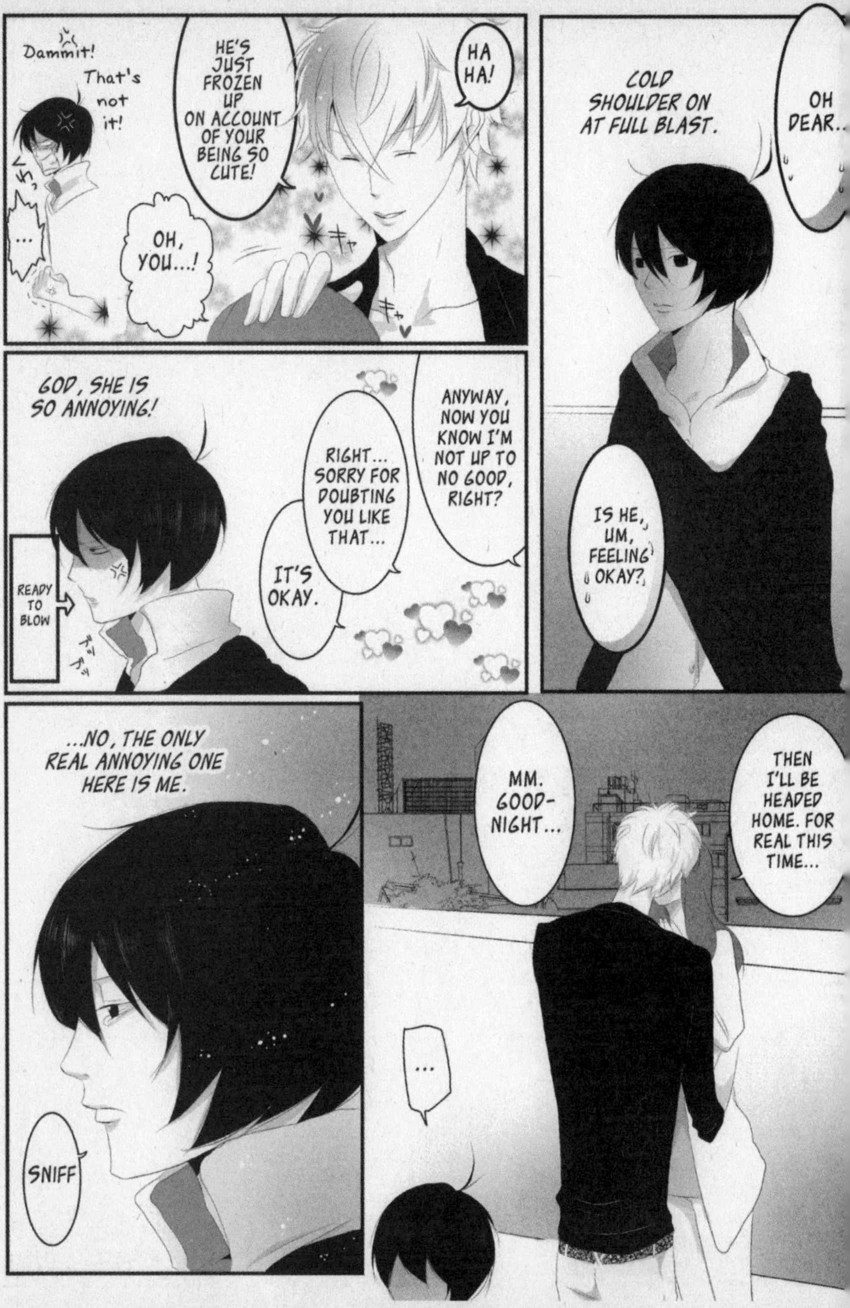
OH DEAR...
COLD SHOULDER ON AT FULL BLAST.
IS HE, UM, FEELING OKAY?
HA HA!
HE'S JUST FROZEN UP ON ACCOUNT OF YOUR BEING SO CUTE!
Dammit! That's not it!
OH, YOU...!
...
ANYWAY, NOW YOU KNOW I'M NOT UP TO NO GOOD, RIGHT?
RIGHT... SORRY FOR DOUBTING YOU LIKE THAT...
IT'S OKAY.
GOD, SHE IS SO ANNOYING!
READY TO BLOW
THEN I'LL BE HEADED HOME. FOR REAL THIS TIME...
MM. GOOD-NIGHT...
...
...NO, THE ONLY REAL ANNOYING ONE HERE IS ME.
SNIFF

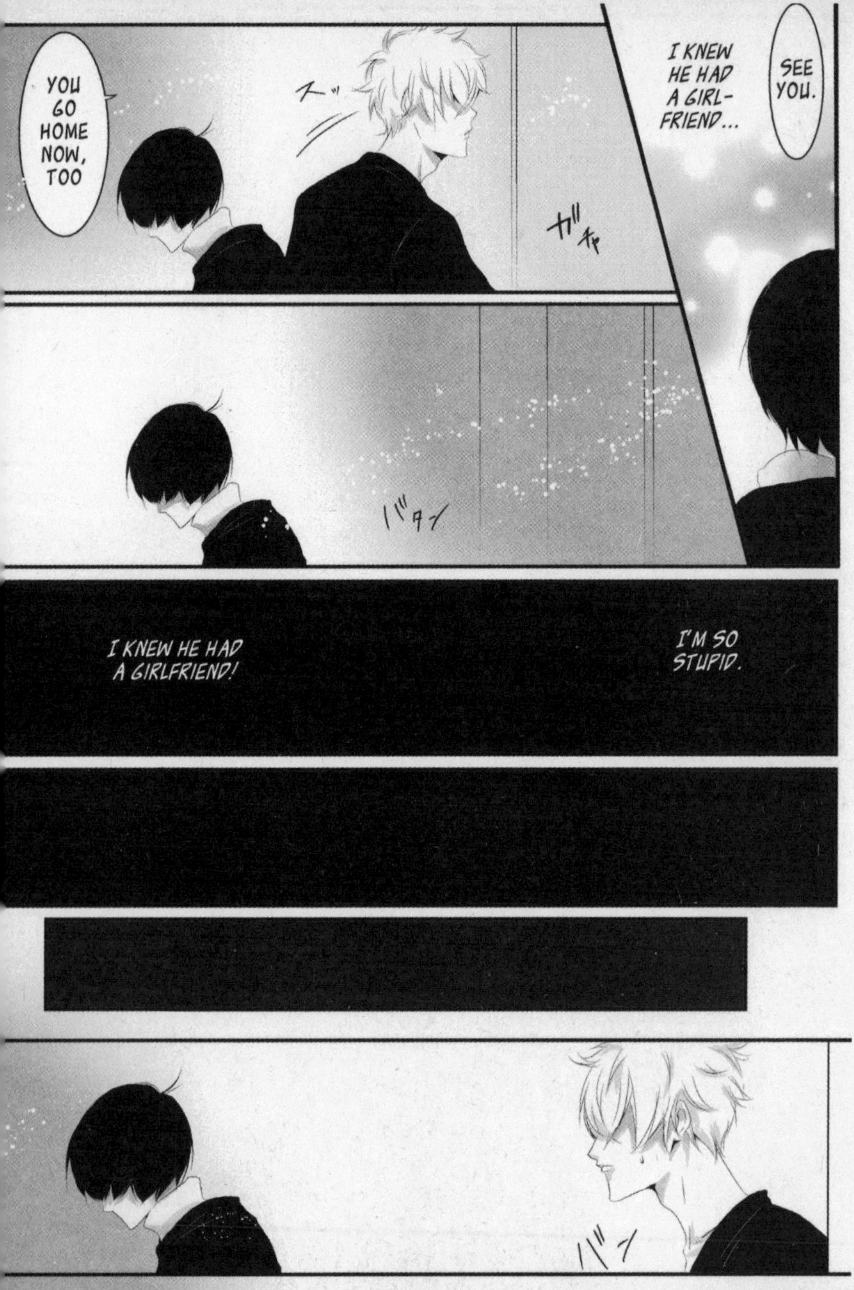
SEE YOU.
I KNEW HE HAD A GIRL-FRIEND...
ガチャ
スッ
YOU GO HOME NOW, TOO
バタン
I'M SO STUPID.
I KNEW HE HAD A GIRLFRIEND!
バン

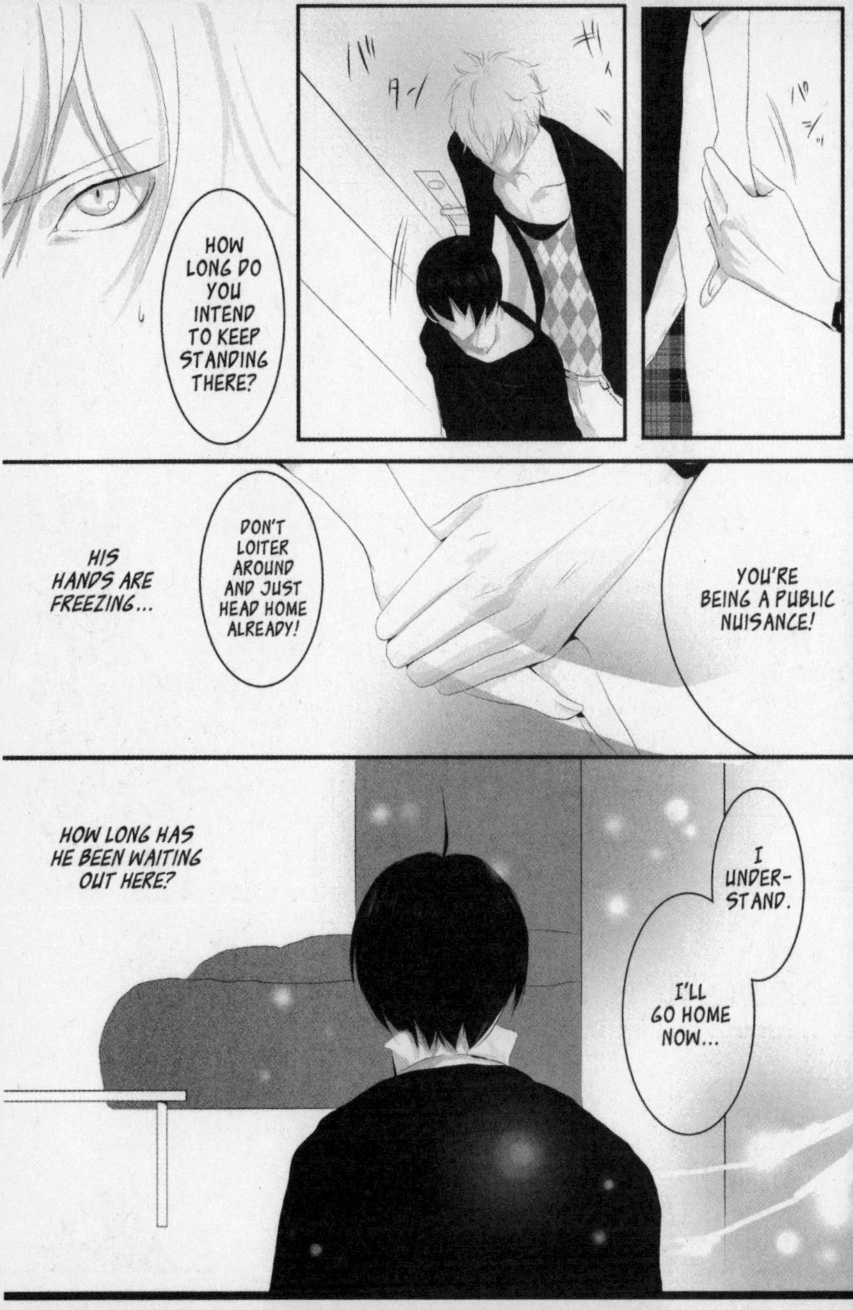
HOW LONG DO YOU INTEND TO KEEP STANDING THERE?
YOU'RE BEING A PUBLIC NUISANCE!
DON'T LOITER AROUND AND JUST HEAD HOME ALREADY!
HIS HANDS ARE FREEZING...
I UNDER-STAND.
I'LL GO HOME NOW...
HOW LONG HAS HE BEEN WAITING OUT HERE?

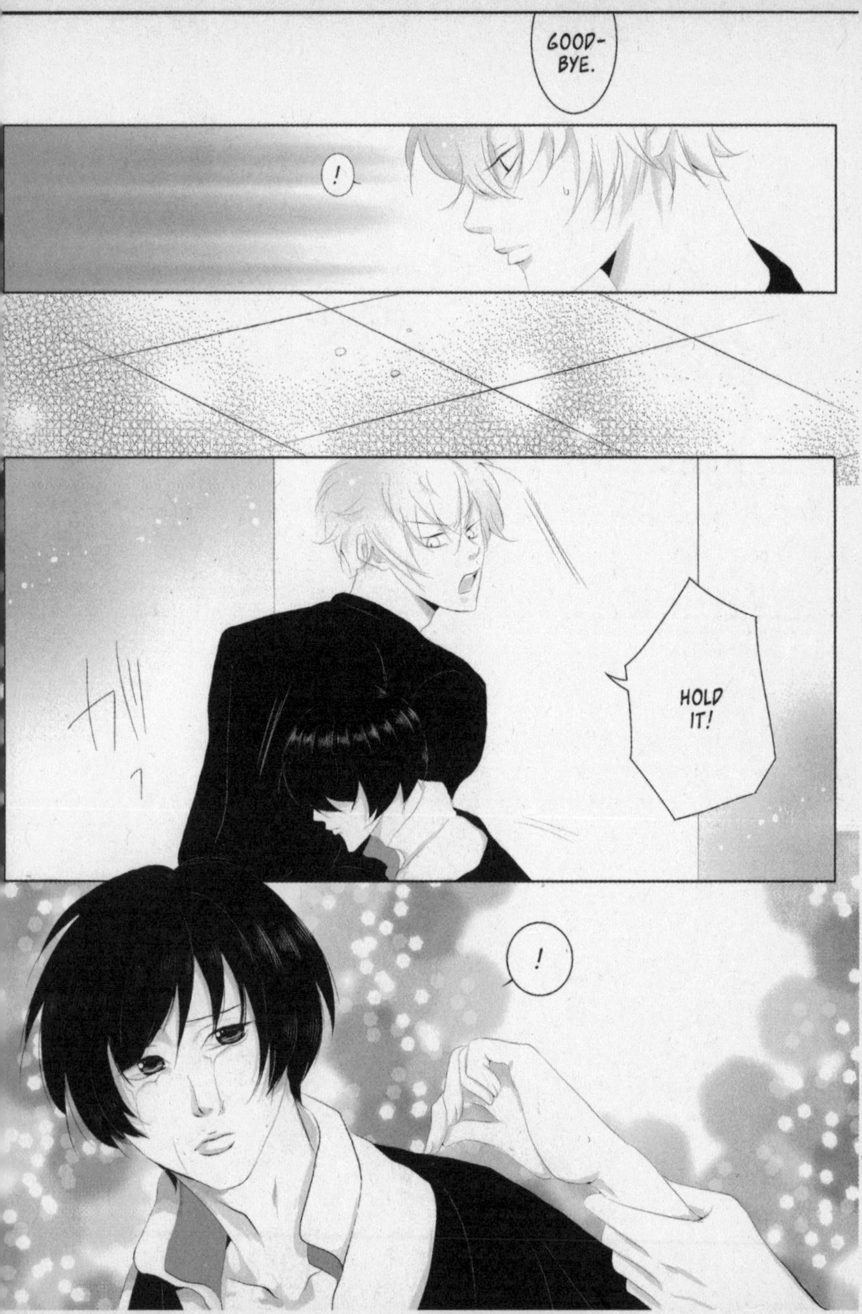
GOOD-BYE.
!
HOLD IT!
!

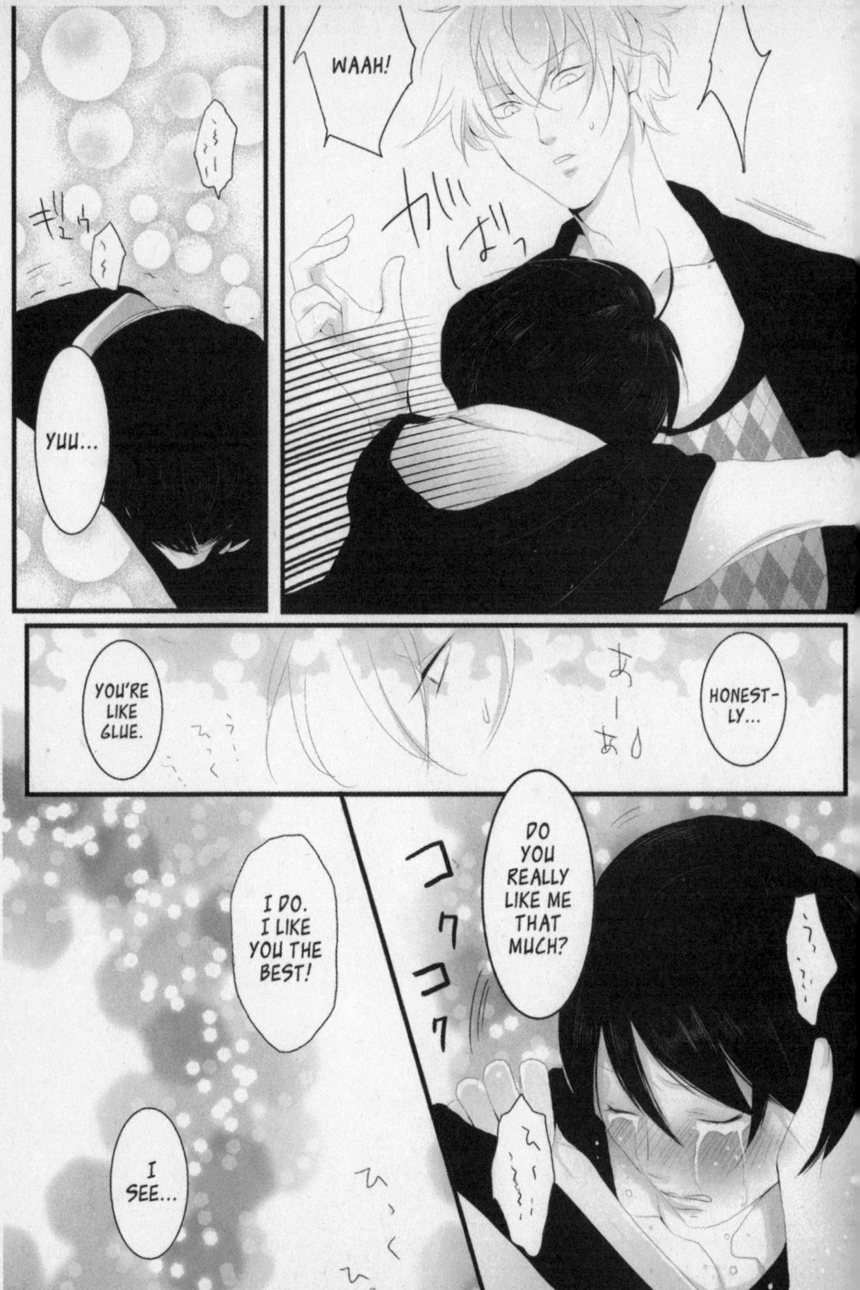
WAAH!
がばっ
YUU...
HONESTLY...
あーあ
YOU'RE LIKE GLUE.
DO YOU REALLY LIKE ME THAT MUCH?
コクコク
I DO. I LIKE YOU THE BEST!
I SEE...

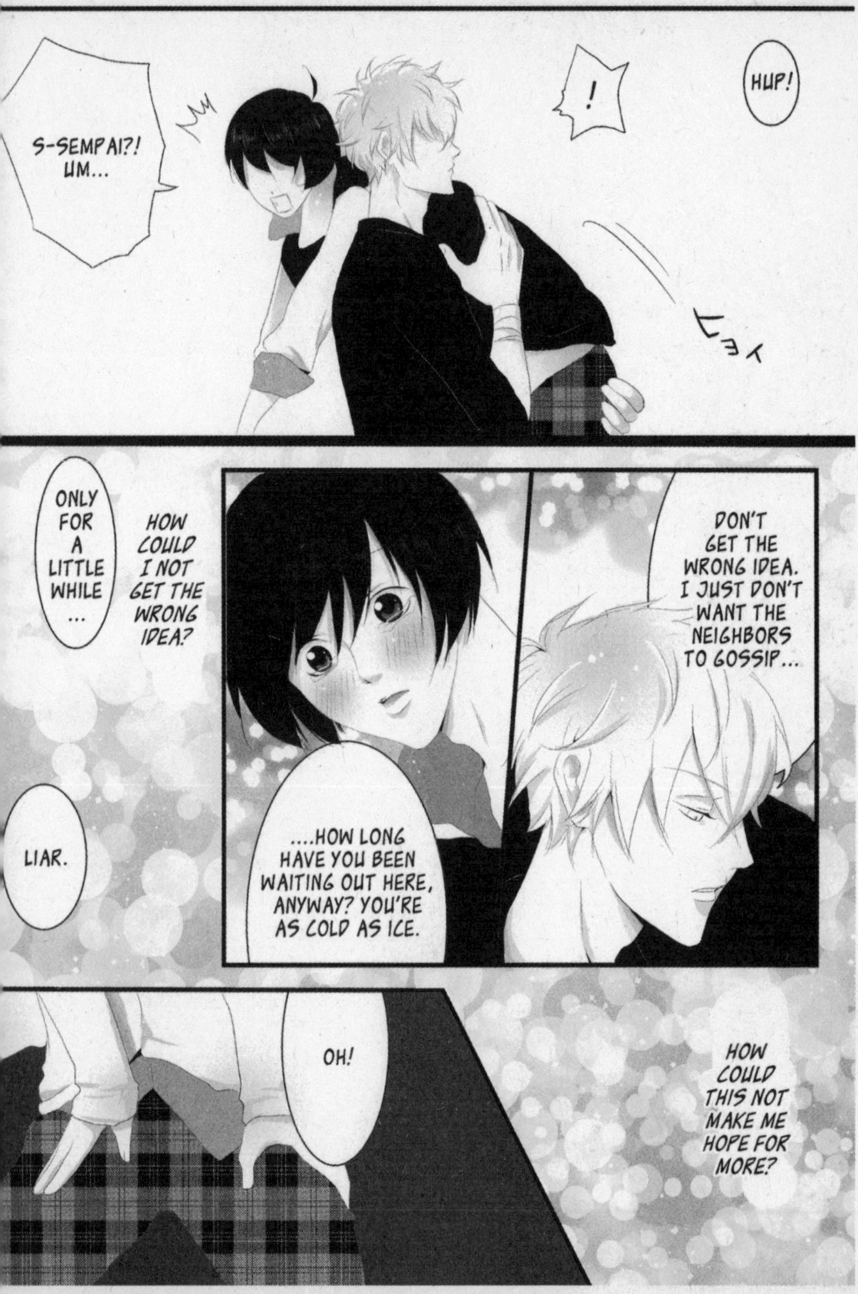
HUP!
!
ヒョイ
S-SEMPAI?! UM...
DON'T GET THE WRONG IDEA. I JUST DON'T WANT THE NEIGHBORS TO GOSSIP...
....HOW LONG HAVE YOU BEEN WAITING OUT HERE, ANYWAY? YOU'RE AS COLD AS ICE.
HOW COULD I NOT GET THE WRONG IDEA?
ONLY FOR A LITTLE WHILE ...
LIAR.
HOW COULD THIS NOT MAKE ME HOPE FOR MORE?
OH!

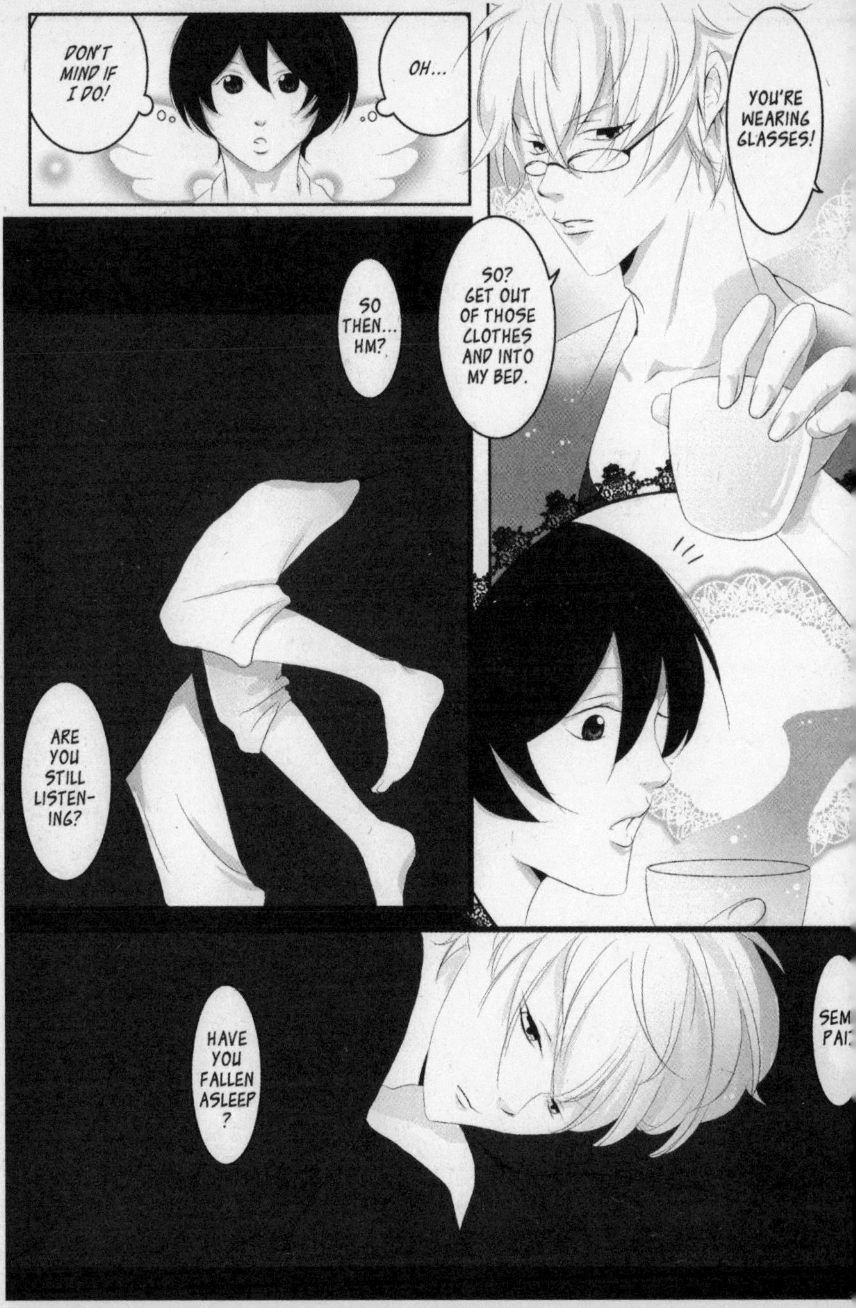
YOU'RE WEARING GLASSES!
SO? GET OUT OF THOSE CLOTHES AND INTO MY BED.
OH...
DON'T MIND IF I DO!
SO THEN... HM?
ARE YOU STILL LISTEN-ING?
SEM PAI
HAVE YOU FALLEN ASLEEP?

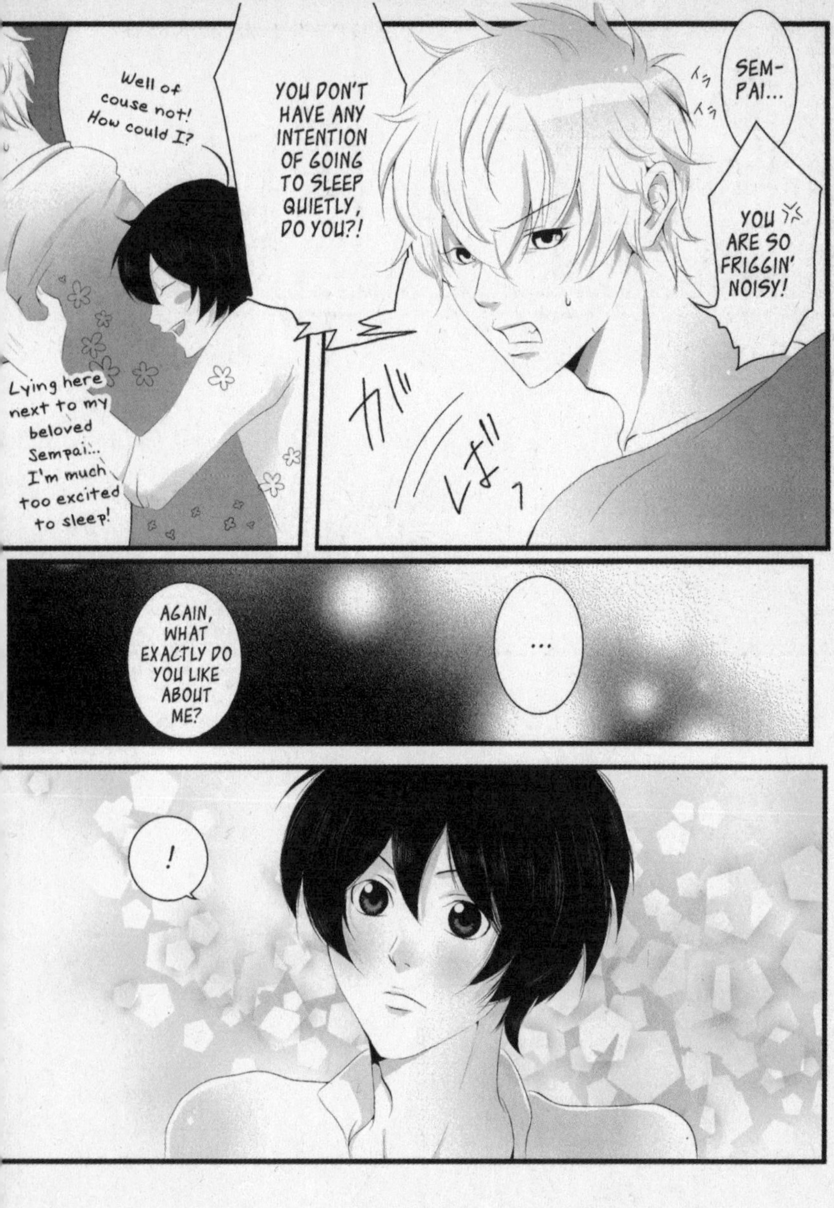
SEM-PAI...
イラ イラ
YOU ARE SO FRIGGIN' NOISY!
YOU DON'T HAVE ANY INTENTION OF GOING TO SLEEP QUIETLY, DO YOU?!
Well of couse not! How could I?
Lying here next to my beloved Sempai... I'm much too excited to sleep!
...
AGAIN, WHAT EXACTLY DO YOU LIKE ABOUT ME?
!

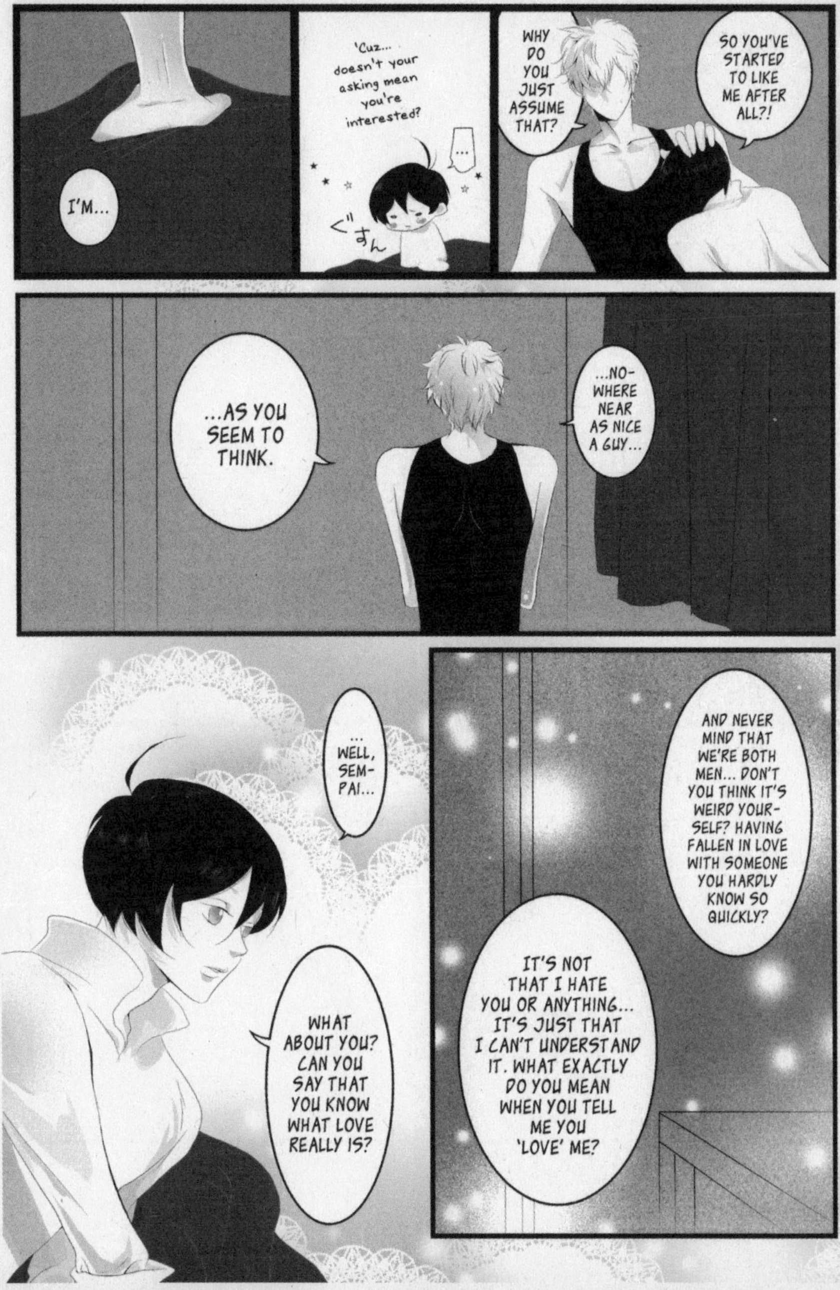
SO YOU'VE STARTED TO LIKE ME AFTER ALL?!
WHY DO YOU JUST ASSUME THAT?
'Cuz... doesn't your asking mean you're interested?
...
ぐずん
I'M...
...NO-WHERE NEAR AS NICE A GUY...
...AS YOU SEEM TO THINK.
AND NEVER MIND THAT WE'RE BOTH MEN... DON'T YOU THINK IT'S WEIRD YOUR-SELF? HAVING FALLEN IN LOVE WITH SOMEONE YOU HARDLY KNOW SO QUICKLY?
IT'S NOT THAT I HATE YOU OR ANYTHING... IT'S JUST THAT I CAN'T UNDERSTAND IT. WHAT EXACTLY DO YOU MEAN WHEN YOU TELL ME YOU 'LOVE' ME?
... WELL, SEM-PAI...
WHAT ABOUT YOU? CAN YOU SAY THAT YOU KNOW WHAT LOVE REALLY IS?

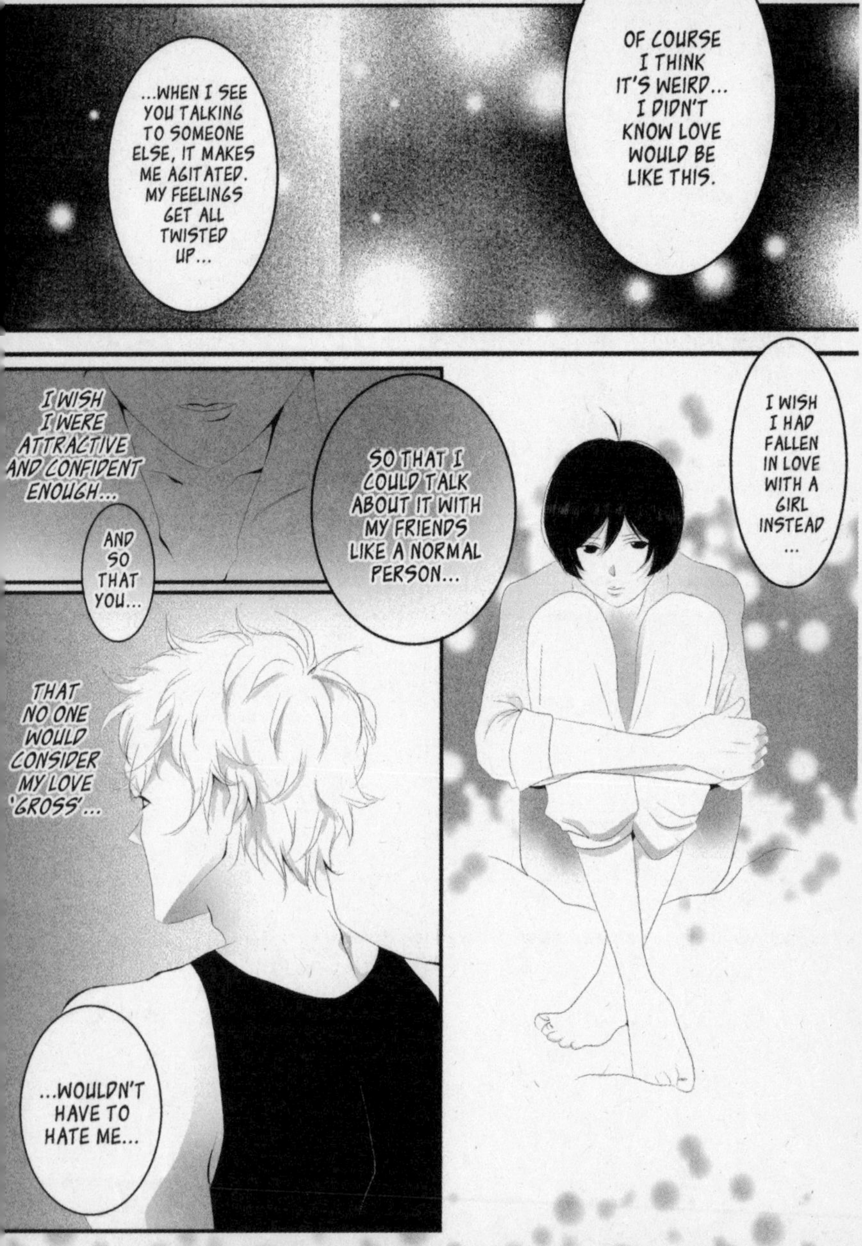
OF COURSE I THINK IT'S WEIRD... I DIDN'T KNOW LOVE WOULD BE LIKE THIS.
...WHEN I SEE YOU TALKING TO SOMEONE ELSE, IT MAKES ME AGITATED. MY FEELINGS GET ALL TWISTED UP...
I WISH I HAD FALLEN IN LOVE WITH A GIRL INSTEAD...
I WISH I WERE ATTRACTIVE AND CONFIDENT ENOUGH...
SO THAT I COULD TALK ABOUT IT WITH MY FRIENDS LIKE A NORMAL PERSON...
AND SO THAT YOU...
THAT NO ONE WOULD CONSIDER MY LOVE 'GROSS'...
...WOULDN'T HAVE TO HATE ME...

...SO MUCH ...
...
...
STRIKE THAT, I WISH I WERE A GIRL.
BUT I'M NOT. AT ALL.
THEN MAYBE YOU'D GO OUT WITH ME..BUT EVEN IF I WERE, ACTING LIKE THIS WOULD PUT YOU OFF, RIGHT?
THERE'S SOMETHING WRONG WITH ME. EVEN I DON'T LIKE ME LIKE THIS.
THIS ISN'T WHAT I WANTED TO SAY TO HIM... WAS IT?
...
I'M SORRY FOR RUINING YOUR NIGHT WITH YOUR GIRLFRIEND ...
I JUST DON'T KNOW ANYMORE!

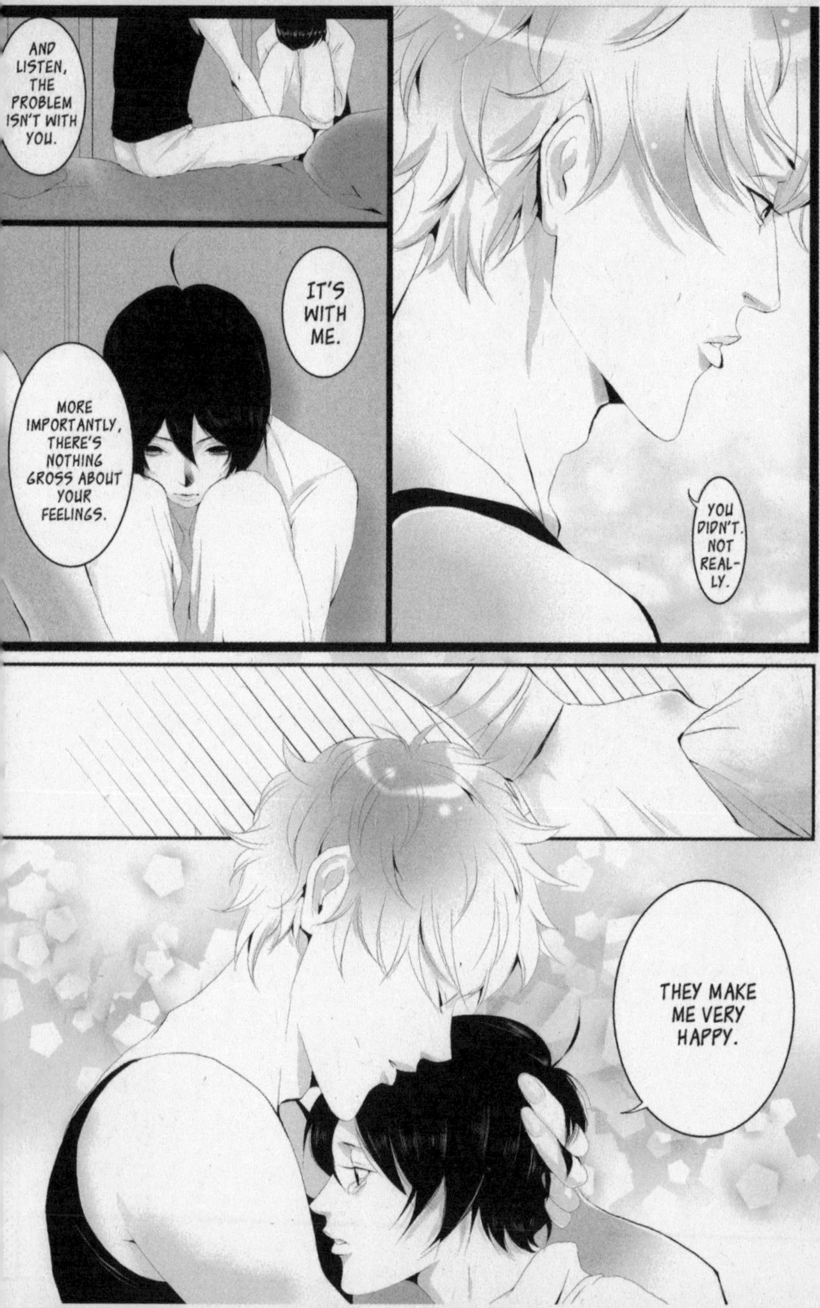
YOU DIDN'T. NOT REAL-LY.
AND LISTEN, THE PROBLEM ISN'T WITH YOU.
IT'S WITH ME.
MORE IMPORTANTLY, THERE'S NOTHING GROSS ABOUT YOUR FEELINGS.
THEY MAKE ME VERY HAPPY.

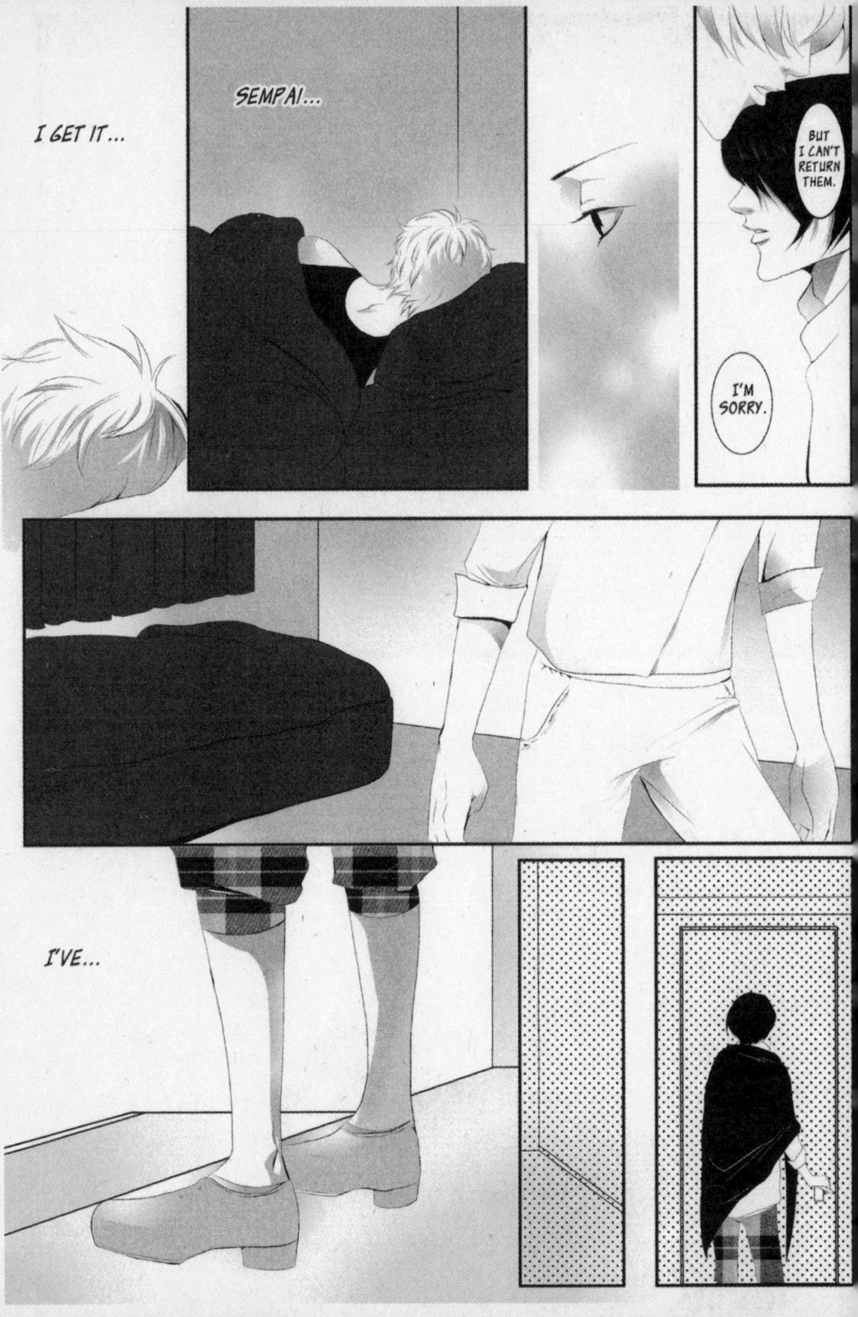
BUT I CAN'T RETURN THEM.
I'M SORRY.
SEMPAI...
I GET IT...
I'VE...

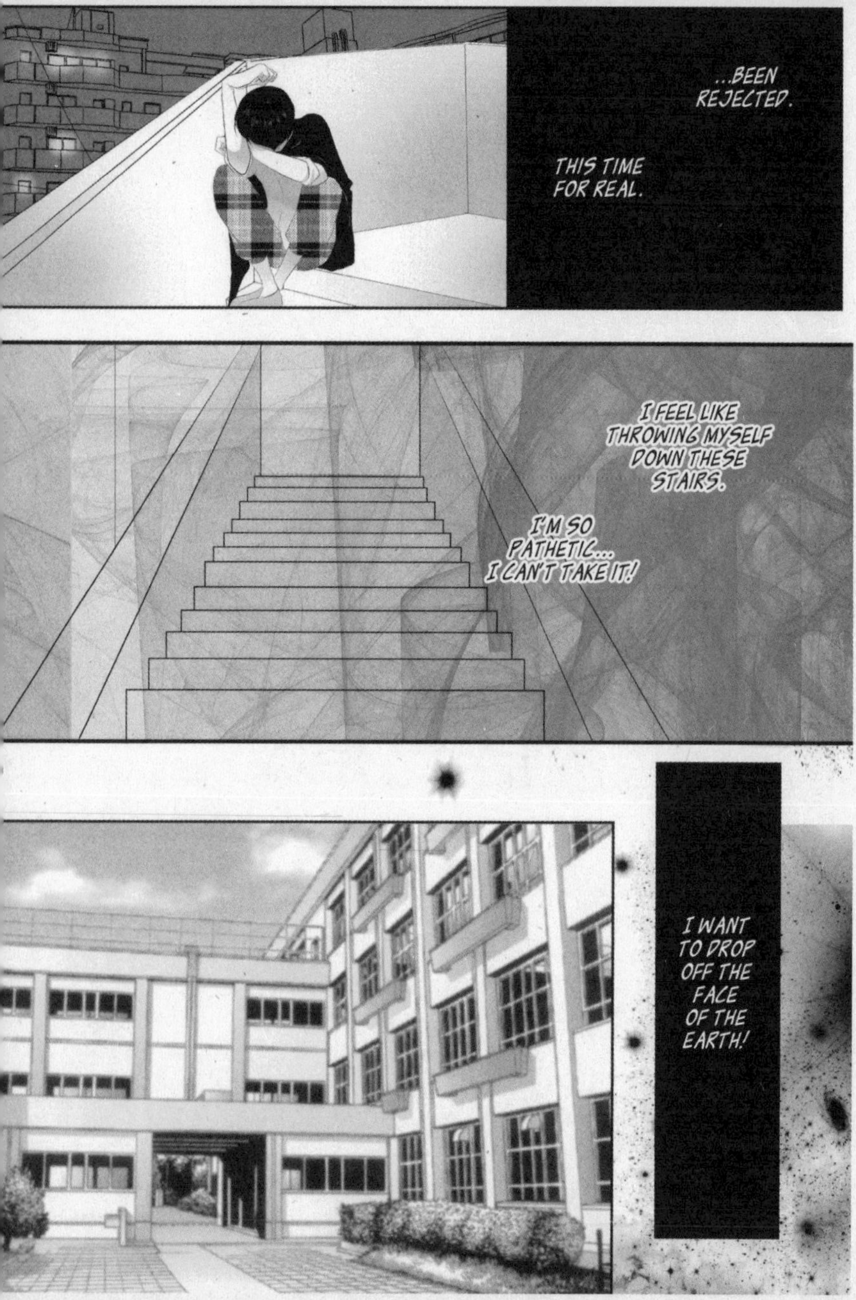
...BEEN REJECTED.
THIS TIME FOR REAL.
I FEEL LIKE THROWING MYSELF DOWN THESE STAIRS.
I'M SO PATHETIC... I CAN'T TAKE IT!
I WANT TO DROP OFF THE FACE OF THE EARTH!

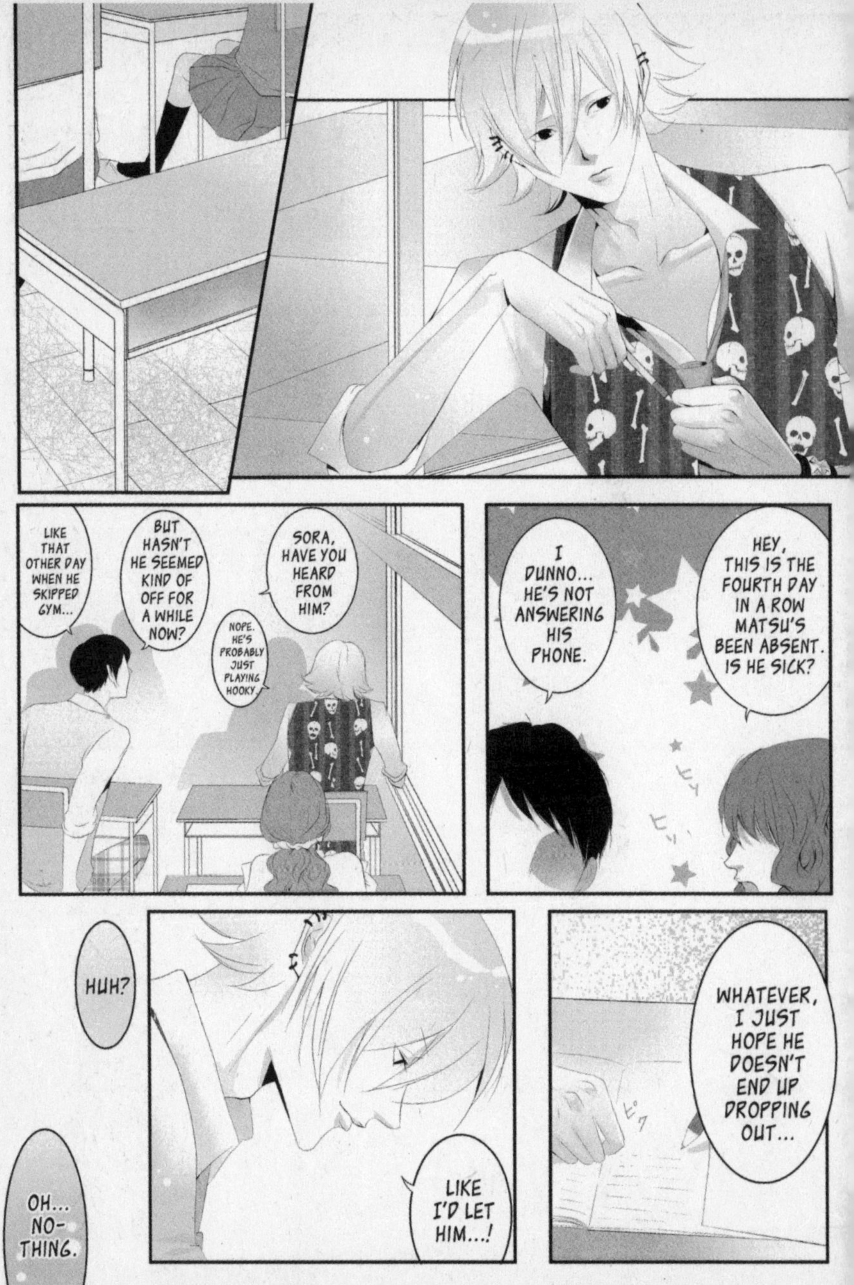
HEY, THIS IS THE FOURTH DAY IN A ROW MATSU'S BEEN ABSENT. IS HE SICK?
I DUNNO... HE'S NOT ANSWERING HIS PHONE.
SORA, HAVE YOU HEARD FROM HIM?
NOPE. HE'S PROBABLY JUST PLAYING HOOKY.
BUT HASN'T HE SEEMED KIND OF OFF FOR A WHILE NOW?
LIKE THAT OTHER DAY WHEN HE SKIPPED GYM...
WHATEVER, I JUST HOPE HE DOESN'T END UP DROPPING OUT...
LIKE I'D LET HIM...!
HUH?
OH... NO-THING.

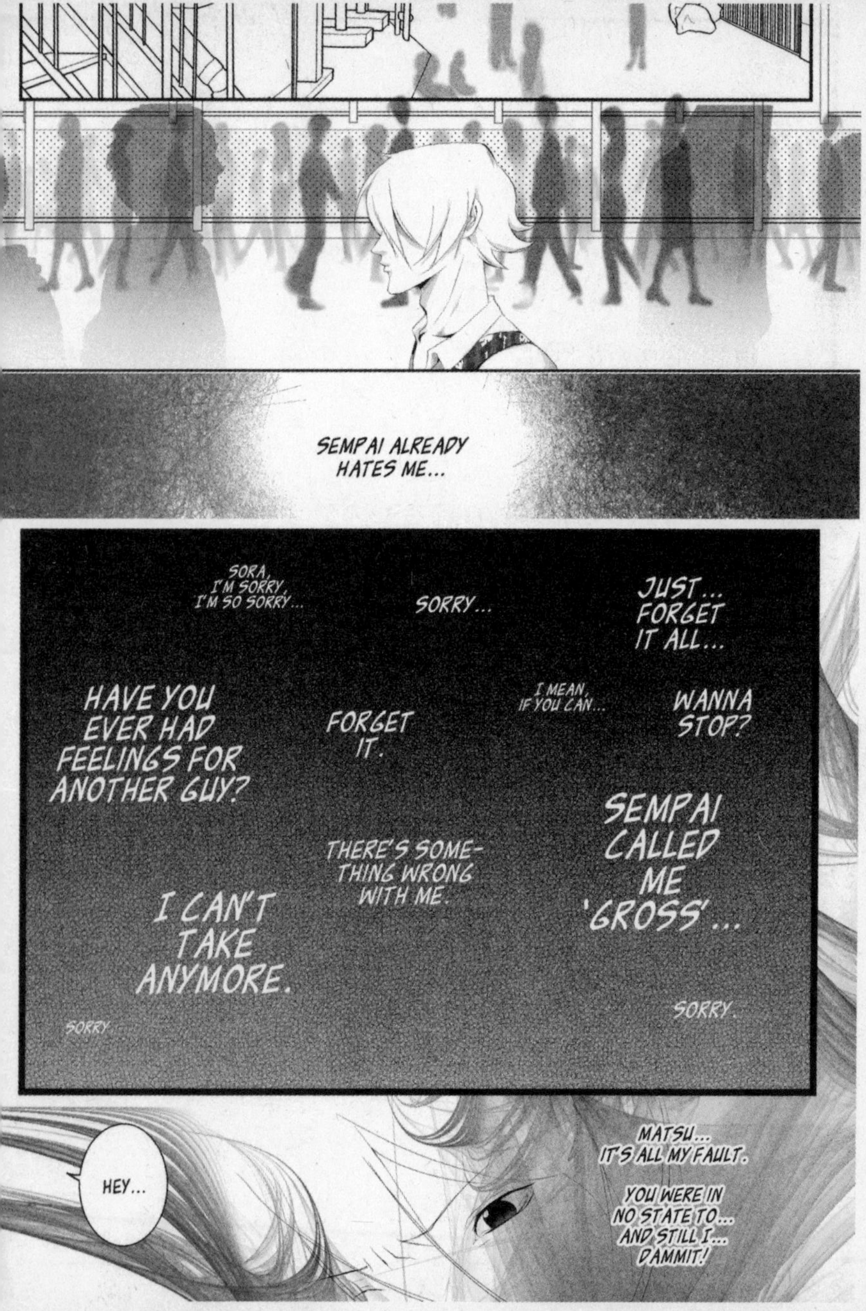
SEMPAI ALREADY HATES ME...
JUST... FORGET IT ALL...
SORRY...
SORA, I'M SORRY, I'M SO SORRY...
WANNA STOP?
I MEAN, IF YOU CAN...
FORGET IT.
HAVE YOU EVER HAD FEELINGS FOR ANOTHER GUY?
SEMPAI CALLED ME 'GROSS'...
THERE'S SOME-THING WRONG WITH ME.
I CAN'T TAKE ANYMORE.
SORRY.
SORRY.
MATSU... IT'S ALL MY FAULT.
YOU WERE IN NO STATE TO... AND STILL I... DAMMIT!
HEY...

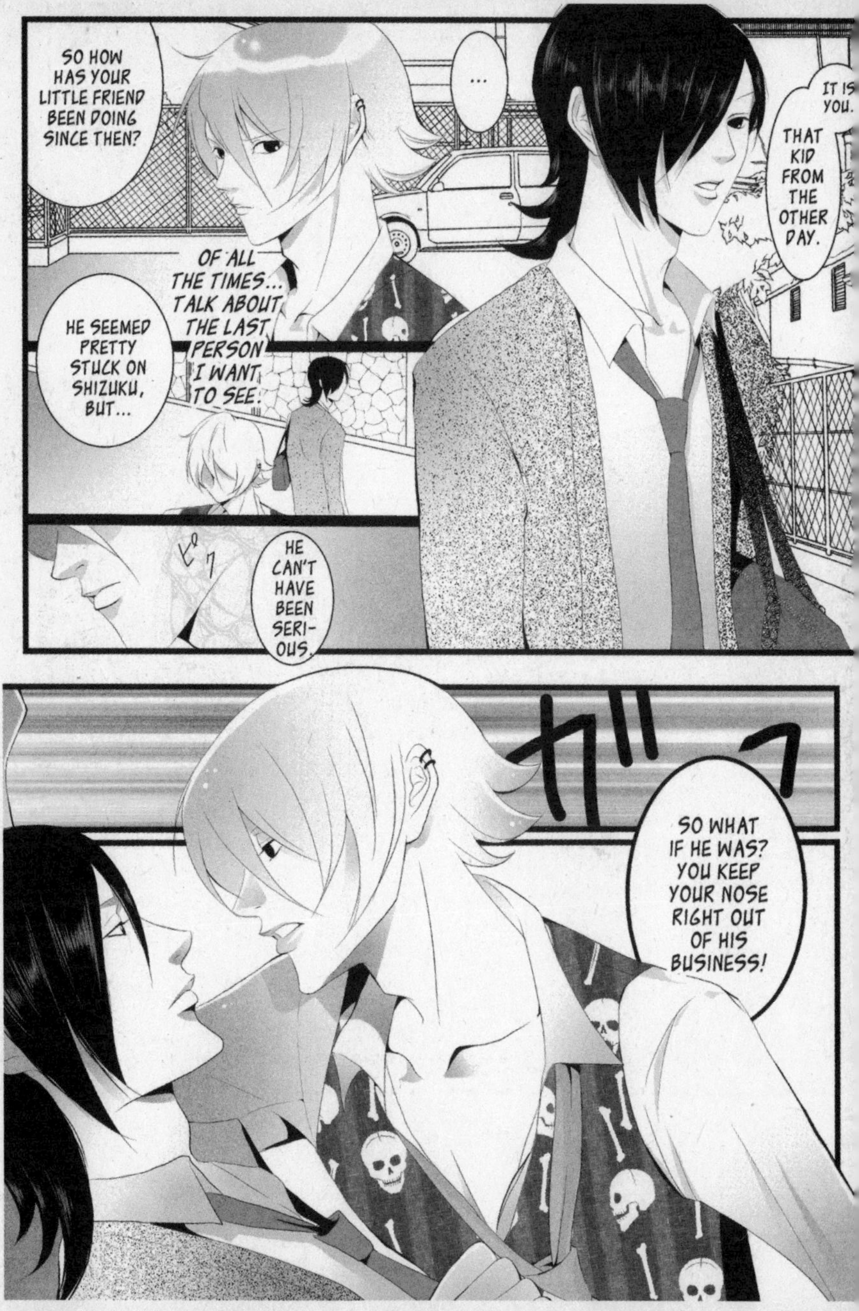
IT IS YOU.
THAT KID FROM THE OTHER DAY.
...
SO HOW HAS YOUR LITTLE FRIEND BEEN DOING SINCE THEN?
OF ALL THE TIMES... TALK ABOUT THE LAST PERSON I WANT TO SEE.
HE SEEMED PRETTY STUCK ON SHIZUKU, BUT...
ピク
HE CAN'T HAVE BEEN SERIOUS.
ガッ
SO WHAT IF HE WAS? YOU KEEP YOUR NOSE RIGHT OUT OF HIS BUSINESS!

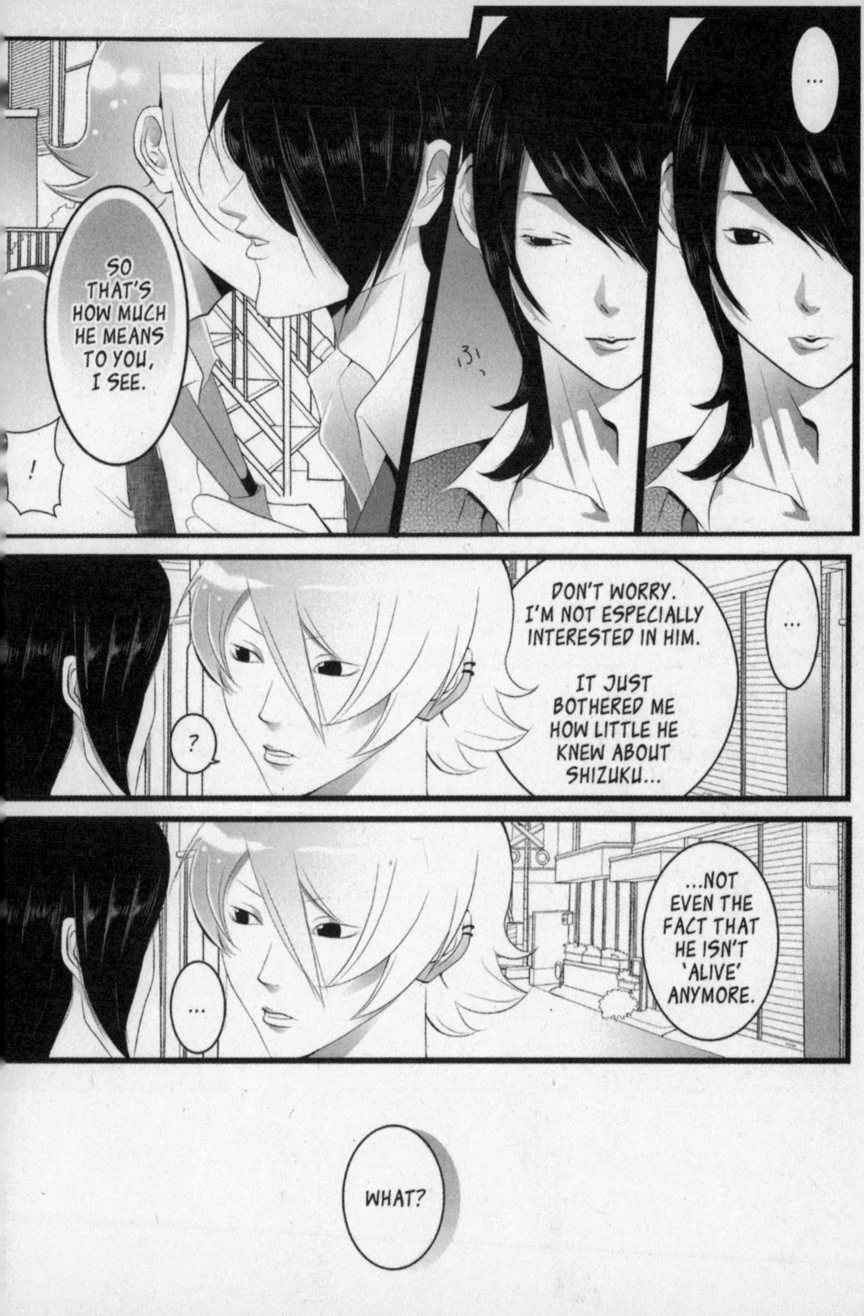
...
SO THAT'S HOW MUCH HE MEANS TO YOU, I SEE.
!
...
DON'T WORRY. I'M NOT ESPECIALLY INTERESTED IN HIM.
IT JUST BOTHERED ME HOW LITTLE HE KNEW ABOUT SHIZUKU...
?
...NOT EVEN THE FACT THAT HE ISN'T 'ALIVE' ANYMORE.
...
WHAT?

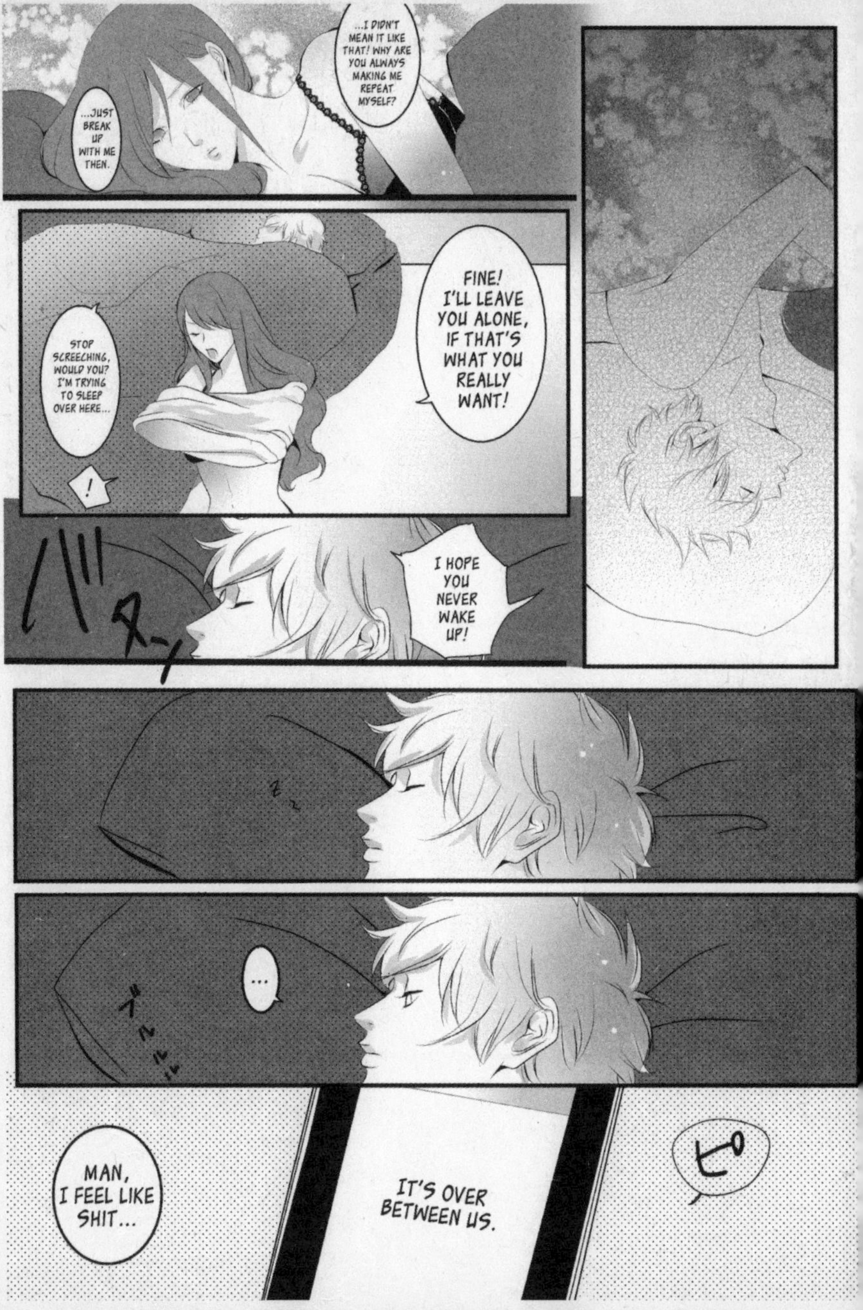
...I DIDN'T MEAN IT LIKE THAT! WHY ARE YOU ALWAYS MAKING ME REPEAT MYSELF?
...JUST BREAK UP WITH ME THEN.
FINE! I'LL LEAVE YOU ALONE, IF THAT'S WHAT YOU REALLY WANT!
STOP SCREECHING, WOULD YOU? I'M TRYING TO SLEEP OVER HERE...
!
I HOPE YOU NEVER WAKE UP!
Z z
...
ピ
IT'S OVER BETWEEN US.
MAN, I FEEL LIKE SHIT...

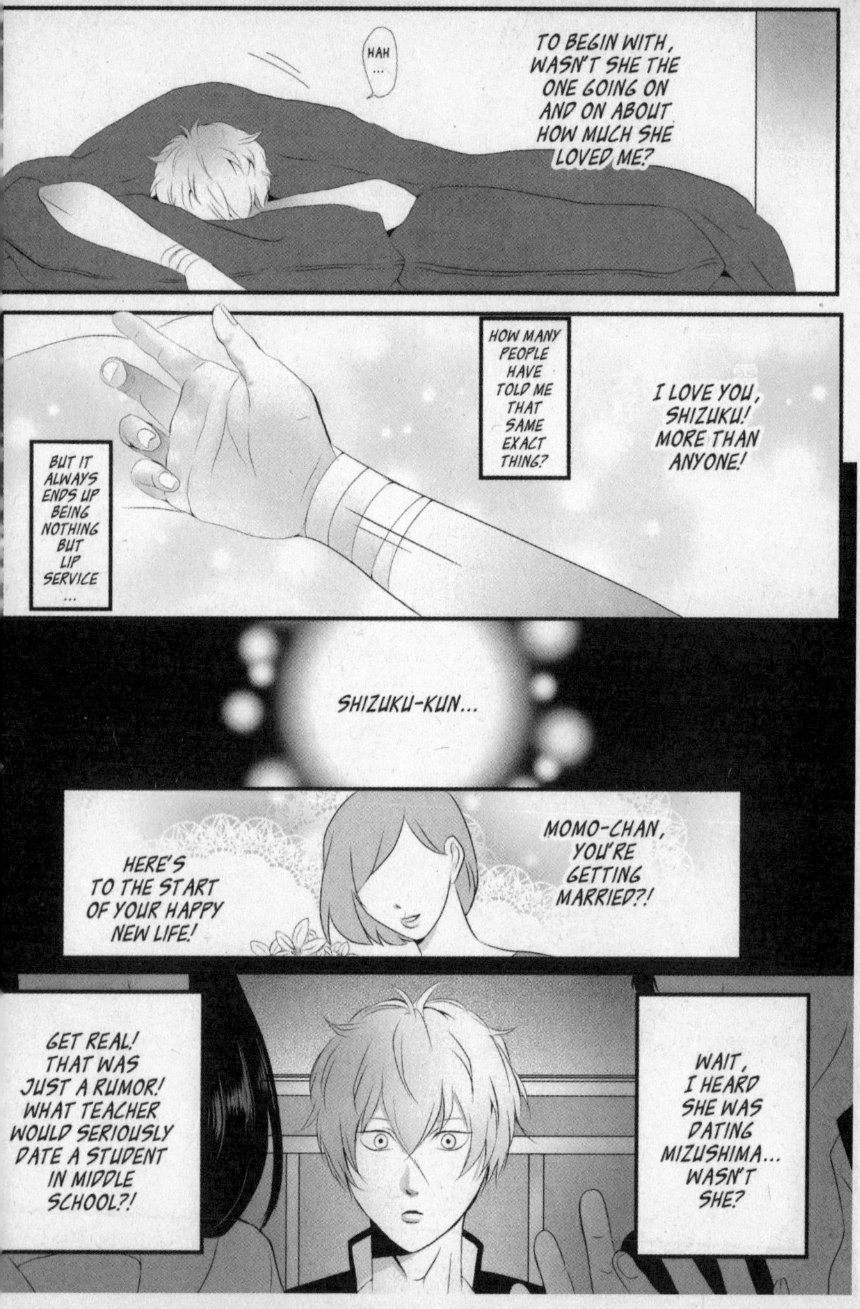
TO BEGIN WITH, WASN'T SHE THE ONE GOING ON AND ON ABOUT HOW MUCH SHE LOVED ME?
HAH ...
I LOVE YOU, SHIZUKU! MORE THAN ANYONE!
HOW MANY PEOPLE HAVE TOLD ME THAT SAME EXACT THING?
BUT IT ALWAYS ENDS UP BEING NOTHING BUT LIP SERVICE ...
SHIZUKU-KUN...
MOMO-CHAN, YOU'RE GETTING MARRIED?!
HERE'S TO THE START OF YOUR HAPPY NEW LIFE!
WAIT, I HEARD SHE WAS DATING MIZUSHIMA... WASN'T SHE?
GET REAL! THAT WAS JUST A RUMOR! WHAT TEACHER WOULD SERIOUSLY DATE A STUDENT IN MIDDLE SCHOOL?!

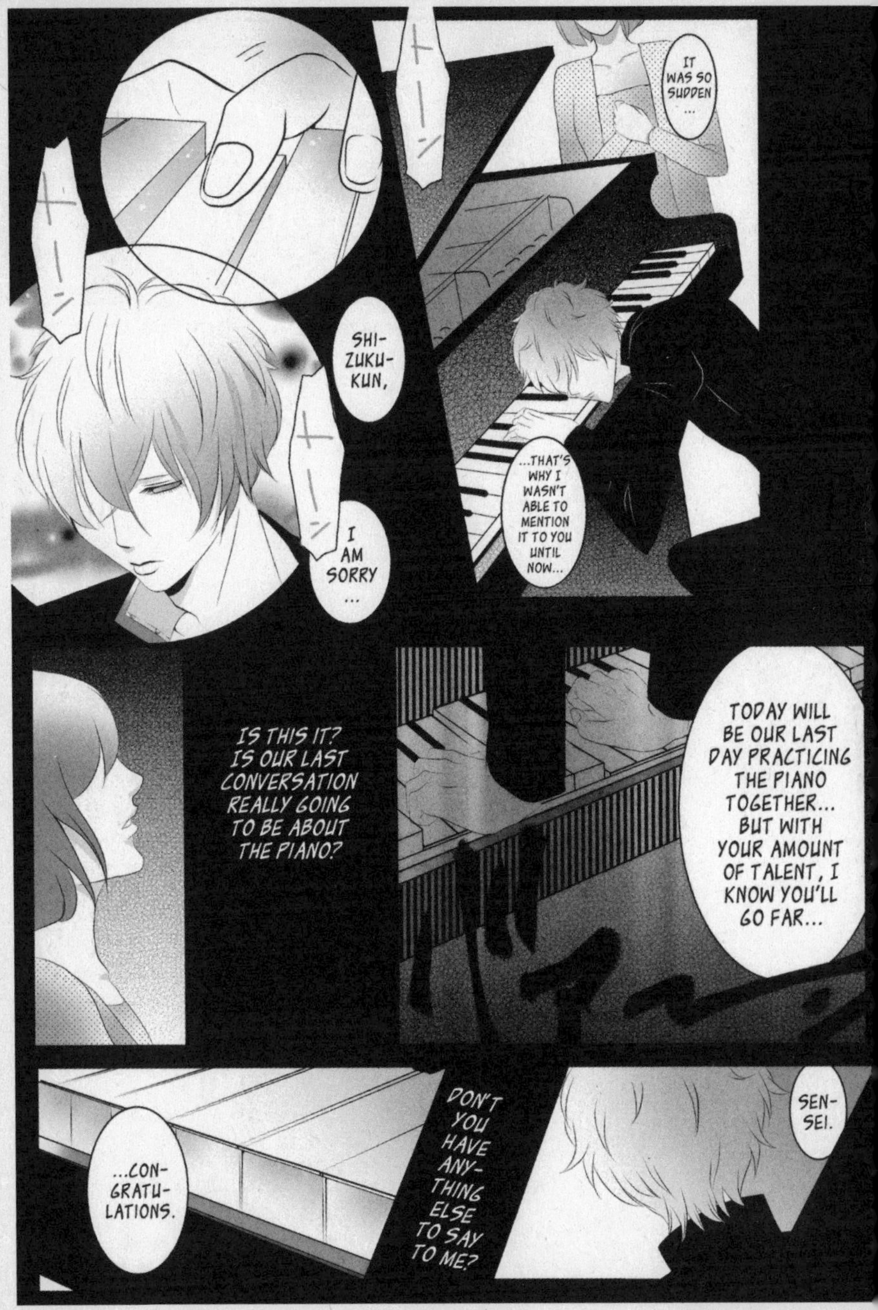
IT WAS SO SUDDEN...
...THAT'S WHY I WASN'T ABLE TO MENTION IT TO YOU UNTIL NOW...
SHI-ZUKU-KUN,
I AM SORRY...
TODAY WILL BE OUR LAST DAY PRACTICING THE PIANO TOGETHER... BUT WITH YOUR AMOUNT OF TALENT, I KNOW YOU'LL GO FAR...
IS THIS IT? IS OUR LAST CONVERSATION REALLY GOING TO BE ABOUT THE PIANO?
SEN-SEI.
DON'T YOU HAVE ANY-THING ELSE TO SAY TO ME?
...CON-GRATU-LATIONS.

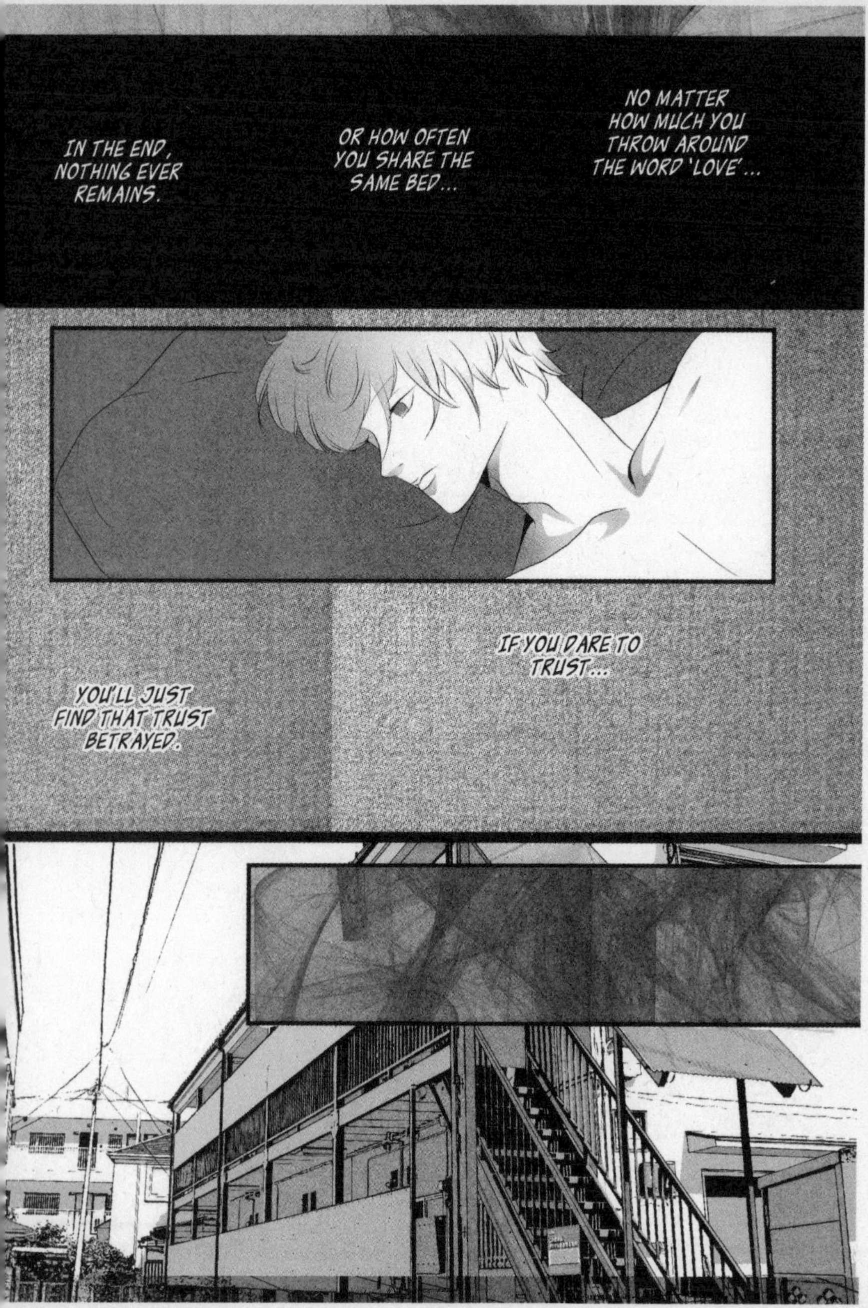
NO MATTER HOW MUCH YOU THROW AROUND THE WORD 'LOVE'...
OR HOW OFTEN YOU SHARE THE SAME BED...
IN THE END, NOTHING EVER REMAINS.
IF YOU DARE TO TRUST...
YOU'LL JUST FIND THAT TRUST BETRAYED.

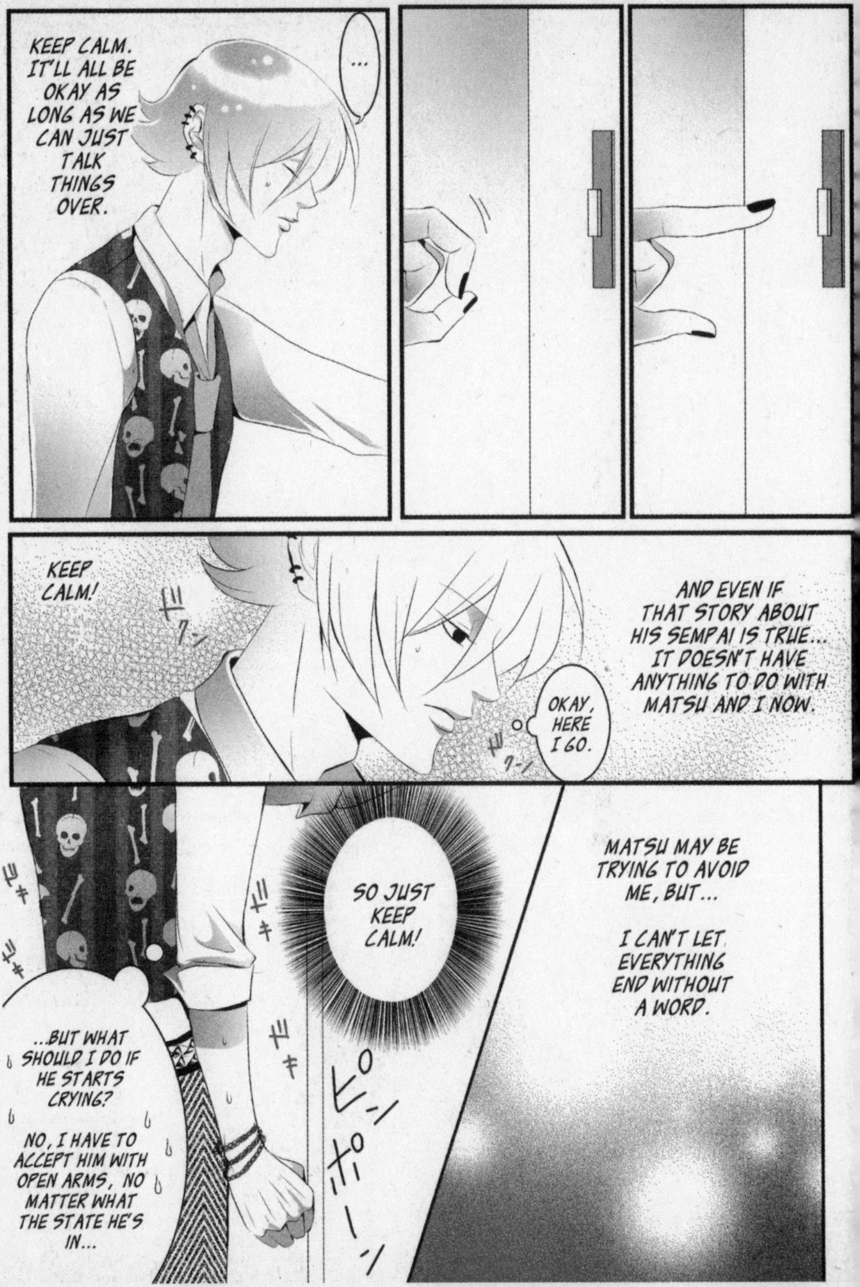
...
KEEP CALM. IT'LL ALL BE OKAY AS LONG AS WE CAN JUST TALK THINGS OVER.
AND EVEN IF THAT STORY ABOUT HIS SEMPAI IS TRUE... IT DOESN'T HAVE ANYTHING TO DO WITH MATSU AND I NOW.
OKAY, HERE I GO.
ドクン
KEEP CALM!
ドクン
MATSU MAY BE TRYING TO AVOID ME, BUT...
I CAN'T LET EVERYTHING END WITHOUT A WORD.
ピーンポーン
SO JUST KEEP CALM!
ドキ
ドキ
ドキ
ドキ
...BUT WHAT SHOULD I DO IF HE STARTS CRYING?
NO, I HAVE TO ACCEPT HIM WITH OPEN ARMS, NO MATTER WHAT THE STATE HE'S IN...

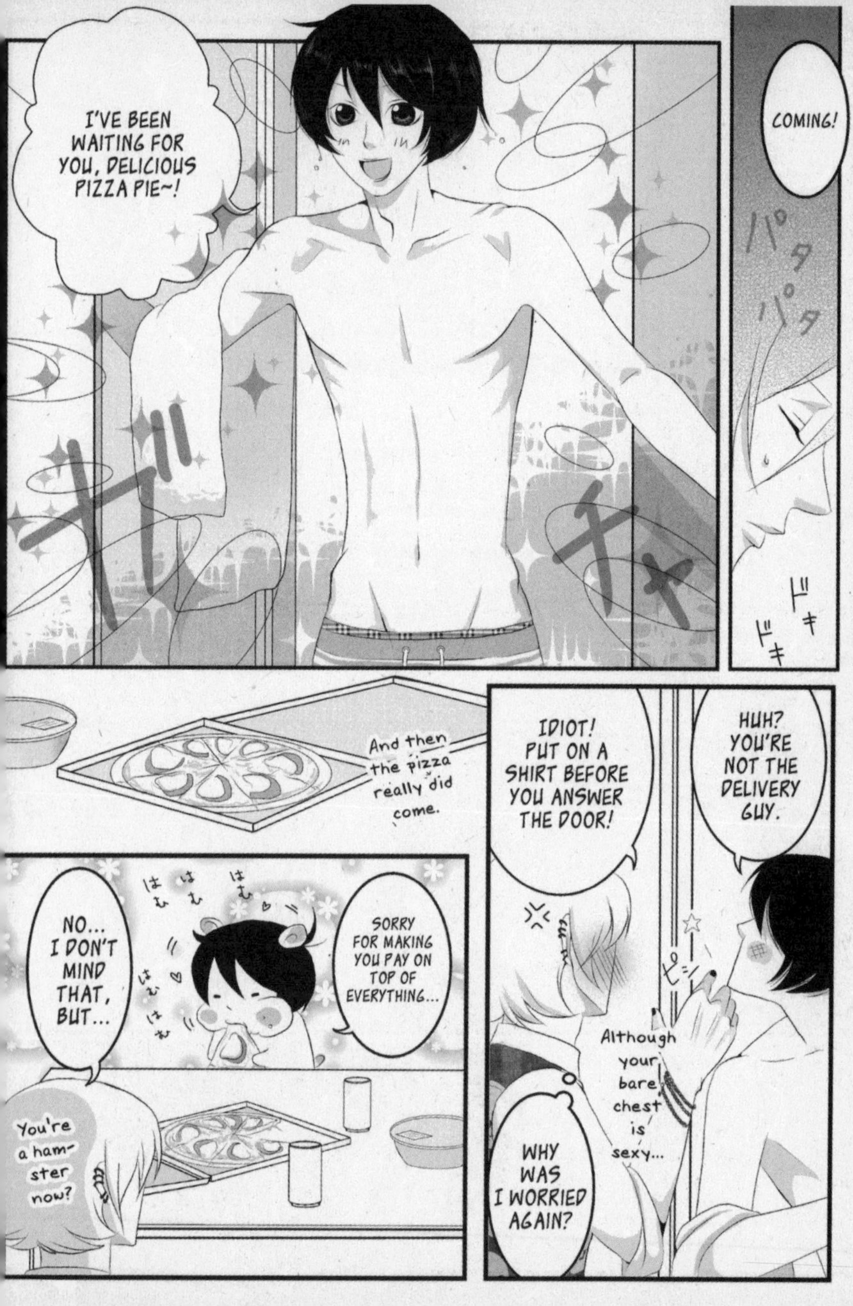
COMING!
パタパタ
ドキドキ
I'VE BEEN WAITING FOR YOU, DELICIOUS PIZZA PIE~!
ガチャ
HUH? YOU'RE NOT THE DELIVERY GUY.
IDIOT! PUT ON A SHIRT BEFORE YOU ANSWER THE DOOR!
Although your bare chest is sexy...
WHY WAS I WORRIED AGAIN?
And then the pizza really did come.
SORRY FOR MAKING YOU PAY ON TOP OF EVERYTHING...
はむはむ
はむ
はむはむ
NO... I DON'T MIND THAT, BUT...
You're a ham-ster now?

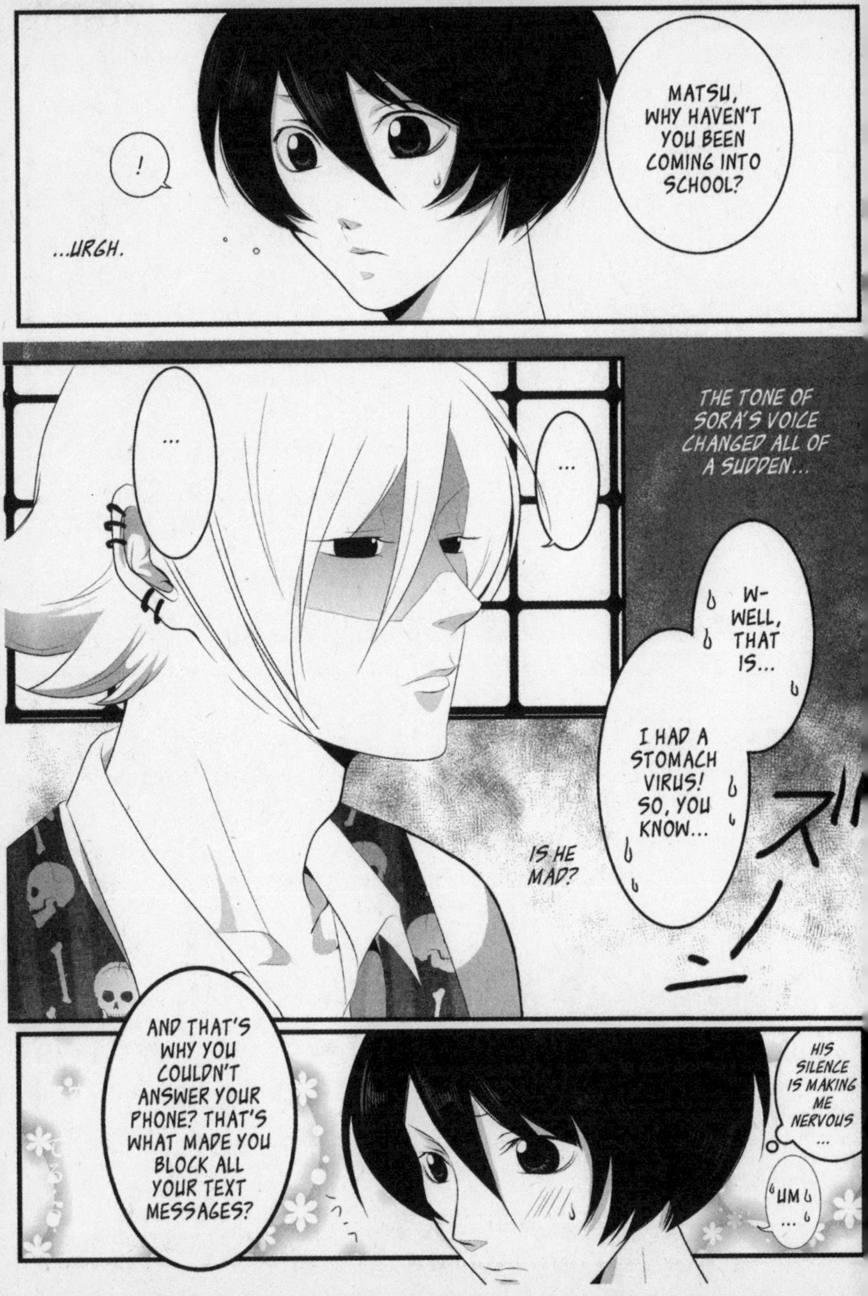
MATSU, WHY HAVEN'T YOU BEEN COMING INTO SCHOOL?
!
...URGH.
THE TONE OF SORA'S VOICE CHANGED ALL OF A SUDDEN...
...
...
W-WELL, THAT IS...
I HAD A STOMACH VIRUS! SO, YOU KNOW...
IS HE MAD?
HIS SILENCE IS MAKING ME NERVOUS...
AND THAT'S WHY YOU COULDN'T ANSWER YOUR PHONE? THAT'S WHAT MADE YOU BLOCK ALL YOUR TEXT MESSAGES?
UM...

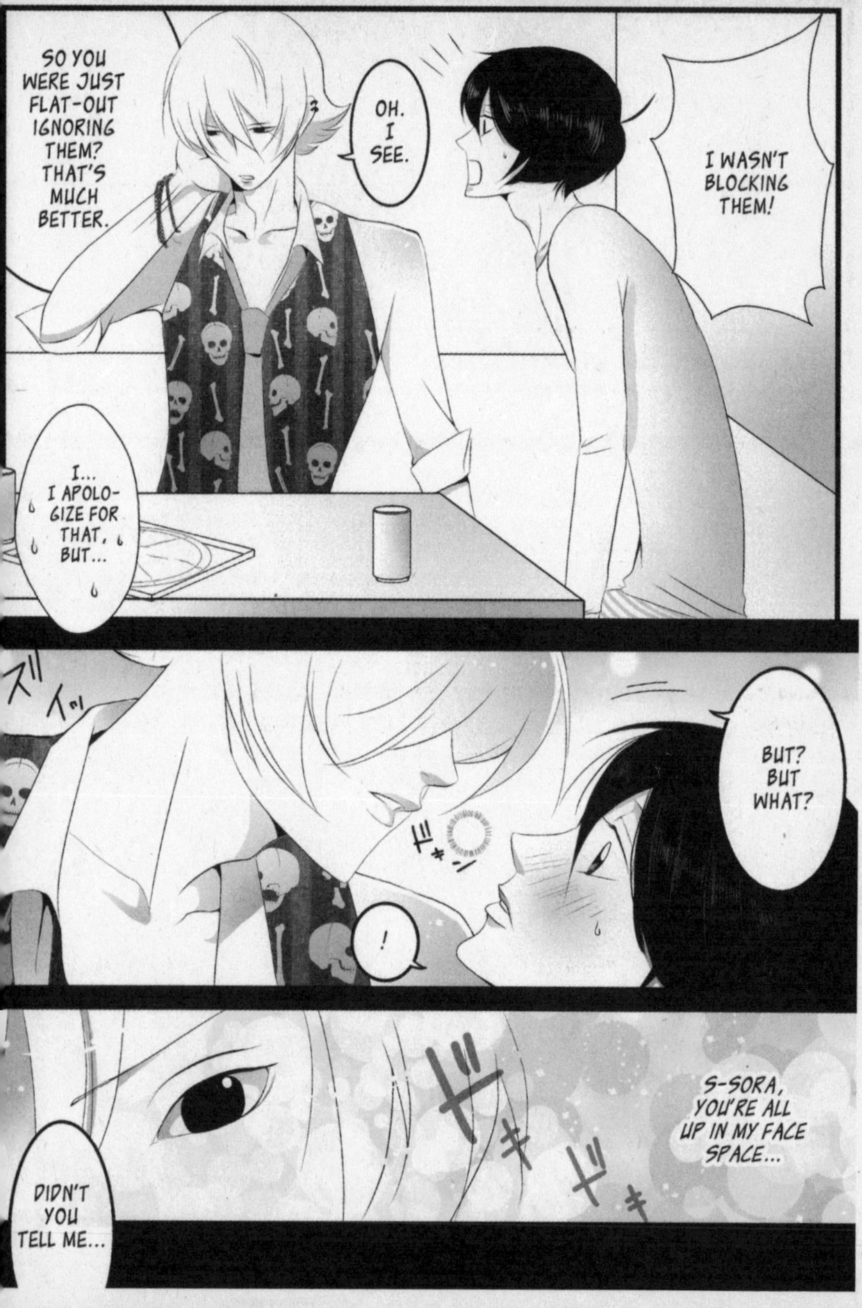
I WASN'T BLOCKING THEM!
OH. I SEE.
SO YOU WERE JUST FLAT-OUT IGNORING THEM? THAT'S MUCH BETTER.
I... I APOLOGIZE FOR THAT, BUT...
BUT? BUT WHAT?
ドキン
!
ズイッ
S-SORA, YOU'RE ALL UP IN MY FACE SPACE...
ドキドキ
DIDN'T YOU TELL ME...

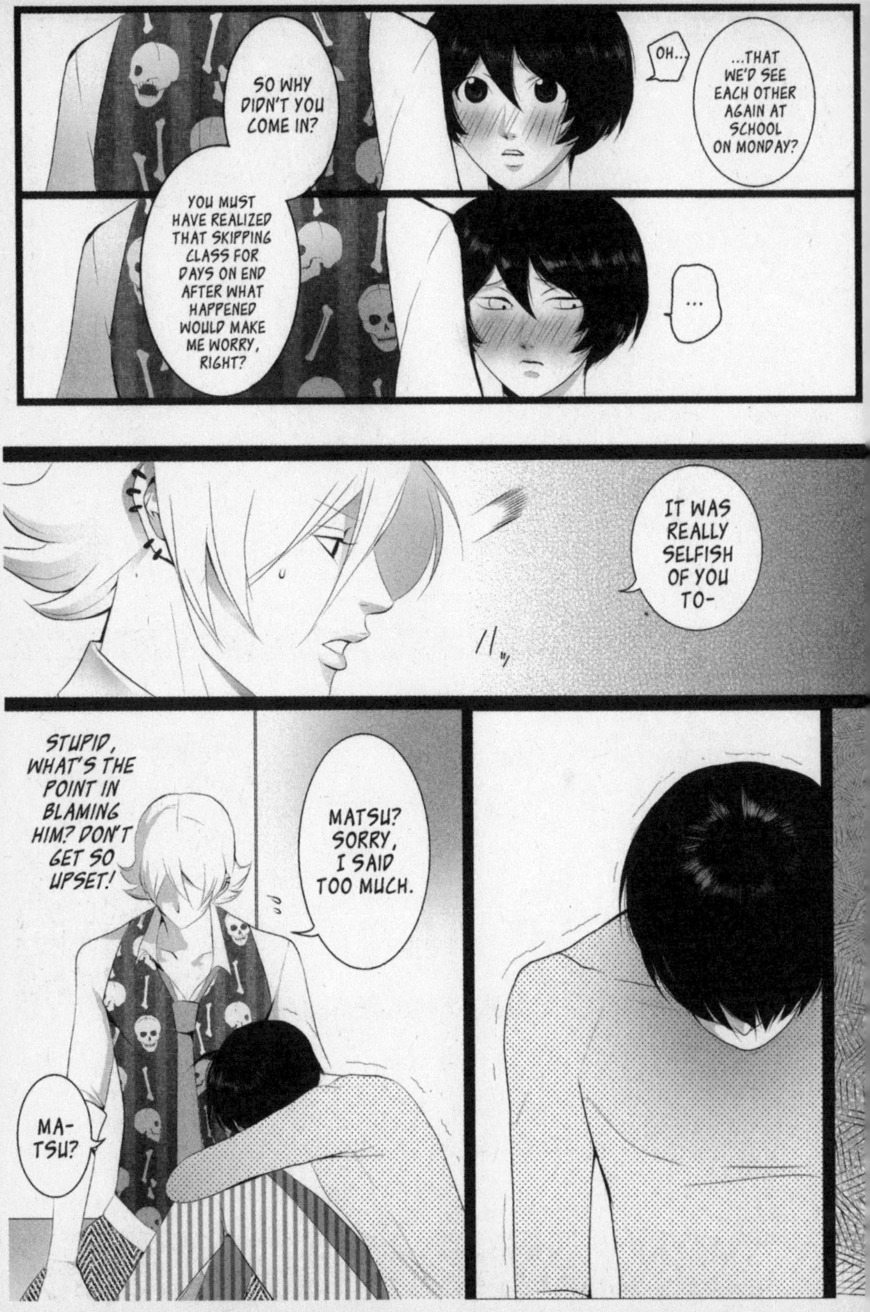
...THAT WE'D SEE EACH OTHER AGAIN AT SCHOOL ON MONDAY?
OH...
SO WHY DIDN'T YOU COME IN?
...
YOU MUST HAVE REALIZED THAT SKIPPING CLASS FOR DAYS ON END AFTER WHAT HAPPENED WOULD MAKE ME WORRY, RIGHT?
IT WAS REALLY SELFISH OF YOU TO-
ハッ
MATSU? SORRY, I SAID TOO MUCH.
STUPID, WHAT'S THE POINT IN BLAMING HIM? DON'T GET SO UPSET!
MA-TSU?

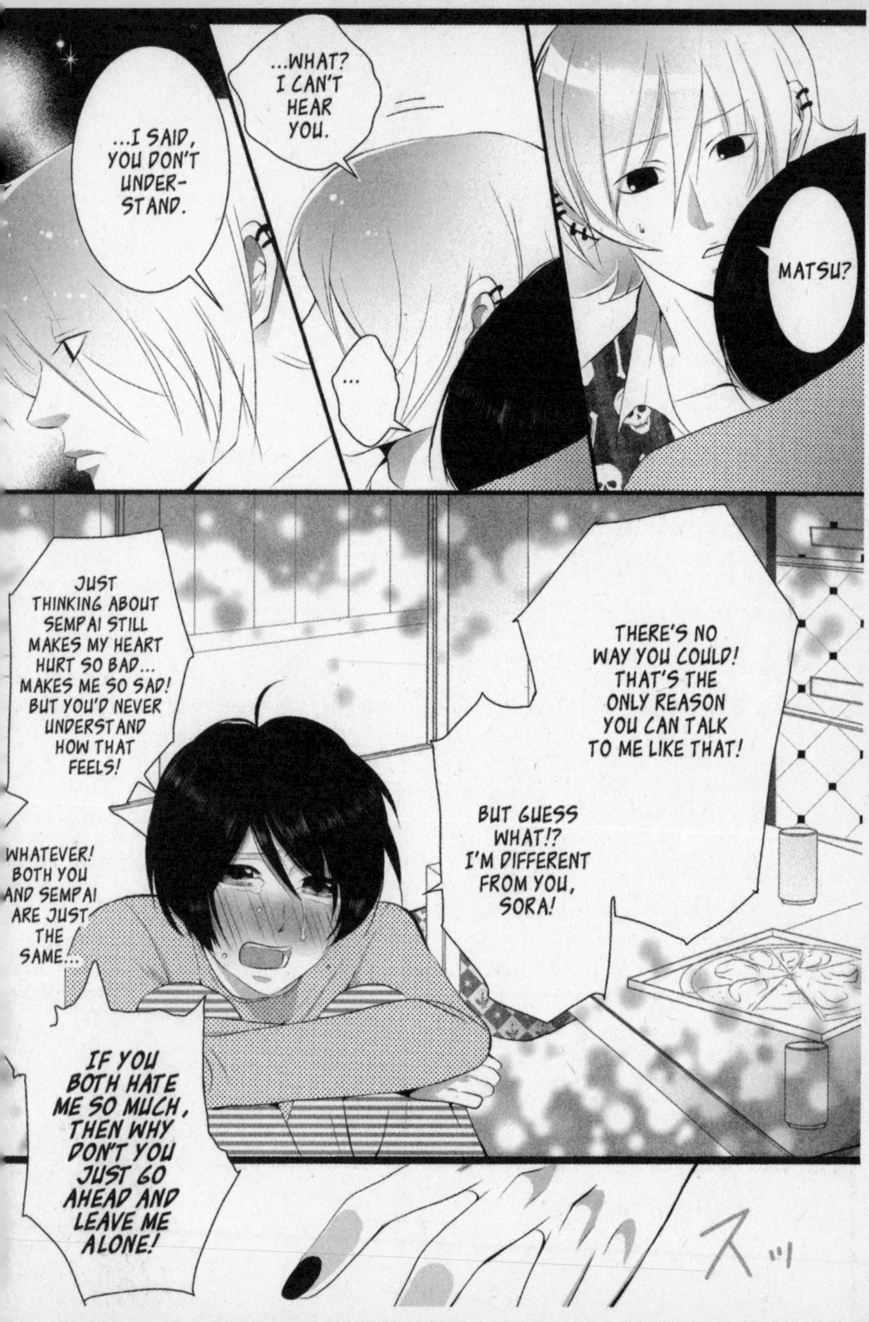
MATSU?
...WHAT? I CAN'T HEAR YOU.
...
...I SAID, YOU DON'T UNDER-STAND.
THERE'S NO WAY YOU COULD! THAT'S THE ONLY REASON YOU CAN TALK TO ME LIKE THAT!
JUST THINKING ABOUT SEMPAI STILL MAKES MY HEART HURT SO BAD... MAKES ME SO SAD! BUT YOU'D NEVER UNDERSTAND HOW THAT FEELS!
BUT GUESS WHAT!? I'M DIFFERENT FROM YOU, SORA!
WHATEVER! BOTH YOU AND SEMPAI ARE JUST THE SAME...
IF YOU BOTH HATE ME SO MUCH, THEN WHY DON'T YOU JUST GO AHEAD AND LEAVE ME ALONE!
スッ

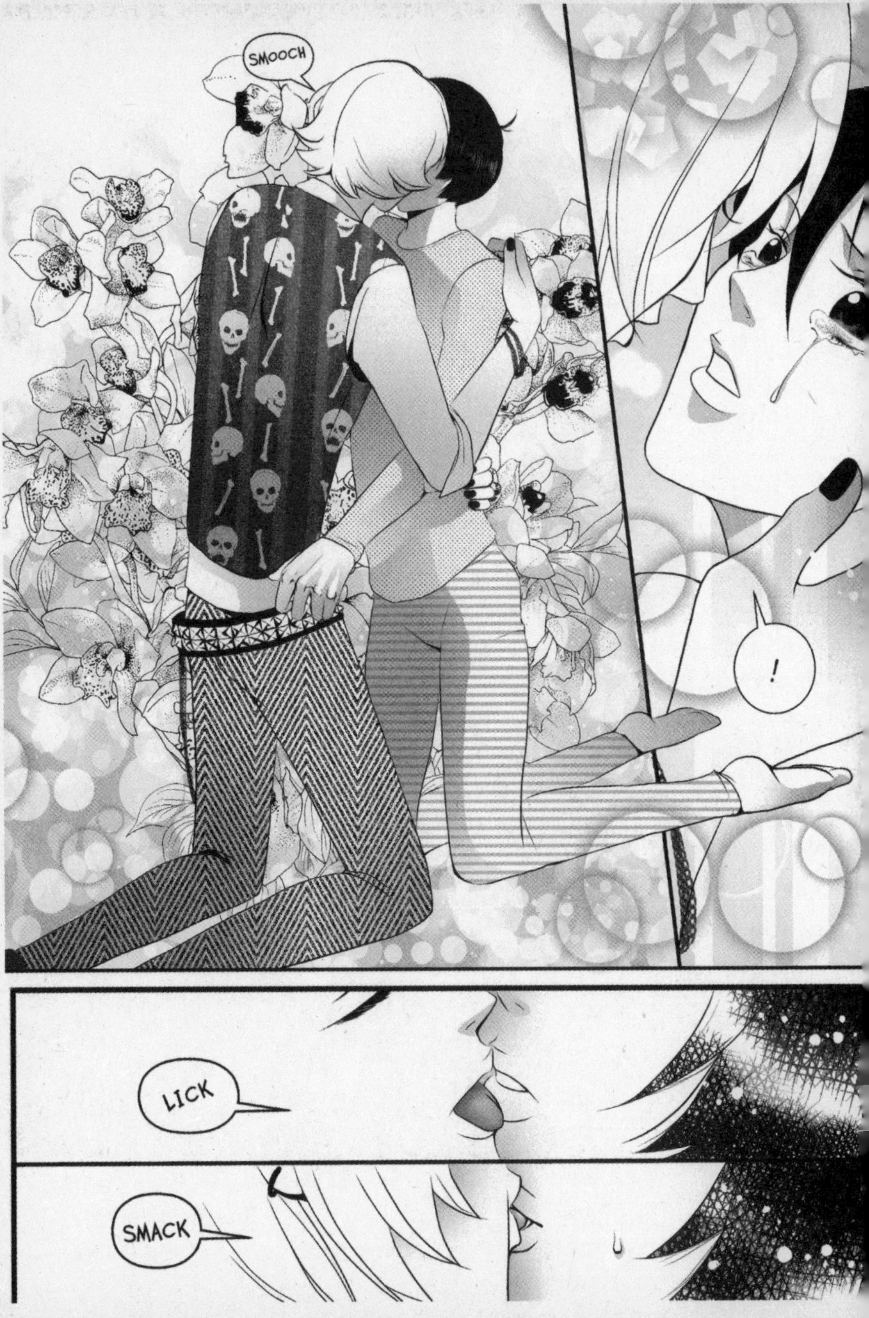
!
SMOOCH
LICK
SMACK

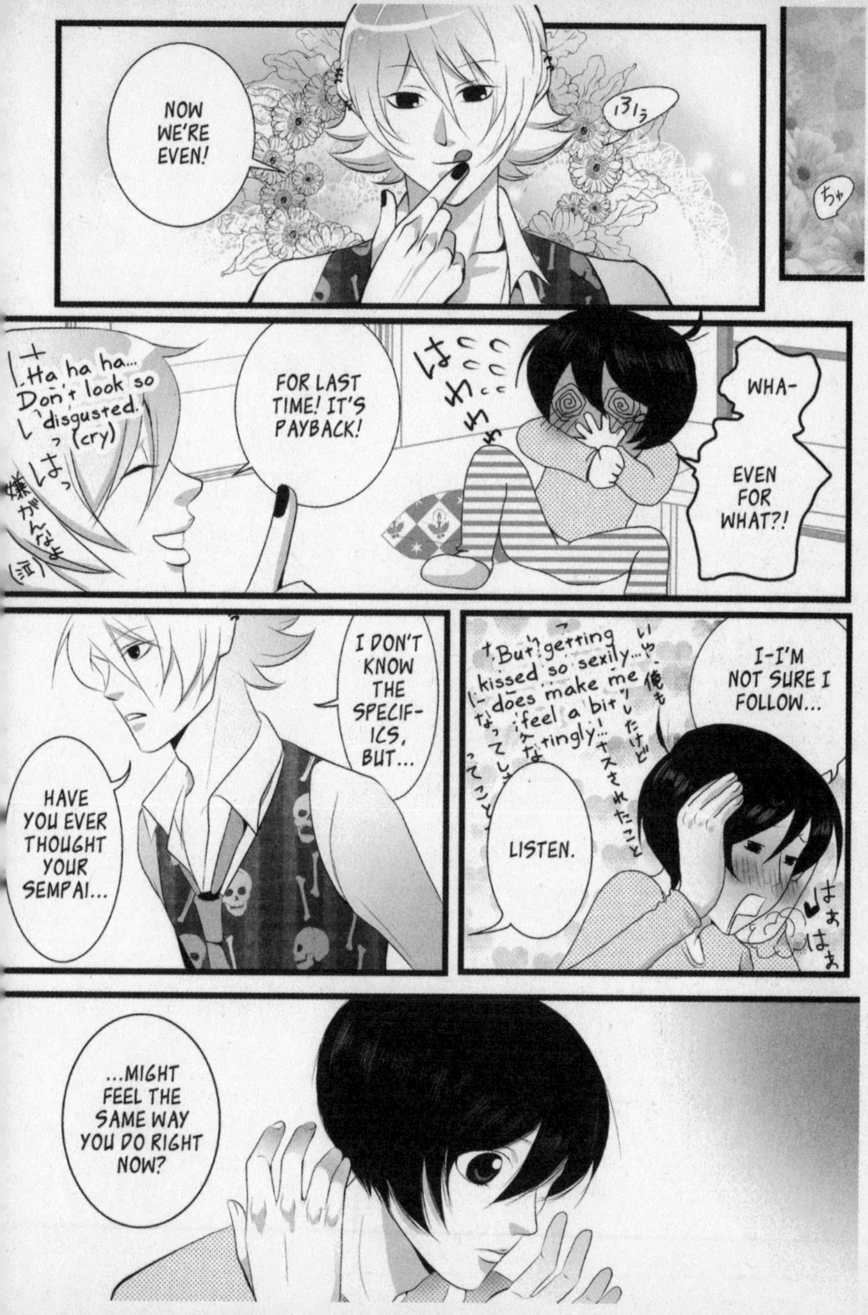
ちゃ
NOW WE'RE EVEN!
WHA-
EVEN FOR WHAT?!
FOR LAST TIME! IT'S PAYBACK!
Ha ha ha... Don't look so disgusted. (cry)
I-I'M NOT SURE I FOLLOW...
But getting kissed so sexily... does make me feel a bit tingly!...
LISTEN.
I DON'T KNOW THE SPECIFICS, BUT...
HAVE YOU EVER THOUGHT YOUR SEMPAI...
...MIGHT FEEL THE SAME WAY YOU DO RIGHT NOW?

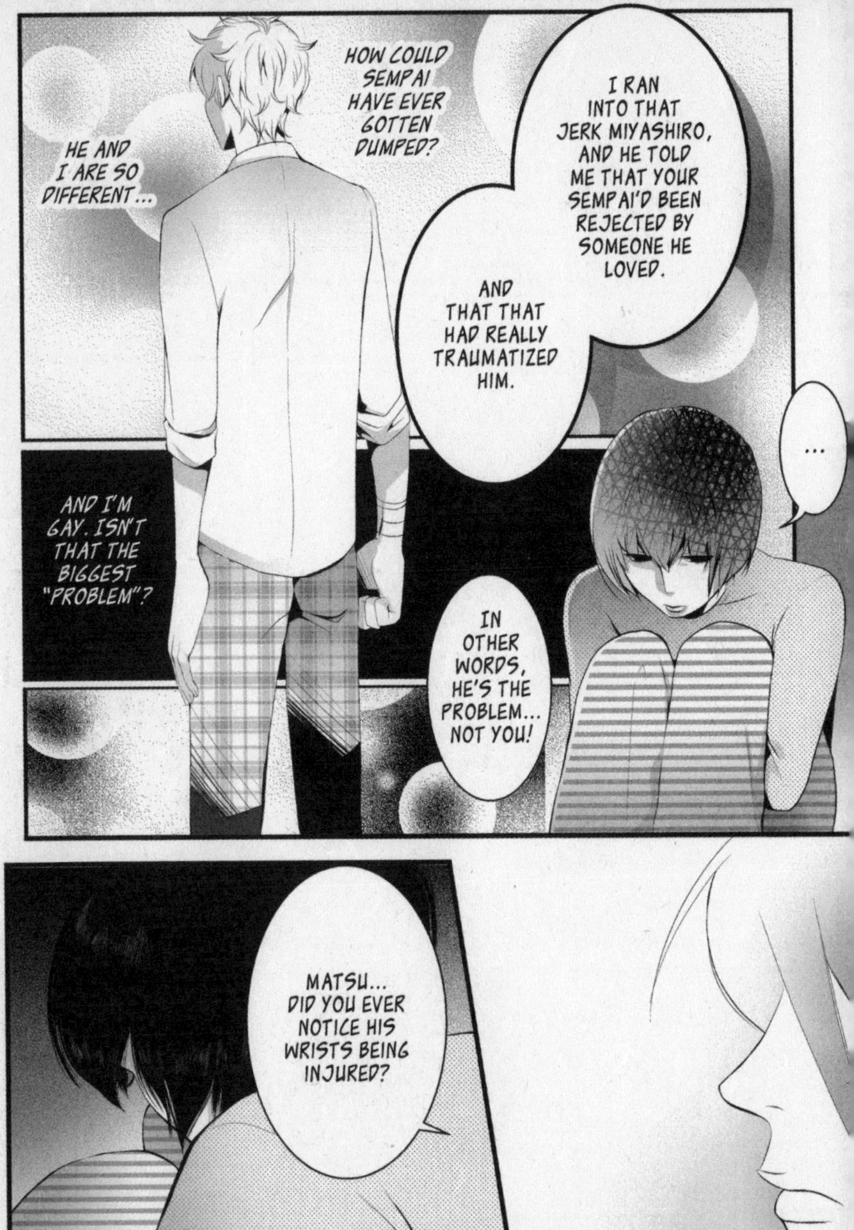
I RAN INTO THAT JERK MIYASHIRO, AND HE TOLD ME THAT YOUR SEMPAI'D BEEN REJECTED BY SOMEONE HE LOVED.
AND THAT THAT HAD REALLY TRAUMATIZED HIM.
HOW COULD SEMPAI HAVE EVER GOTTEN DUMPED?
HE AND I ARE SO DIFFERENT...
...
IN OTHER WORDS, HE'S THE PROBLEM... NOT YOU!
AND I'M GAY. ISN'T THAT THE BIGGEST "PROBLEM"?
MATSU... DID YOU EVER NOTICE HIS WRISTS BEING INJURED?

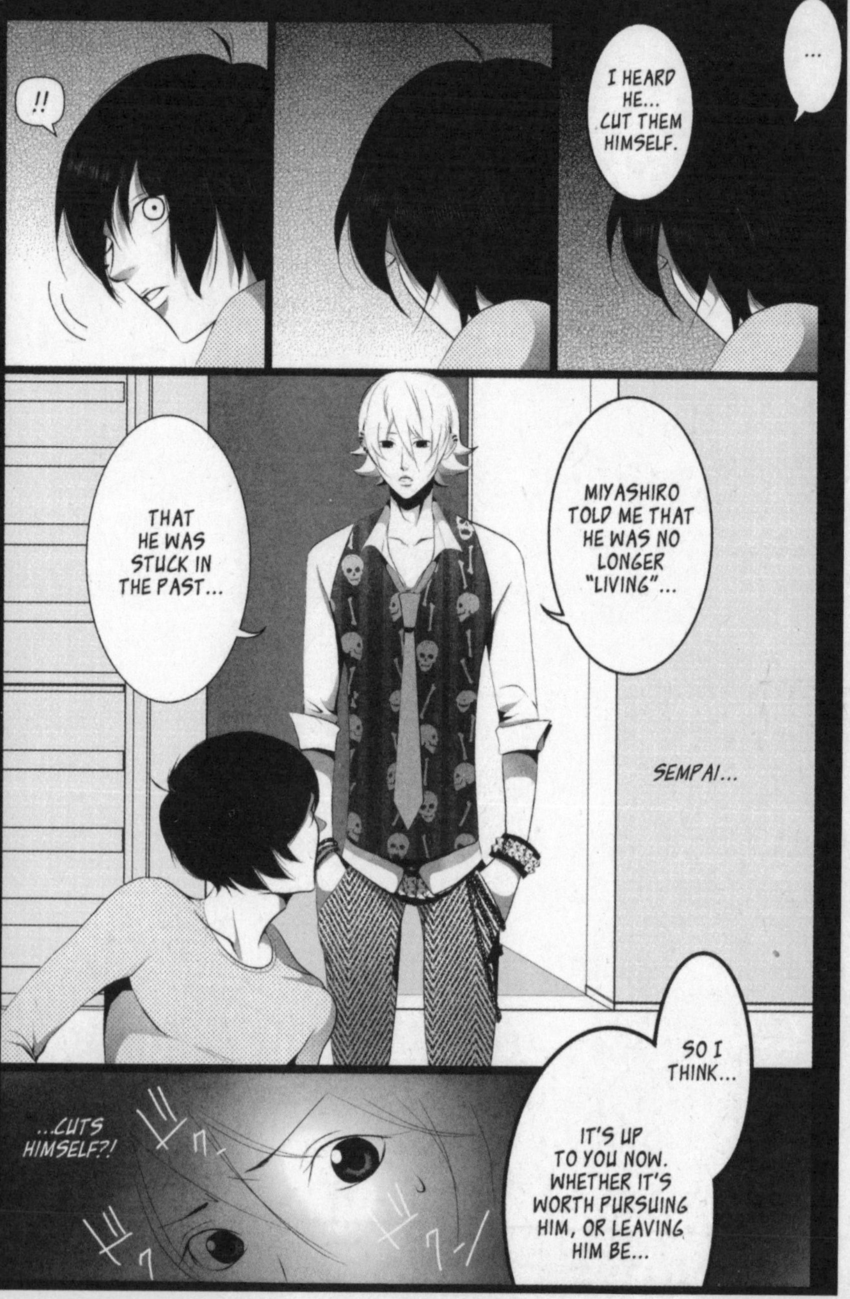
...
I HEARD HE... CUT THEM HIMSELF.
!!
MIYASHIRO TOLD ME THAT HE WAS NO LONGER "LIVING"...
THAT HE WAS STUCK IN THE PAST...
SEMPAI...
SO I THINK...
IT'S UP TO YOU NOW. WHETHER IT'S WORTH PURSUING HIM, OR LEAVING HIM BE...
...CUTS HIMSELF?!

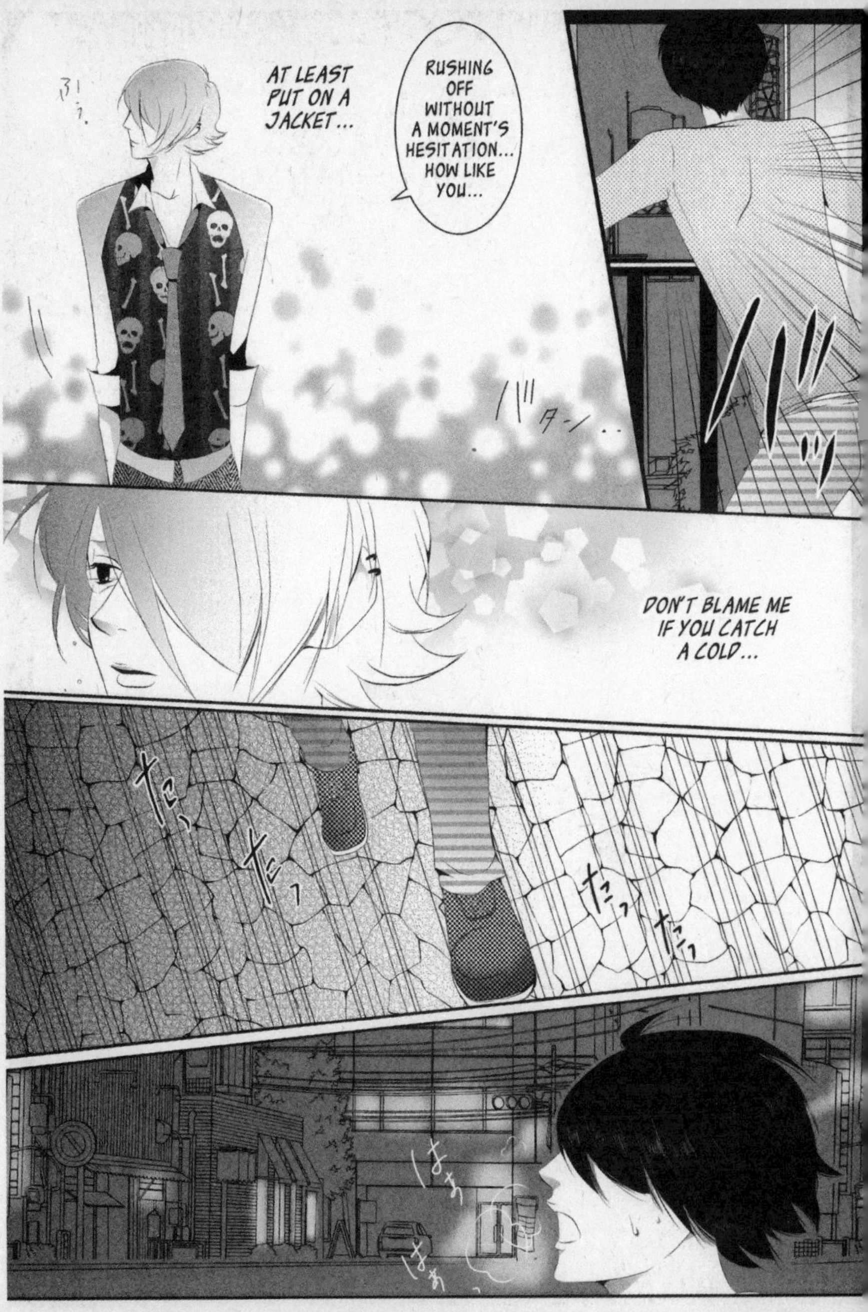
RUSHING OFF WITHOUT A MOMENT'S HESITATION... HOW LIKE YOU...
AT LEAST PUT ON A JACKET...
DON'T BLAME ME IF YOU CATCH A COLD...

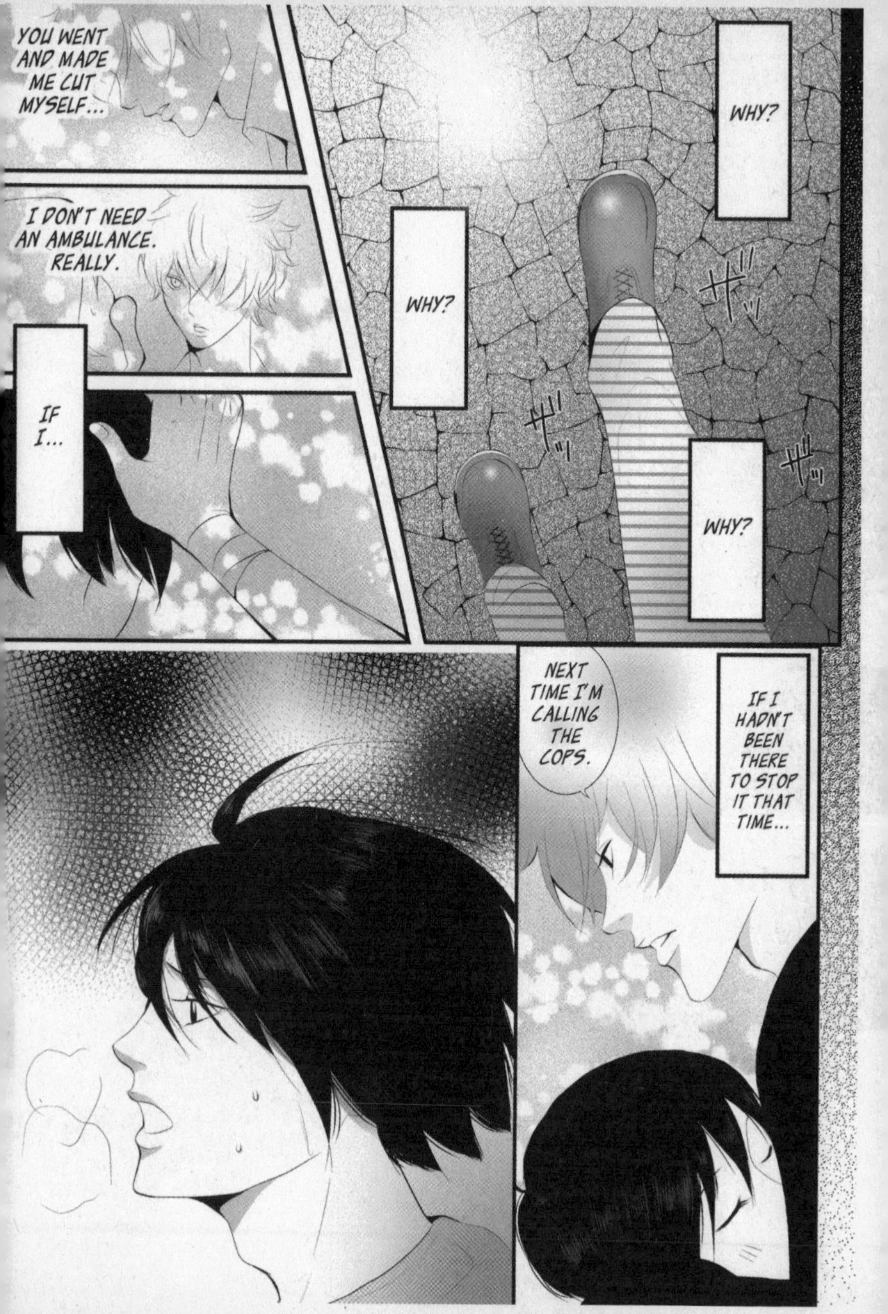
WHY?
ザッ
WHY?
ザッ
WHY?
ザッ
YOU WENT AND MADE ME CUT MYSELF...
I DON'T NEED AN AMBULANCE. REALLY.
IF I...
IF I HADN'T BEEN THERE TO STOP IT THAT TIME...
NEXT TIME I'M CALLING THE COPS.

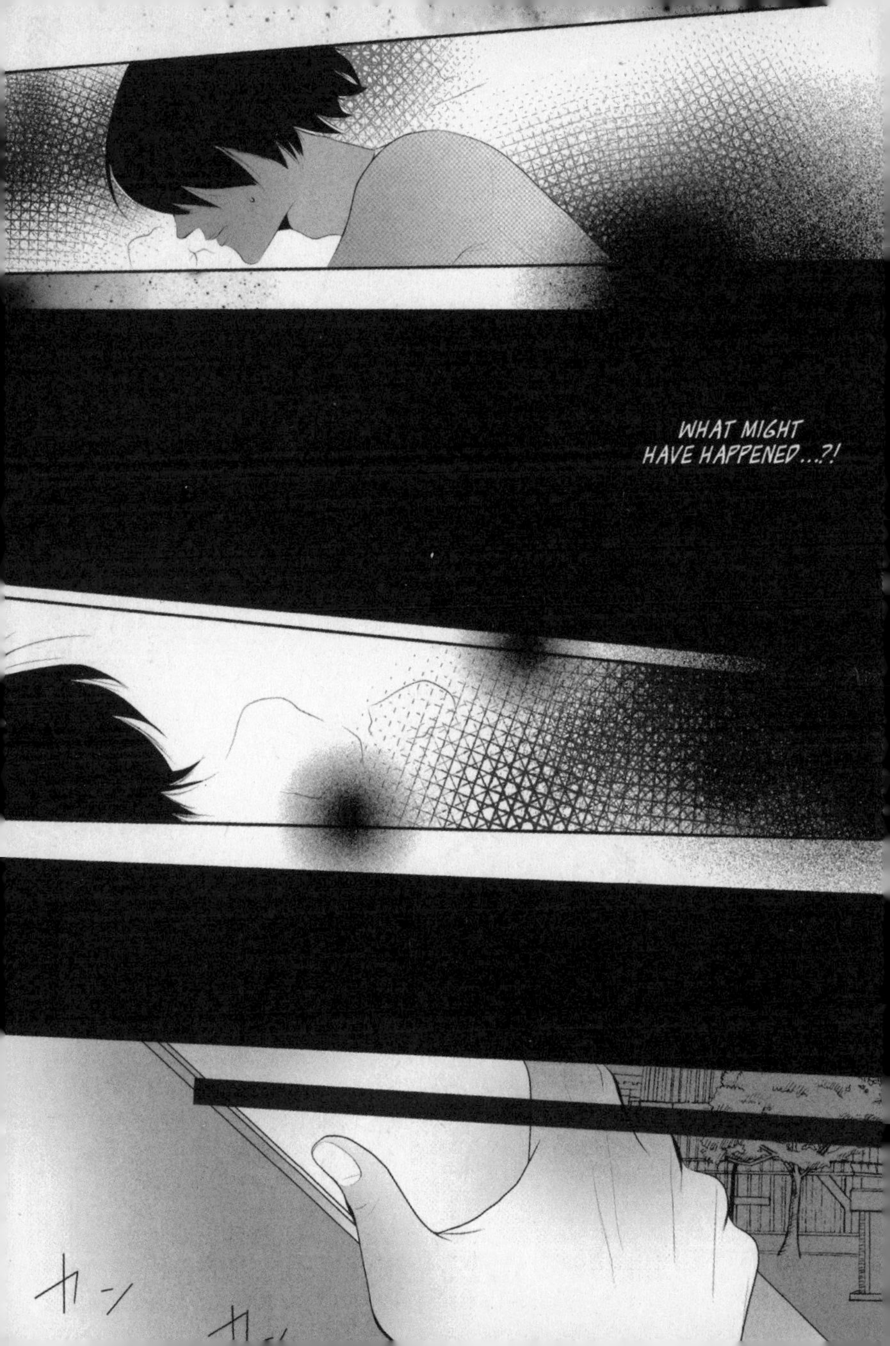
WHAT MIGHT HAVE HAPPENED...?!
カーン

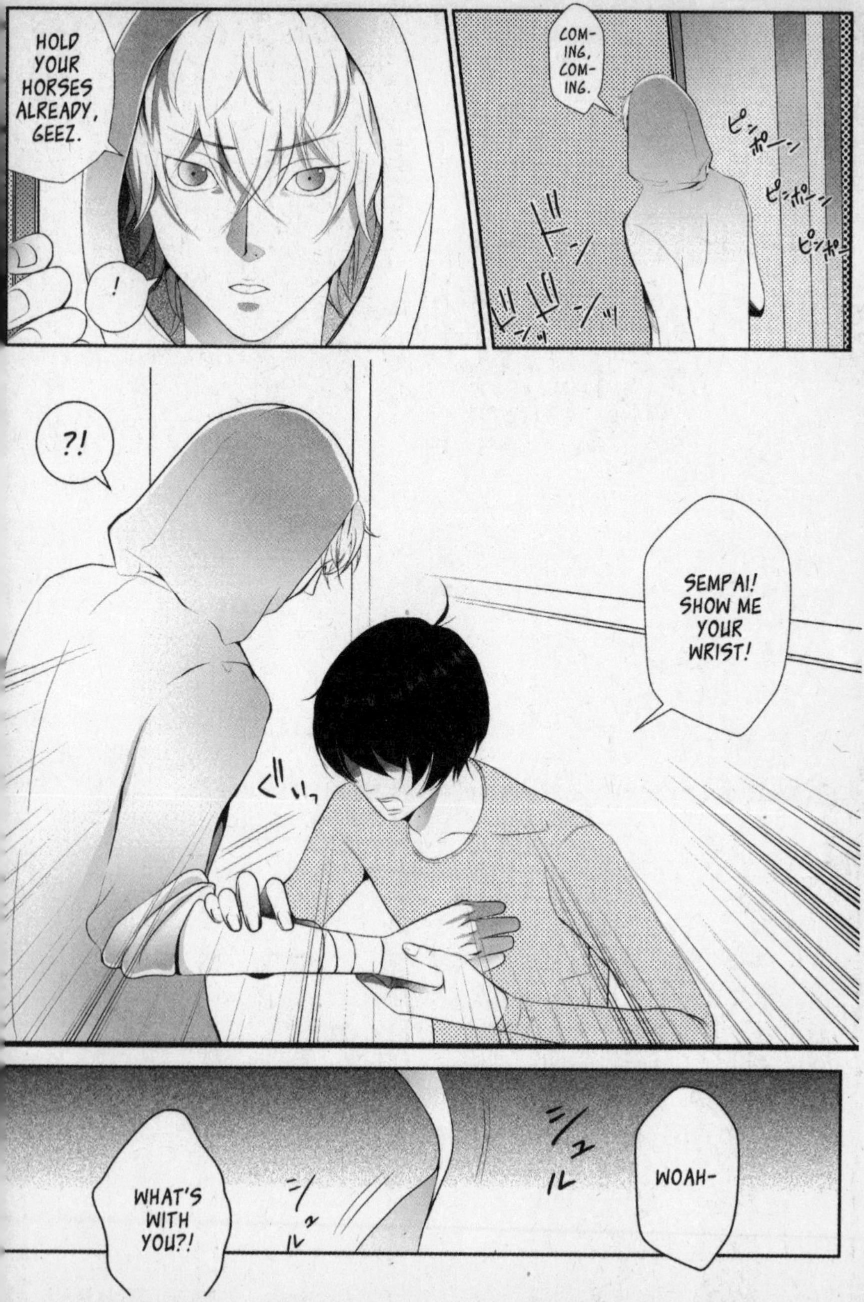
COM-ING, COM-ING.
ピンポーン
ピンポーン
ピンポー
HOLD YOUR HORSES ALREADY, GEEZ.
!
SEMPAI! SHOW ME YOUR WRIST!
?!
ぐいっ
シュル
WOAH-
シュル
WHAT'S WITH YOU?!

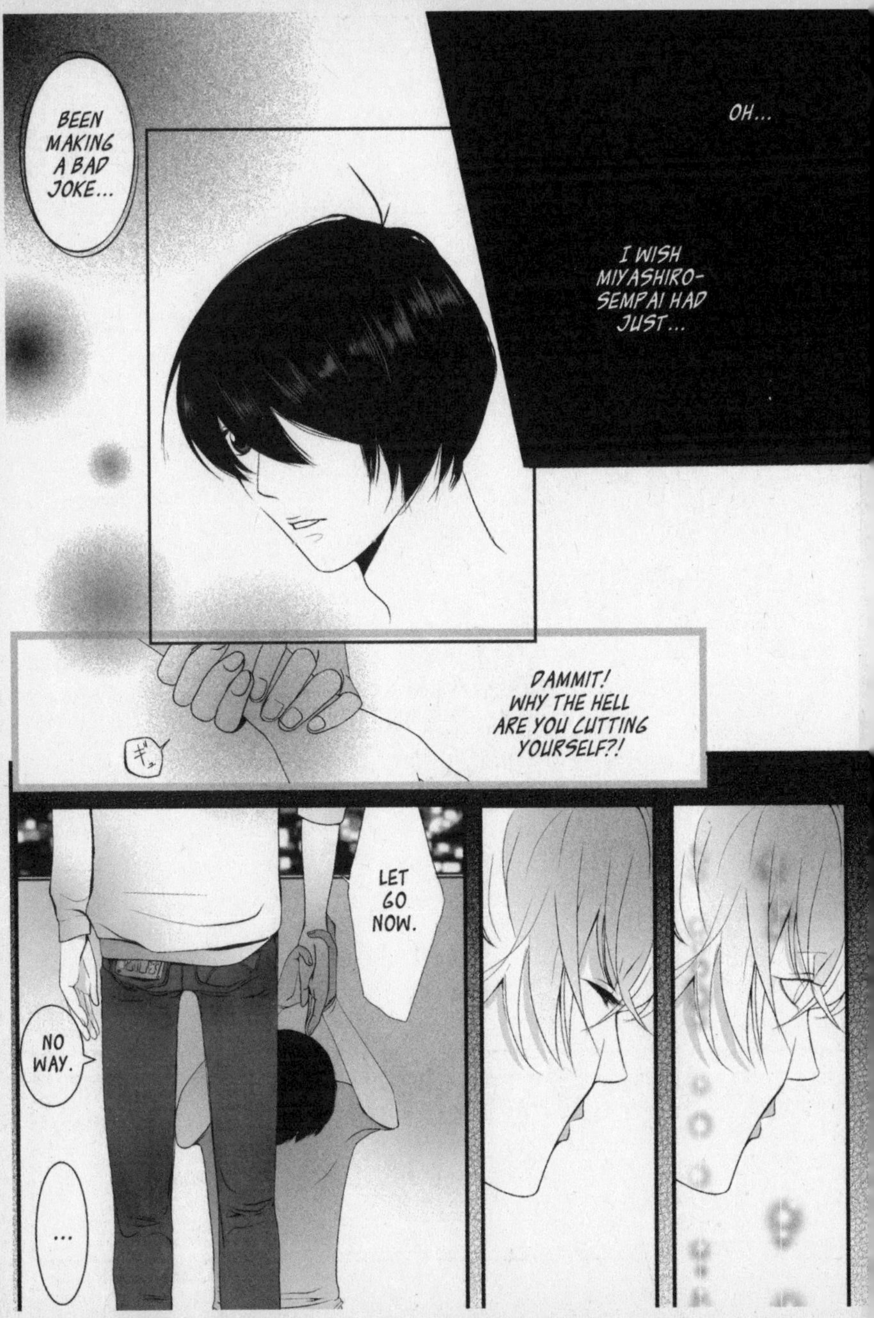
OH...
I WISH MIYASHIRO-SEMPAI HAD JUST...
BEEN MAKING A BAD JOKE...
DAMMIT! WHY THE HELL ARE YOU CUTTING YOURSELF?!
ギュ
LET GO NOW.
NO WAY.
...

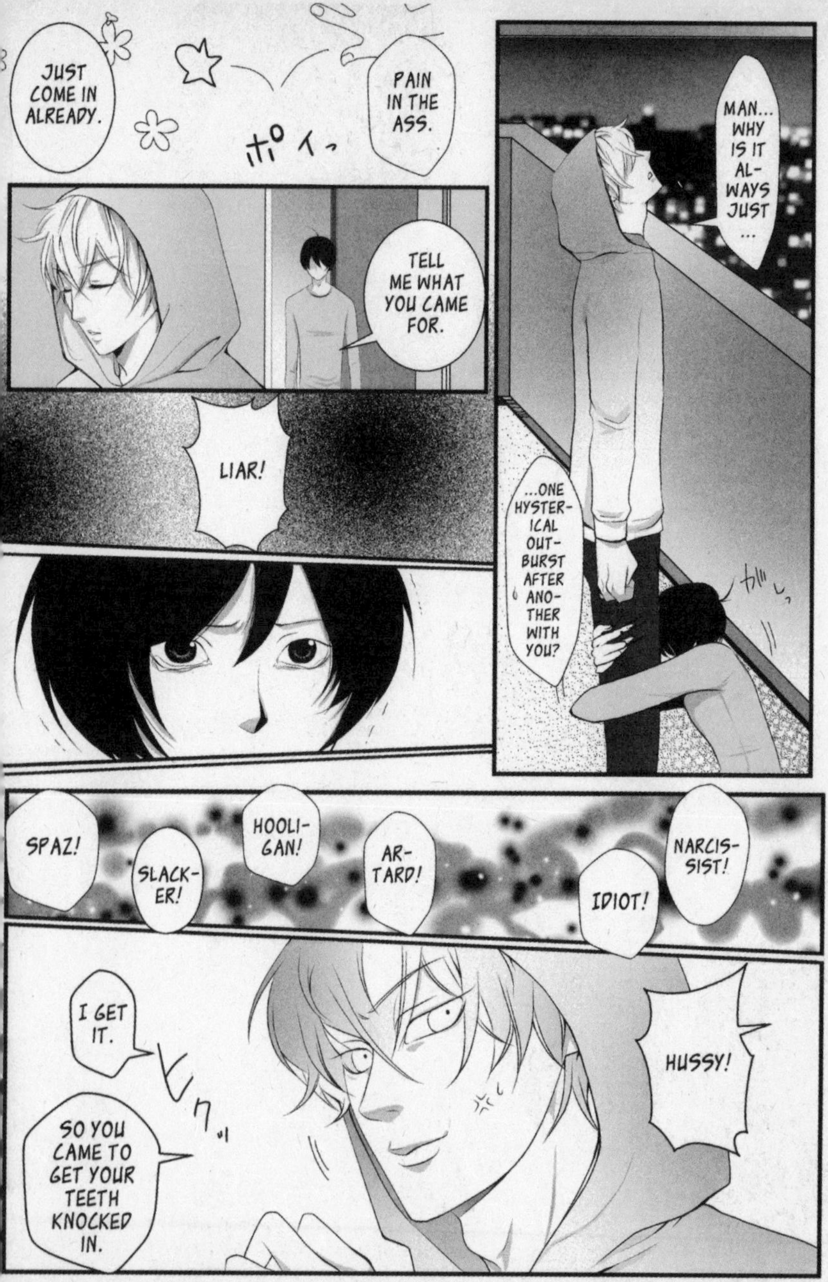
MAN... WHY IS IT ALWAYS JUST ...
...ONE HYSTERICAL OUTBURST AFTER ANOTHER WITH YOU?
PAIN IN THE ASS.
ポイっ
JUST COME IN ALREADY.
TELL ME WHAT YOU CAME FOR.
LIAR!
NARCISSIST!
IDIOT!
ARTARD!
HOOLIGAN!
SLACKER!
SPAZ!
HUSSY!
I GET IT.
SO YOU CAME TO GET YOUR TEETH KNOCKED IN.

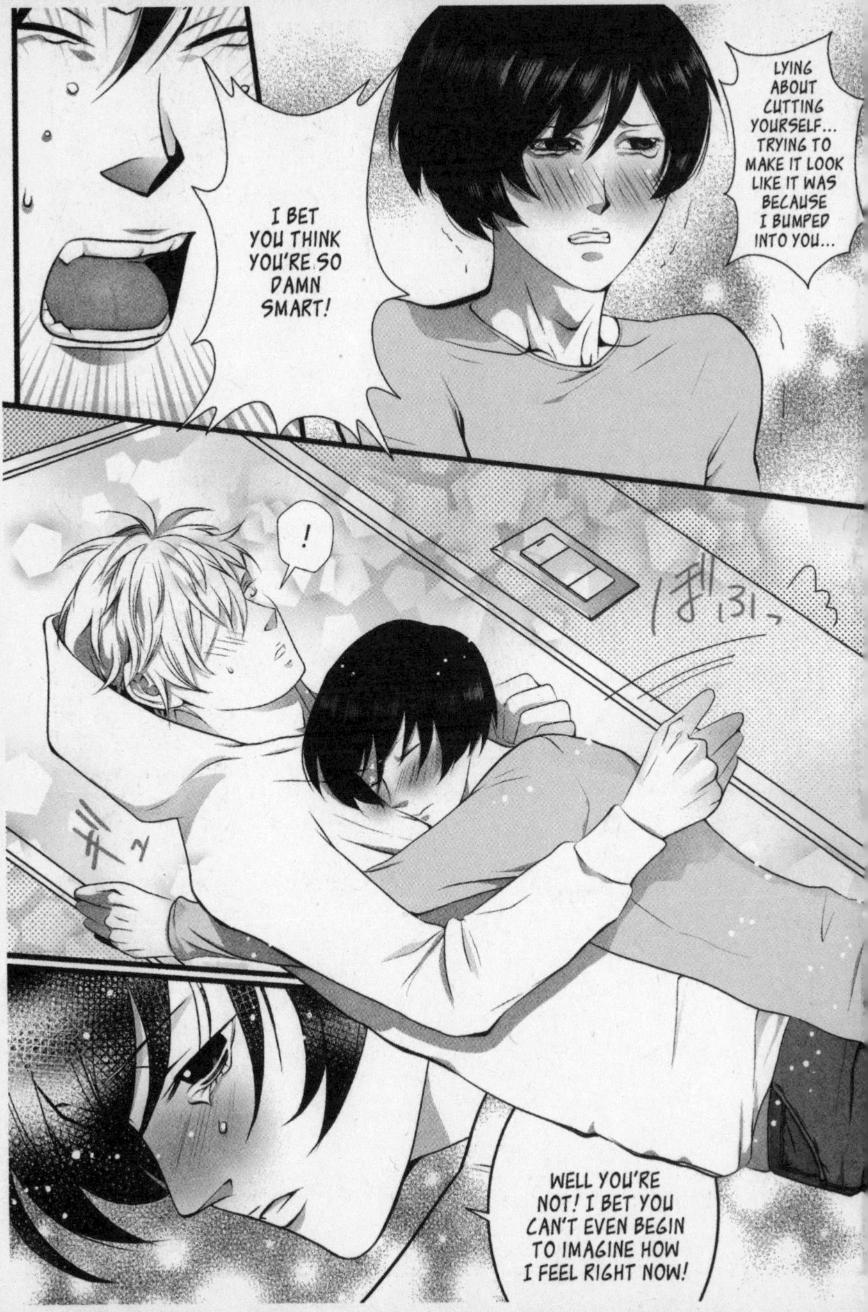
LYING ABOUT CUTTING YOURSELF... TRYING TO MAKE IT LOOK LIKE IT WAS BECAUSE I BUMPED INTO YOU...
I BET YOU THINK YOU'RE SO DAMN SMART!
!
ぽふっ
ギュ
WELL YOU'RE NOT! I BET YOU CAN'T EVEN BEGIN TO IMAGINE HOW I FEEL RIGHT NOW!

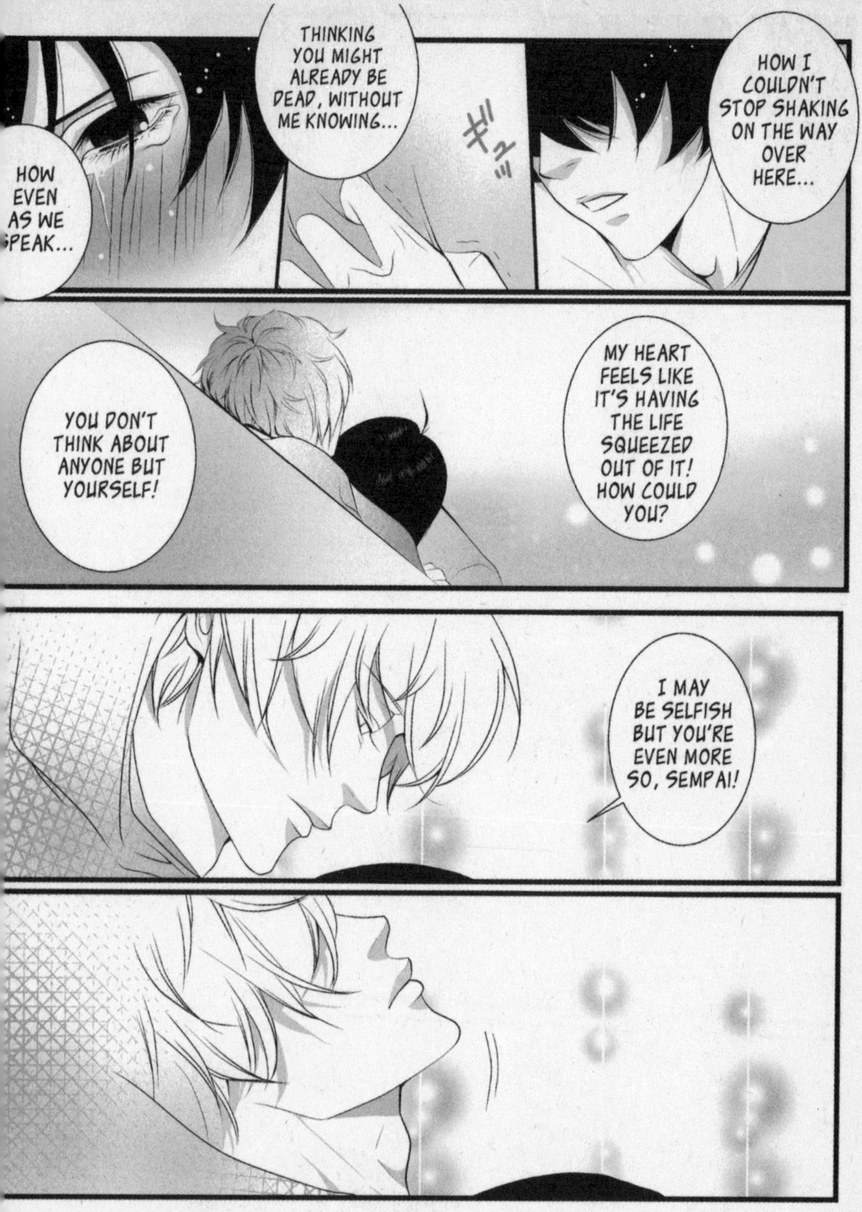
HOW I COULDN'T STOP SHAKING ON THE WAY OVER HERE...
ギュッ
THINKING YOU MIGHT ALREADY BE DEAD, WITHOUT ME KNOWING...
HOW EVEN AS WE SPEAK...
MY HEART FEELS LIKE IT'S HAVING THE LIFE SQUEEZED OUT OF IT! HOW COULD YOU?
YOU DON'T THINK ABOUT ANYONE BUT YOURSELF!
I MAY BE SELFISH BUT YOU'RE EVEN MORE SO, SEMPAI!

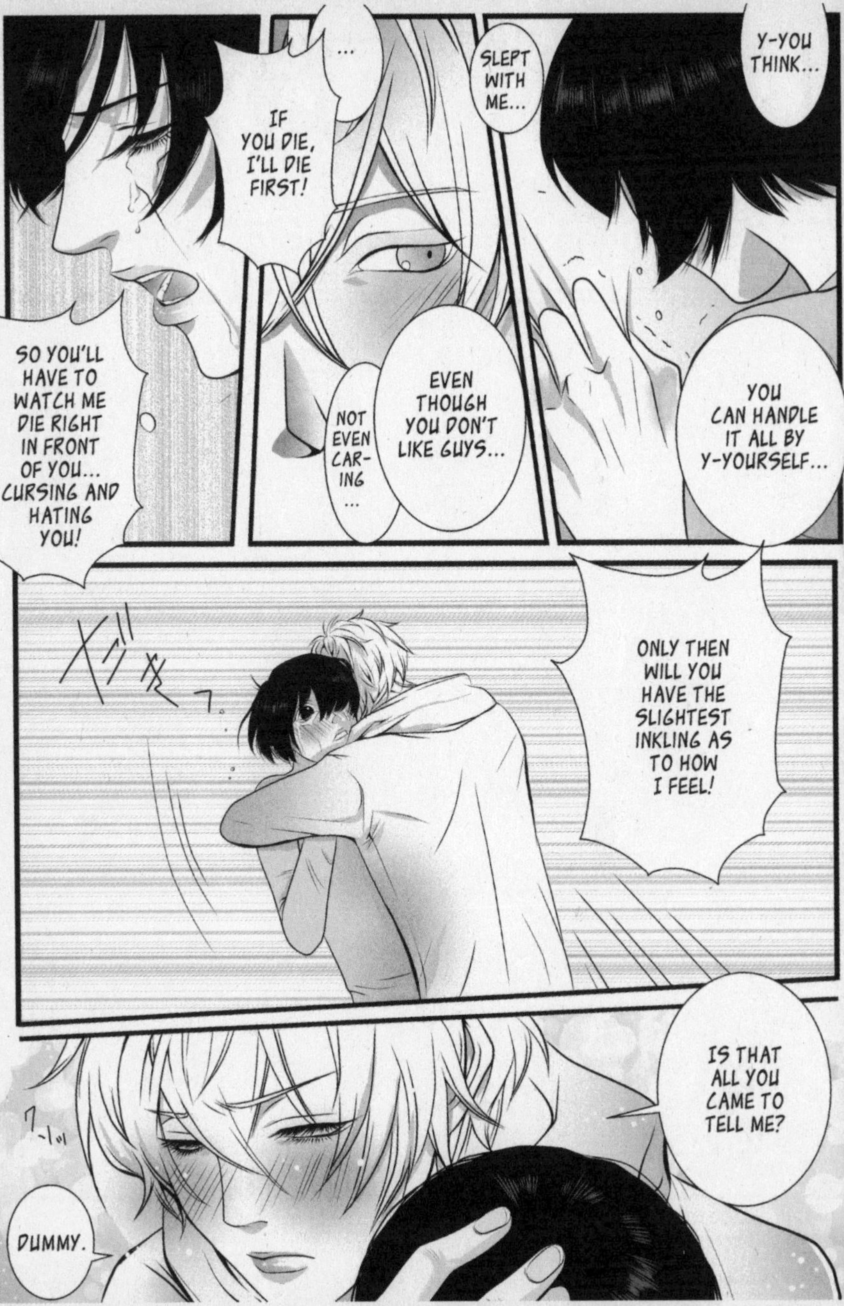
Y-YOU THINK...
YOU CAN HANDLE IT ALL BY Y-YOURSELF...
SLEPT WITH ME...
...
EVEN THOUGH YOU DON'T LIKE GUYS...
NOT EVEN CAR-ING...
IF YOU DIE, I'LL DIE FIRST!
SO YOU'LL HAVE TO WATCH ME DIE RIGHT IN FRONT OF YOU... CURSING AND HATING YOU!
ONLY THEN WILL YOU HAVE THE SLIGHTEST INKLING AS TO HOW I FEEL!
IS THAT ALL YOU CAME TO TELL ME?
DUMMY.

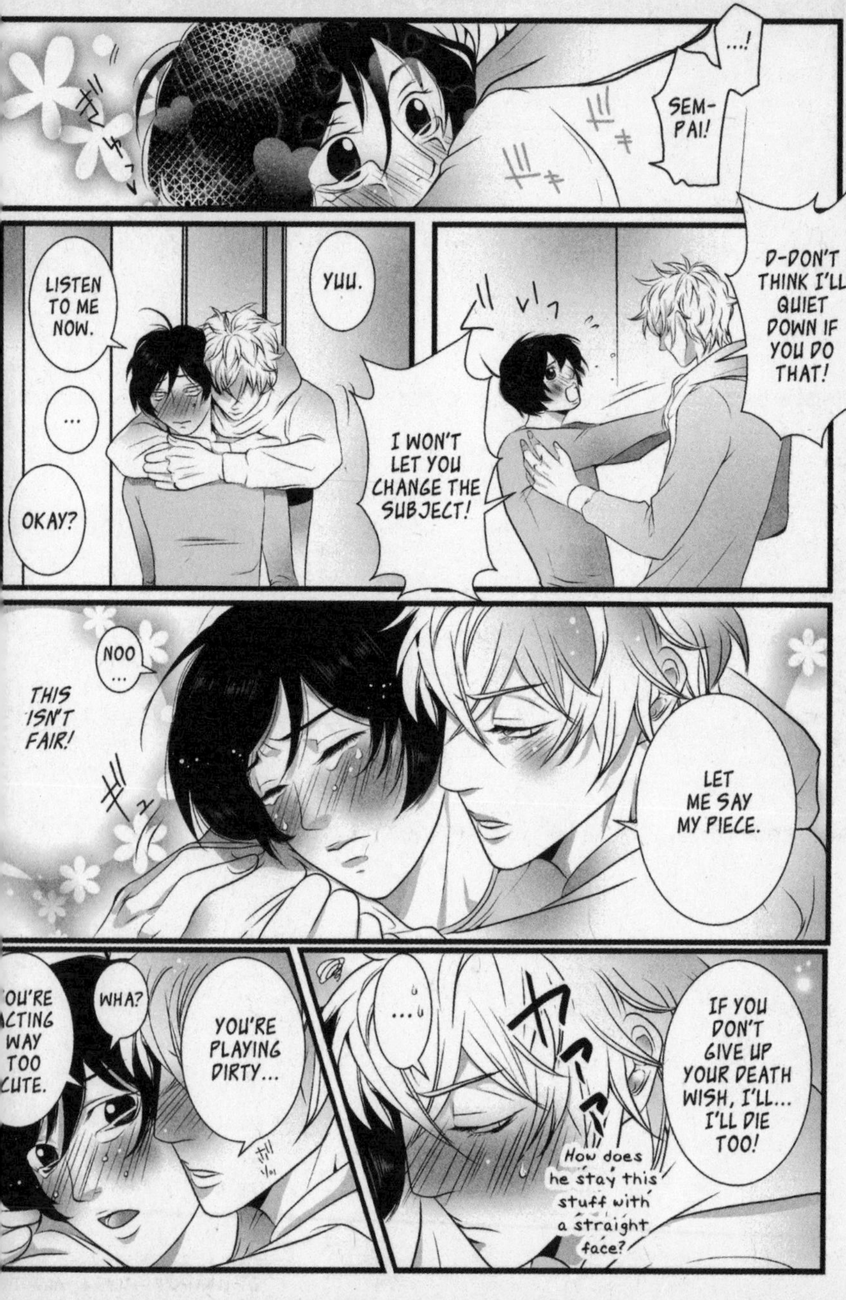
...!
SEM-PAI!
D-DON'T THINK I'LL QUIET DOWN IF YOU DO THAT!
I WON'T LET YOU CHANGE THE SUBJECT!
YUU.
LISTEN TO ME NOW.
...
OKAY?
LET ME SAY MY PIECE.
NOO...
THIS ISN'T FAIR!
...
IF YOU DON'T GIVE UP YOUR DEATH WISH, I'LL... I'LL DIE TOO!
How does he stay this stuff with a straight face?
YOU'RE PLAYING DIRTY...
WHA?
OU'RE ACTING WAY TOO CUTE.

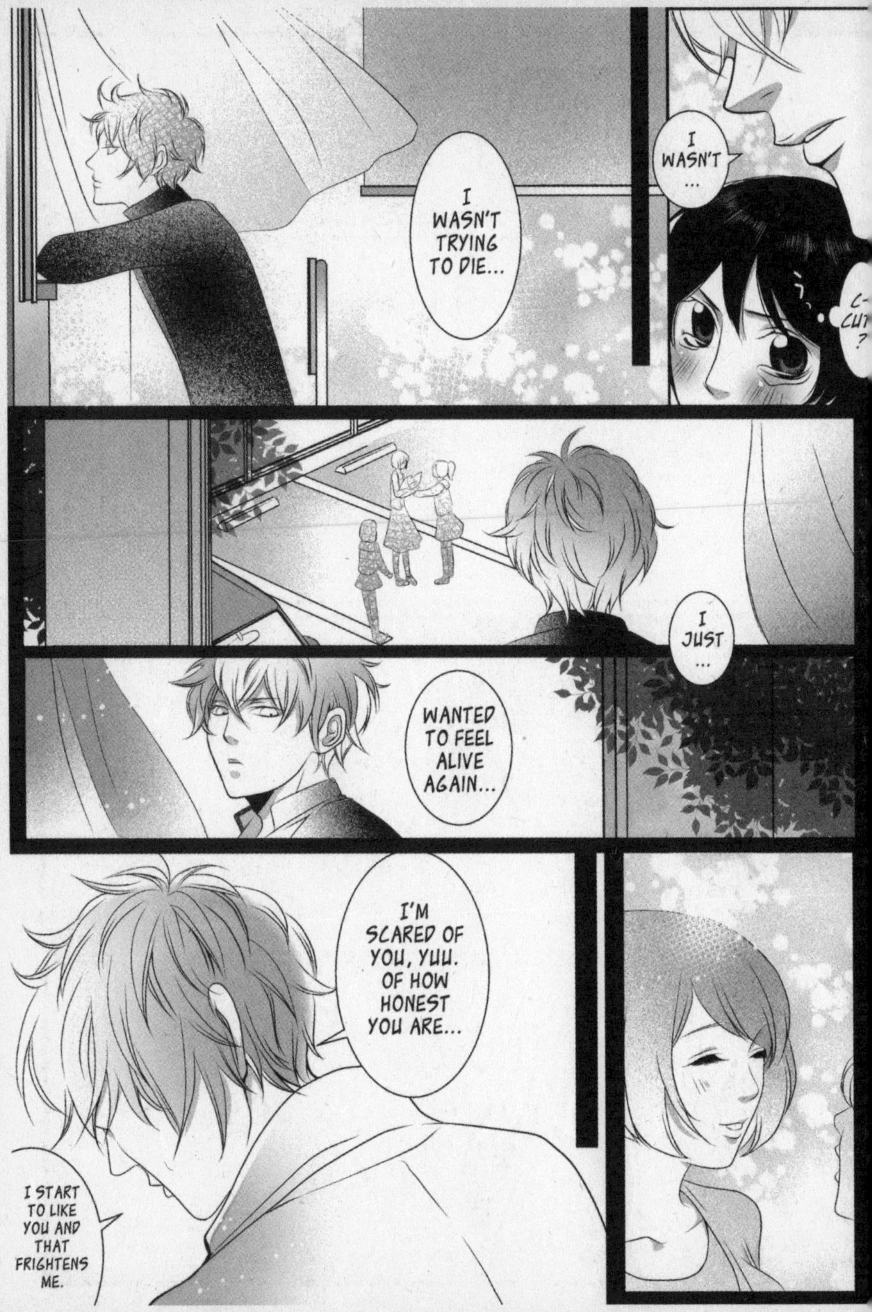
I WASN'T ...
C-CUT?
I WASN'T TRYING TO DIE...
I JUST ...
WANTED TO FEEL ALIVE AGAIN...
I'M SCARED OF YOU, YUU. OF HOW HONEST YOU ARE...
I START TO LIKE YOU AND THAT FRIGHTENS ME.

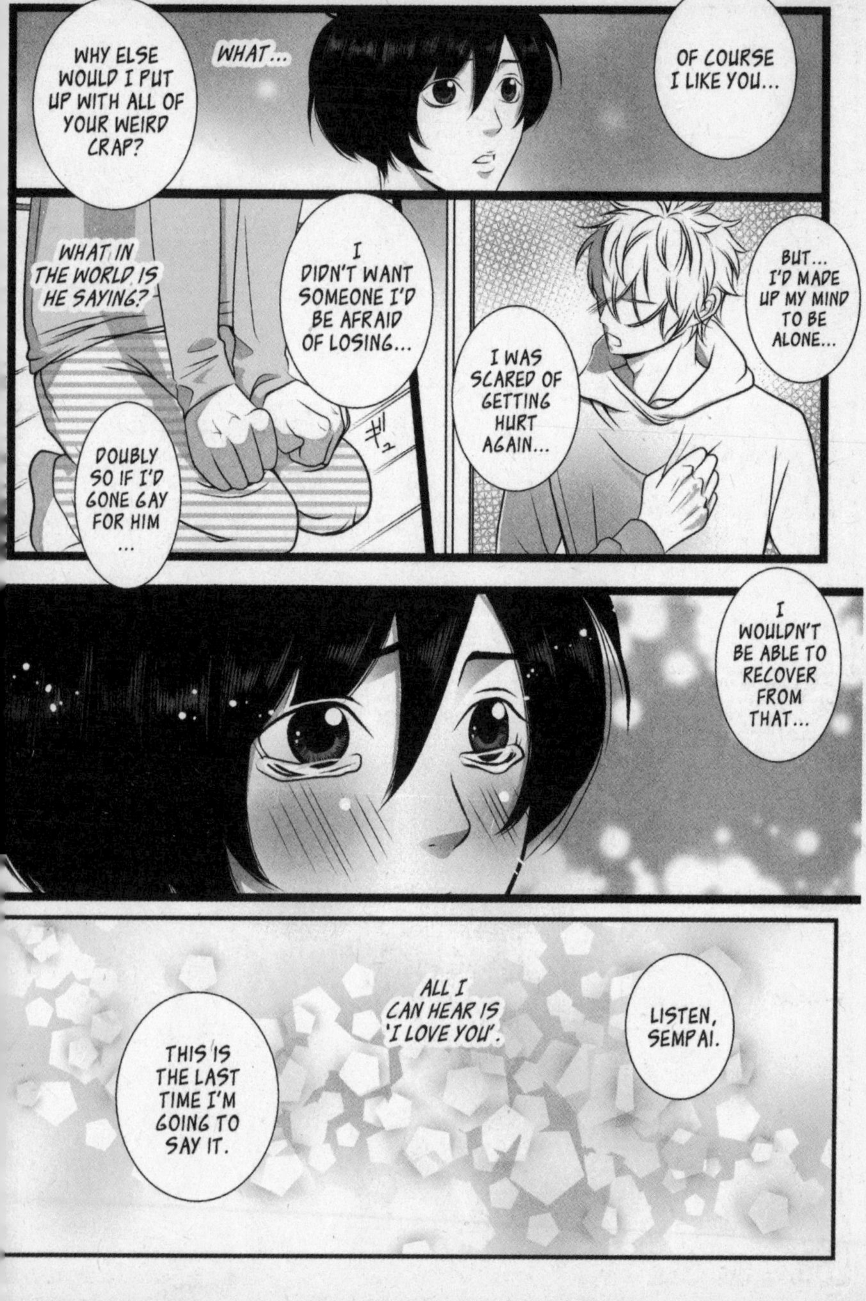
OF COURSE I LIKE YOU...
WHAT...
WHY ELSE WOULD I PUT UP WITH ALL OF YOUR WEIRD CRAP?
BUT... I'D MADE UP MY MIND TO BE ALONE...
I WAS SCARED OF GETTING HURT AGAIN...
I DIDN'T WANT SOMEONE I'D BE AFRAID OF LOSING...
WHAT IN THE WORLD IS HE SAYING?
DOUBLY SO IF I'D GONE GAY FOR HIM ...
I WOULDN'T BE ABLE TO RECOVER FROM THAT...
LISTEN, SEMPAI.
ALL I CAN HEAR IS 'I LOVE YOU'.
THIS IS THE LAST TIME I'M GOING TO SAY IT.

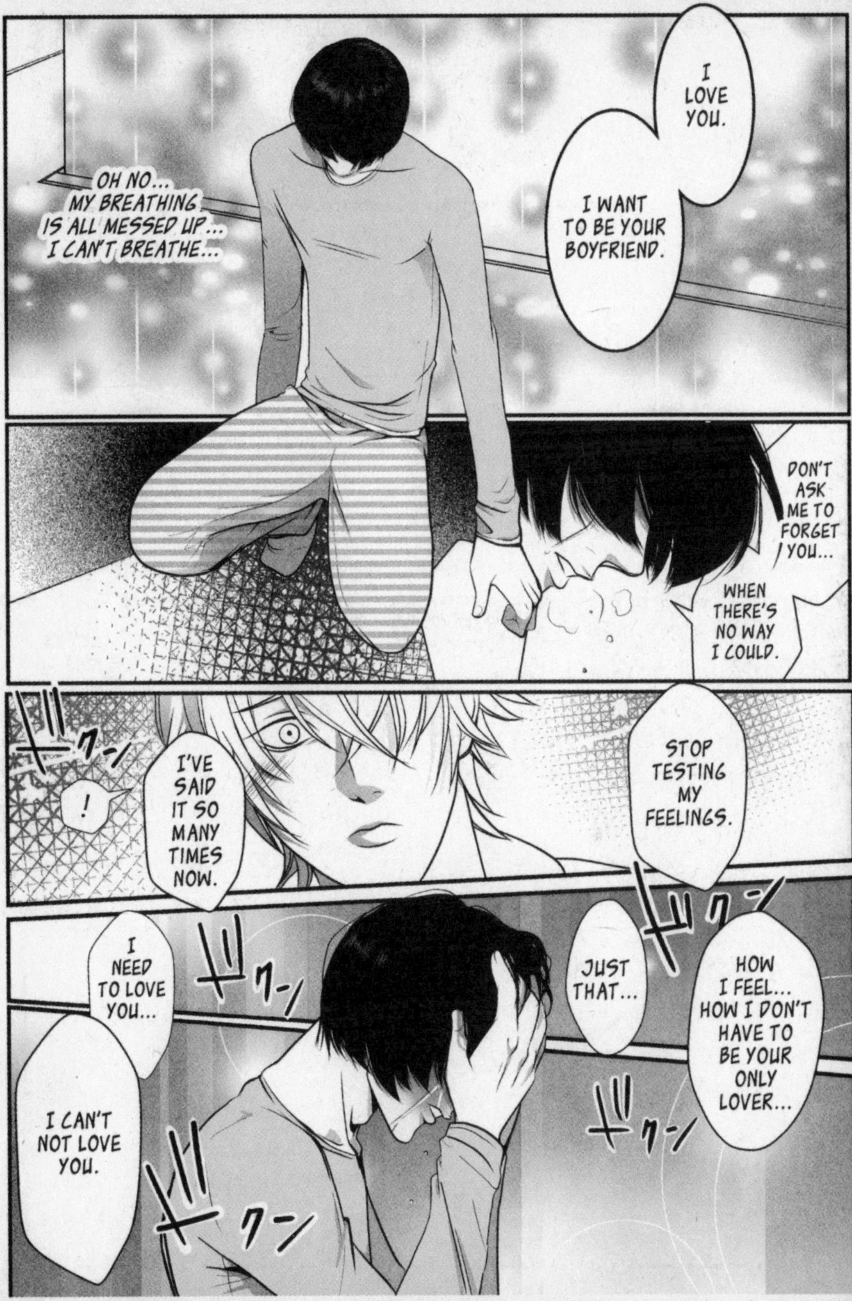
I LOVE YOU.
I WANT TO BE YOUR BOYFRIEND.
OH NO... MY BREATHING IS ALL MESSED UP... I CAN'T BREATHE...
DON'T ASK ME TO FORGET YOU...
WHEN THERE'S NO WAY I COULD.
STOP TESTING MY FEELINGS.
I'VE SAID IT SO MANY TIMES NOW.
!
ドクン
ドクン
HOW I FEEL... HOW I DON'T HAVE TO BE YOUR ONLY LOVER...
JUST THAT...
ドクン
ドクン
I NEED TO LOVE YOU...
I CAN'T NOT LOVE YOU.
ドクン

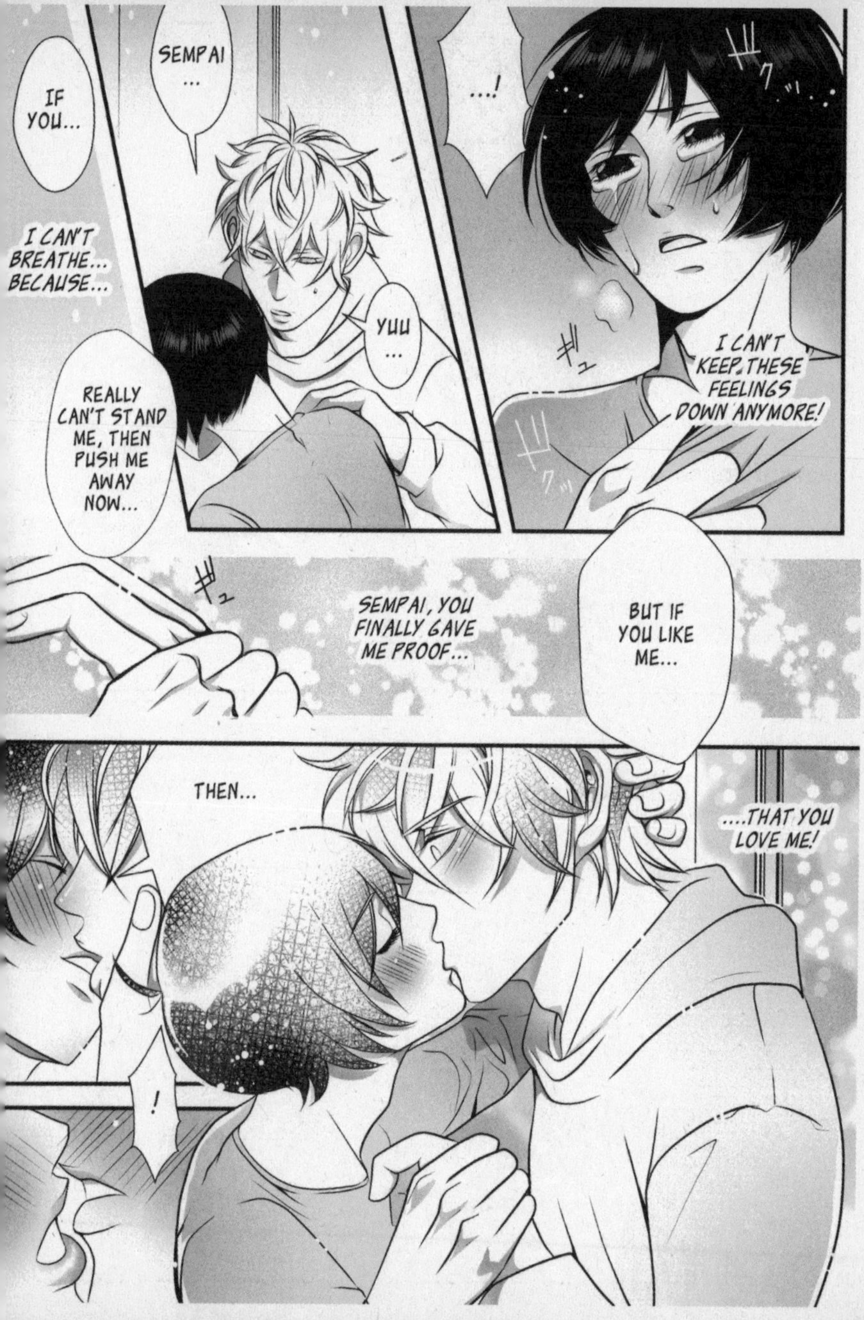
...!
I CAN'T KEEP THESE FEELINGS DOWN ANYMORE!
SEMPAI ...
YUU ...
IF YOU...
I CAN'T BREATHE... BECAUSE...
REALLY CAN'T STAND ME, THEN PUSH ME AWAY NOW...
BUT IF YOU LIKE ME...
SEMPAI, YOU FINALLY GAVE ME PROOF...
....THAT YOU LOVE ME!
THEN...
!

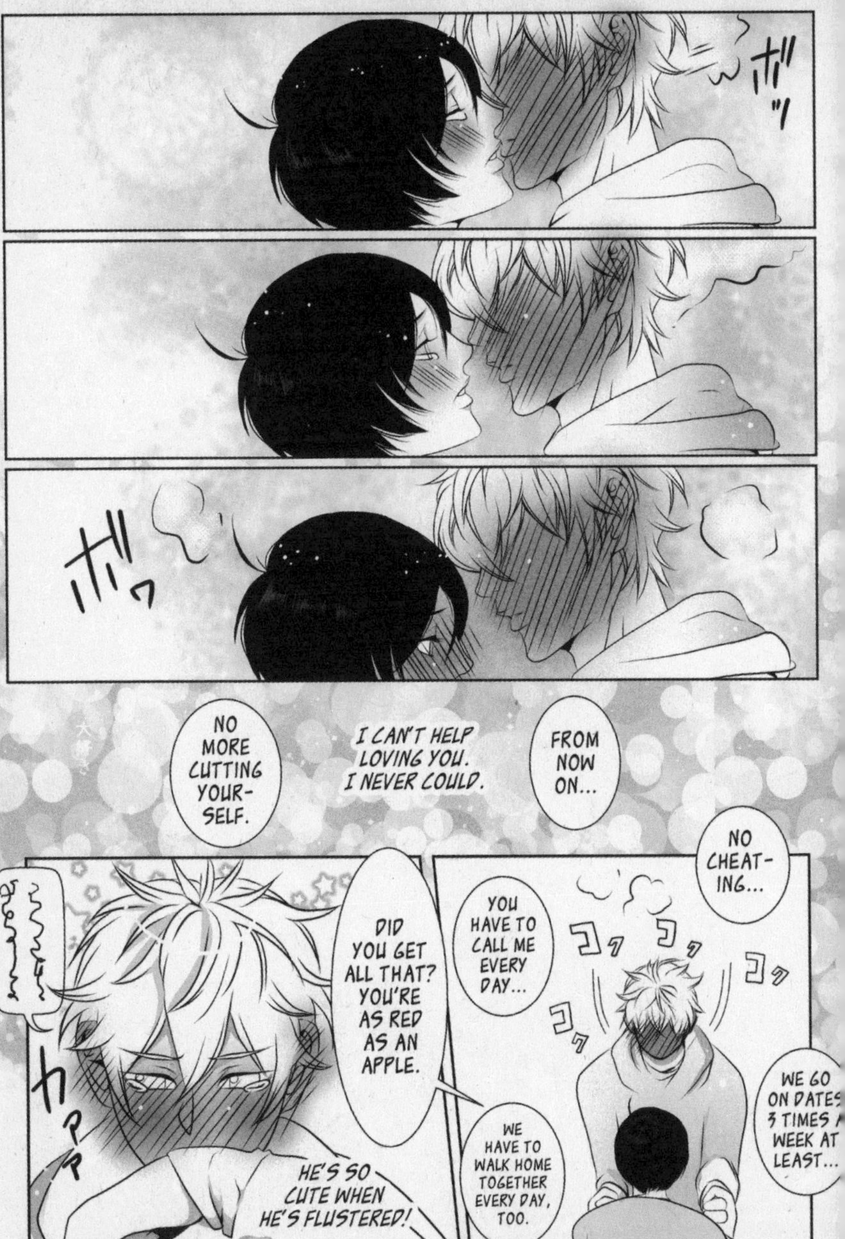
FROM NOW ON...
I CAN'T HELP LOVING YOU. I NEVER COULD.
NO MORE CUTTING YOURSELF.
NO CHEATING...
YOU HAVE TO CALL ME EVERY DAY...
WE GO ON DATES 3 TIMES A WEEK AT LEAST...
WE HAVE TO WALK HOME TOGETHER EVERY DAY, TOO.
DID YOU GET ALL THAT? YOU'RE AS RED AS AN APPLE.
HE'S SO CUTE WHEN HE'S FLUSTERED!

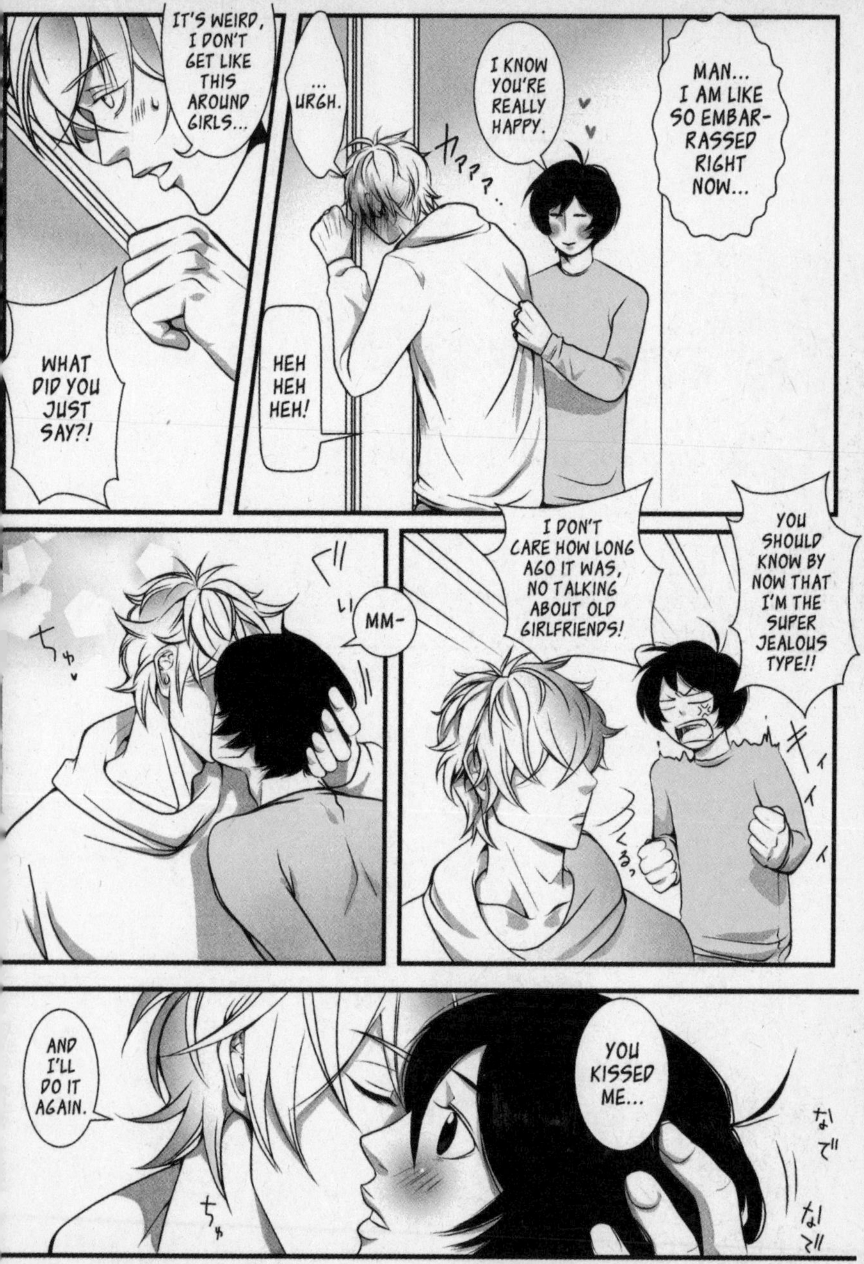
MAN... I AM LIKE SO EMBARRASSED RIGHT NOW...
I KNOW YOU'RE REALLY HAPPY.
... URGH.
HEH HEH HEH!
IT'S WEIRD, I DON'T GET LIKE THIS AROUND GIRLS...
WHAT DID YOU JUST SAY?!
YOU SHOULD KNOW BY NOW THAT I'M THE SUPER JEALOUS TYPE!!
I DON'T CARE HOW LONG AGO IT WAS, NO TALKING ABOUT OLD GIRLFRIENDS!
キィイイ
くるっ
ぐい
MM-
ちゅ
YOU KISSED ME...
なで
なで
AND I'LL DO IT AGAIN.
ちゅ

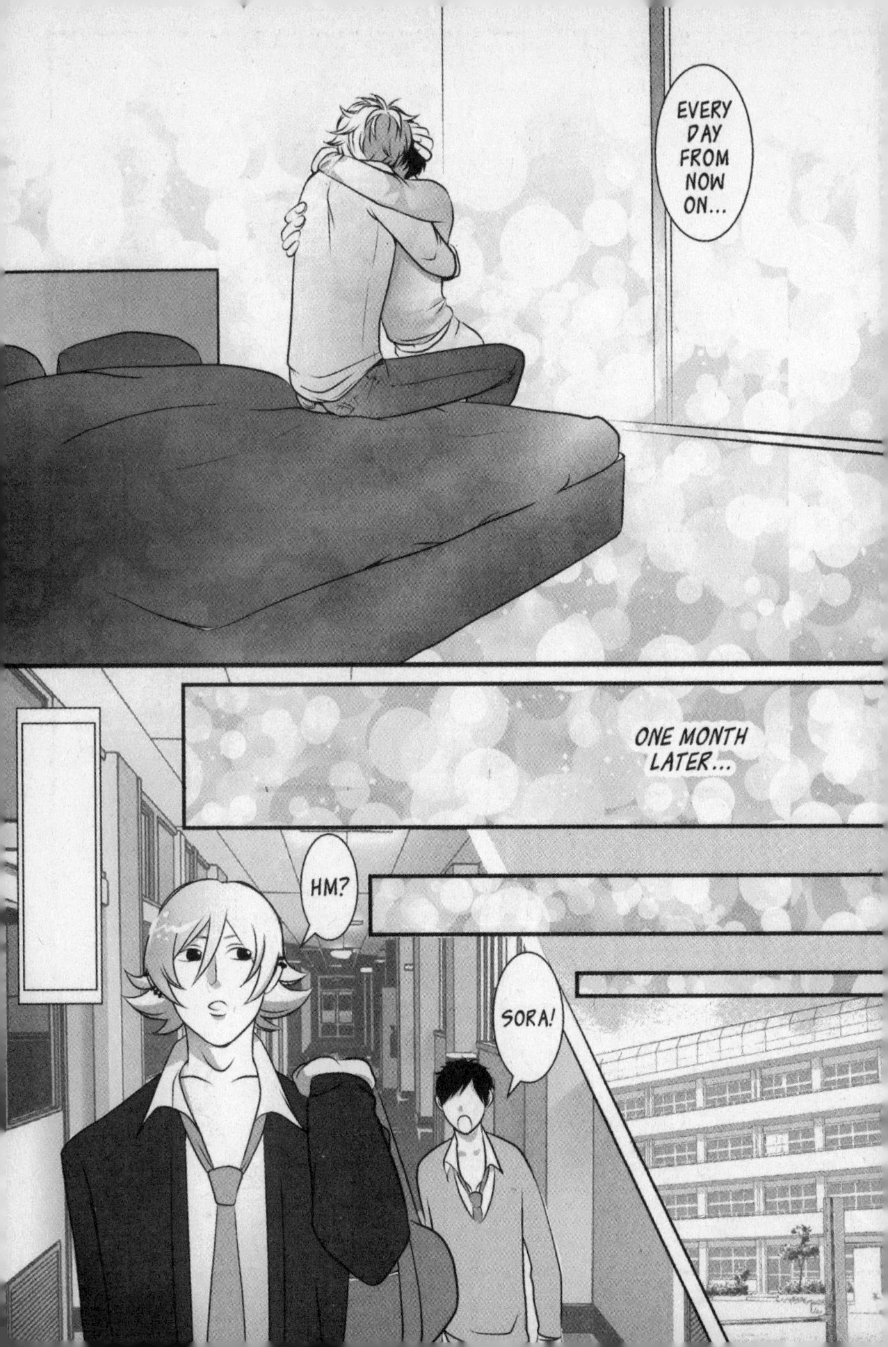
EVERY DAY FROM NOW ON...
ONE MONTH LATER...
SORA!
HM?

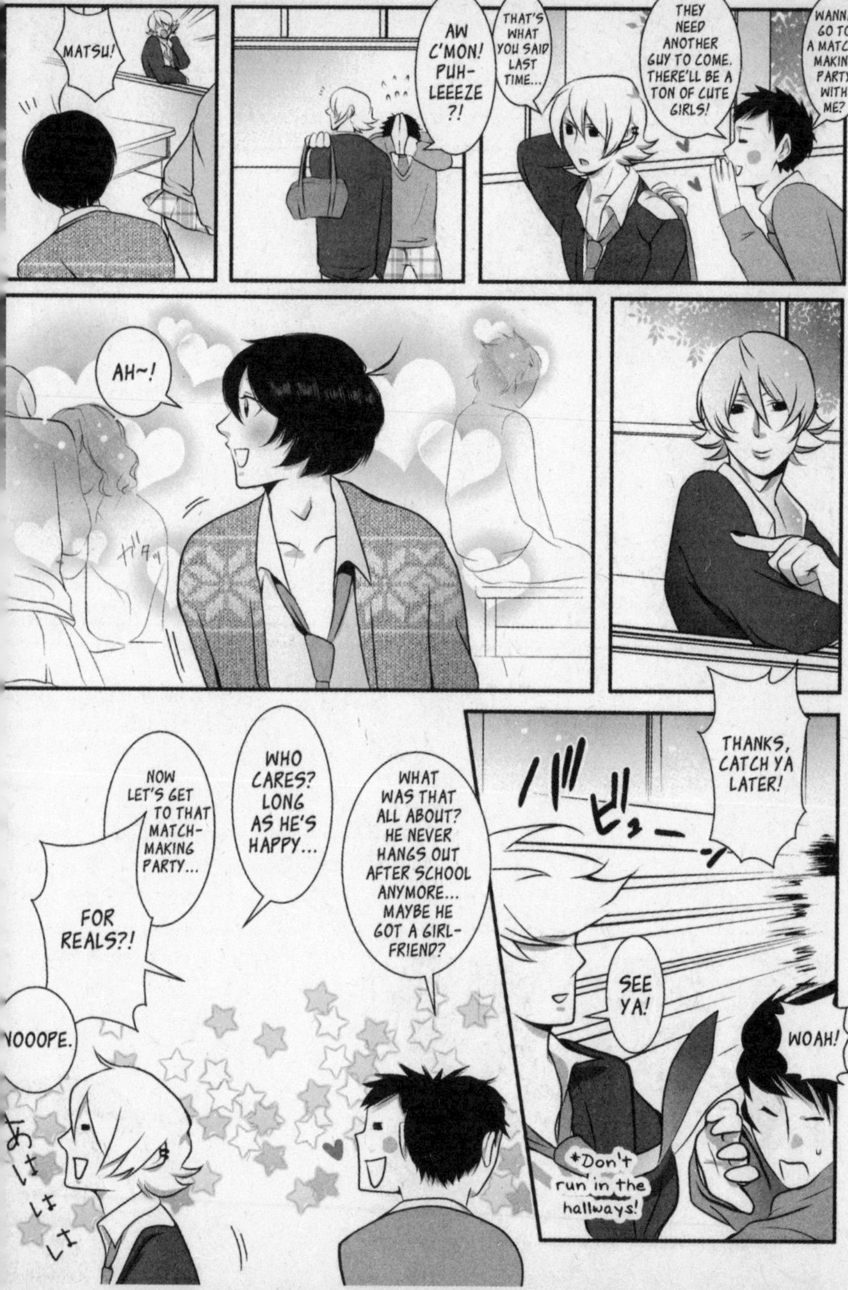
WANNA GO TO A MATCH-MAKING PARTY WITH ME?
THEY NEED ANOTHER GUY TO COME. THERE'LL BE A TON OF CUTE GIRLS!
THAT'S WHAT YOU SAID LAST TIME...
AW C'MON! PUH-LEEEZE?!
MATSU!
AH~!
ガタッ
THANKS, CATCH YA LATER!
バビューッ
SEE YA!
WOAH!
*Don't run in the hallways!
WHAT WAS THAT ALL ABOUT? HE NEVER HANGS OUT AFTER SCHOOL ANYMORE... MAYBE HE GOT A GIRL-FRIEND?
WHO CARES? LONG AS HE'S HAPPY...
NOW LET'S GET TO THAT MATCH-MAKING PARTY...
FOR REALS?!
NOOOPE.
あははは

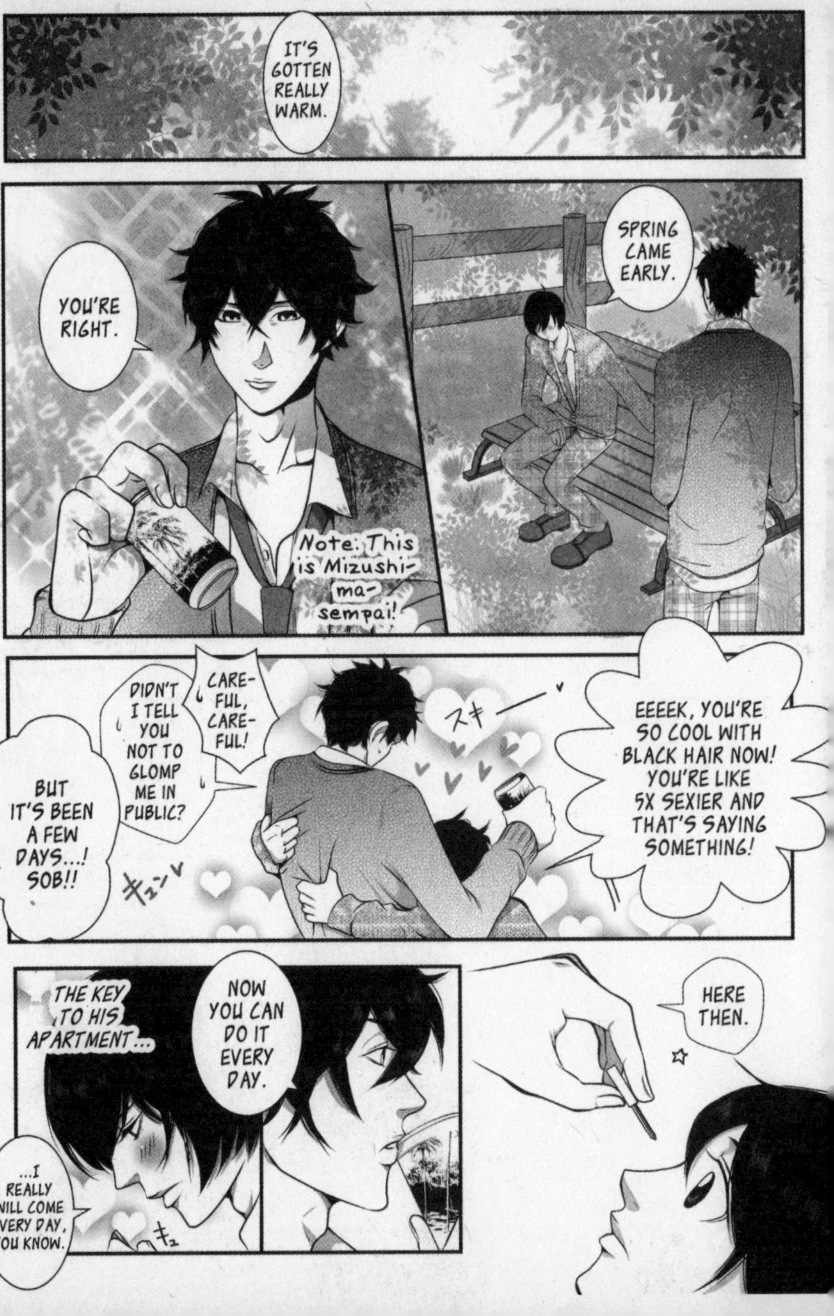
IT'S GOTTEN REALLY WARM.
SPRING CAME EARLY.
YOU'RE RIGHT.
Note: This is Mizushima-sempai!
EEEEK, YOU'RE SO COOL WITH BLACK HAIR NOW! YOU'RE LIKE 5X SEXIER AND THAT'S SAYING SOMETHING!
スキー
CARE-FUL, CARE-FUL!
DIDN'T I TELL YOU NOT TO GLOMP ME IN PUBLIC?
BUT IT'S BEEN A FEW DAYS...! SOB!!
キュン
HERE THEN.
NOW YOU CAN DO IT EVERY DAY.
THE KEY TO HIS APARTMENT...
...I REALLY WILL COME EVERY DAY, YOU KNOW.

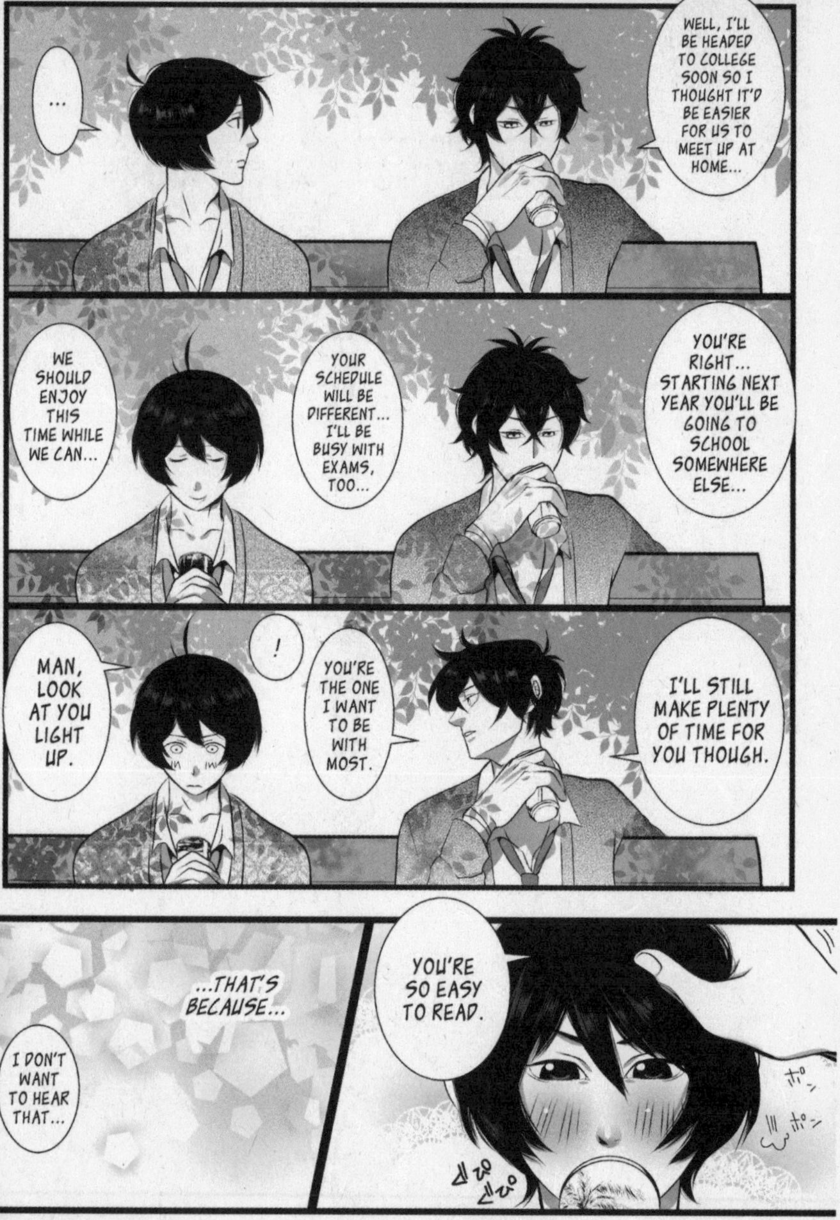
WELL, I'LL BE HEADED TO COLLEGE SOON SO I THOUGHT IT'D BE EASIER FOR US TO MEET UP AT HOME...
...
YOU'RE RIGHT... STARTING NEXT YEAR YOU'LL BE GOING TO SCHOOL SOMEWHERE ELSE...
YOUR SCHEDULE WILL BE DIFFERENT... I'LL BE BUSY WITH EXAMS, TOO...
WE SHOULD ENJOY THIS TIME WHILE WE CAN...
I'LL STILL MAKE PLENTY OF TIME FOR YOU THOUGH.
YOU'RE THE ONE I WANT TO BE WITH MOST.
!
MAN, LOOK AT YOU LIGHT UP.
YOU'RE SO EASY TO READ.
...THAT'S BECAUSE...
I DON'T WANT TO HEAR THAT...

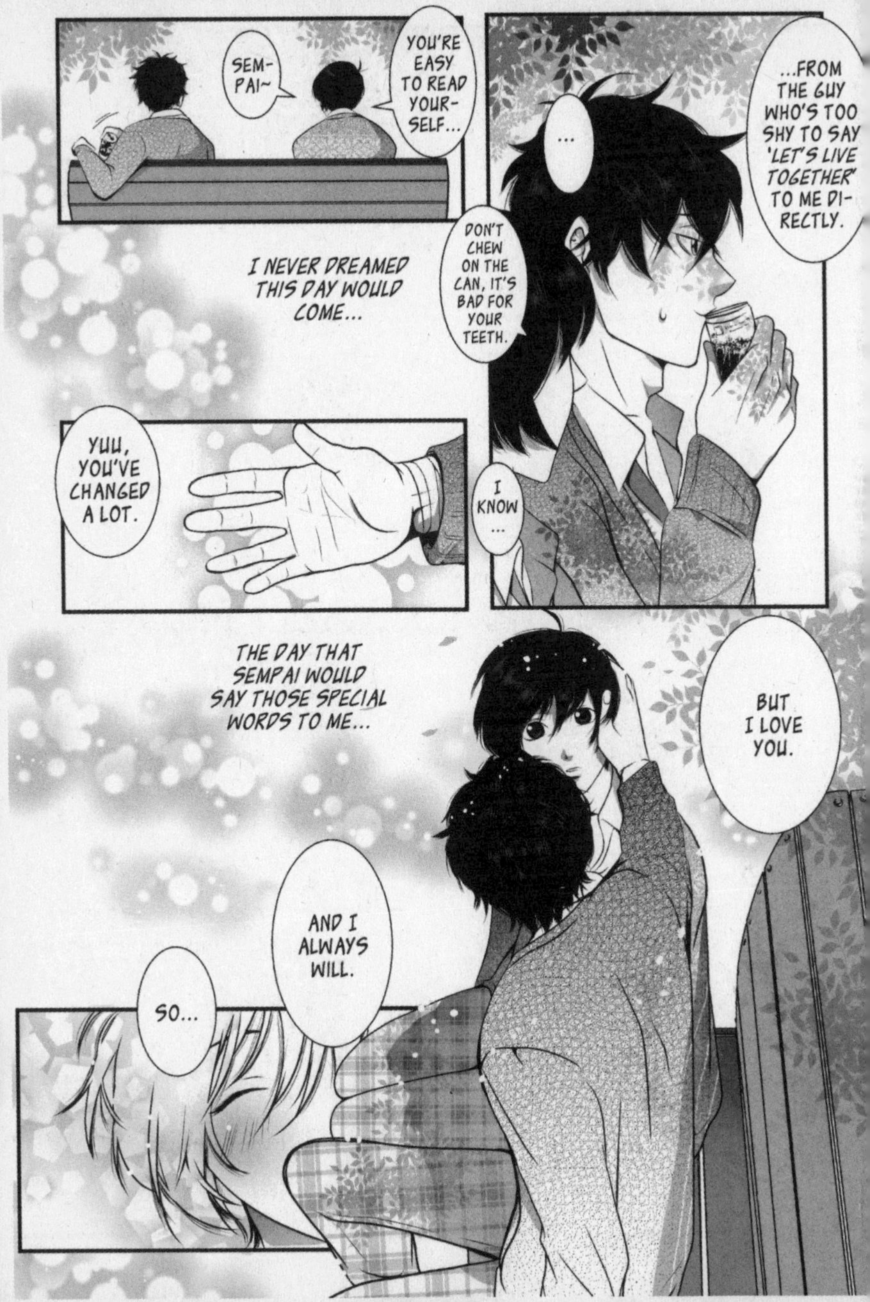
...FROM THE GUY WHO'S TOO SHY TO SAY 'LET'S LIVE TOGETHER' TO ME DIRECTLY.
...
DON'T CHEW ON THE CAN, IT'S BAD FOR YOUR TEETH.
I KNOW ...
YOU'RE EASY TO READ YOURSELF...
SEMPAI~
I NEVER DREAMED THIS DAY WOULD COME...
YUU, YOU'VE CHANGED A LOT.
THE DAY THAT SEMPAI WOULD SAY THOSE SPECIAL WORDS TO ME...
BUT I LOVE YOU.
AND I ALWAYS WILL.
SO...

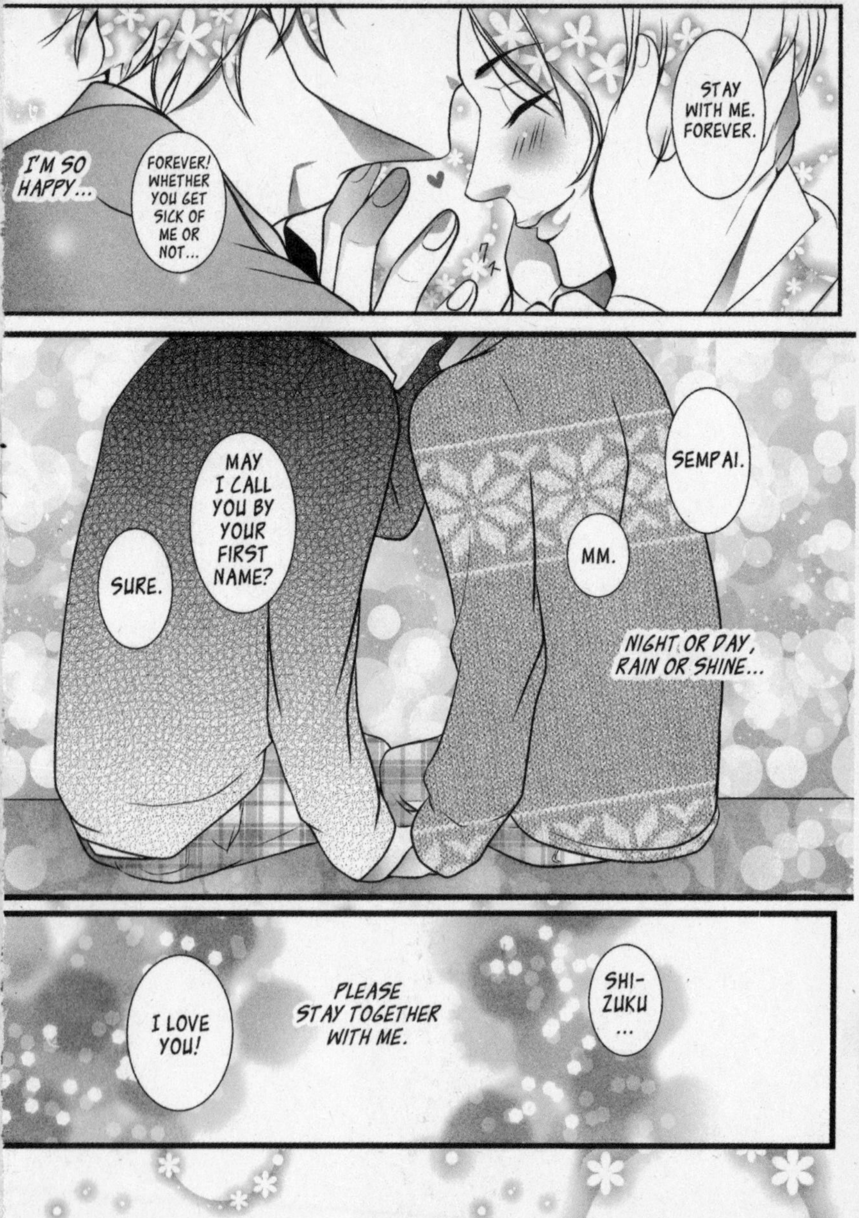
STAY WITH ME. FOREVER.
FOREVER! WHETHER YOU GET SICK OF ME OR NOT...
I'M SO HAPPY...
SEMPAI.
MM.
MAY I CALL YOU BY YOUR FIRST NAME?
SURE.
NIGHT OR DAY, RAIN OR SHINE...
SHI-ZUKU...
PLEASE STAY TOGETHER WITH ME.
I LOVE YOU!
ONE IS ENOUGH: END